T0383035

Embers of the Hands

EMBERS OF THE HANDS

Hidden Histories of the Viking Age

ELEANOR BARRACLOUGH

Profile Books

First published in Great Britain in 2024 by
Profile Books Ltd
29 Cloth Fair
London ECIA 7JQ

www.profilebooks.com

Epigraph on p1 taken from LORDS AND LADIES by Terry Pratchett.
Published by Victor Gollancz Ltd, 1992. Copyright © Terry Pratchett.
Reproduced by permission of the Estate c/o Rogers, Coleridge & White Ltd.,
20 Powis Mews, London W11 1JN

1 3 5 7 9 10 8 6 4 2

Typeset and designed by James Alexander/Jade Design

Printed and bound in Great Britain by
Clays Ltd, Elcograf S.p.A.

A CIP catalogue record for this book is available from the British Library.

ISBN 978 1 78816 6744
eISBN 978 1 78283 7879

For Magnus and Wulfie

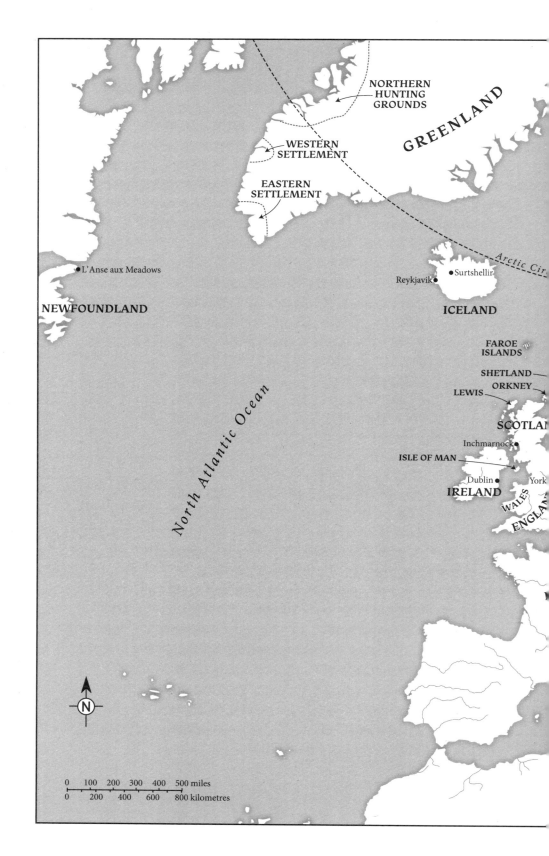

CONTENTS

Prologue

KINDLING

There are very few starts. Oh, some things seem to be
beginnings. The curtain goes up, the first pawn moves, the
first shot is fired – but that's not the start. The play, the game,
the war is just a little window on a ribbon of events that may
extend back thousands of years. The point is, there's always
something before. It's always a case of Now Read On.

Terry Pratchett, *Lords and Ladies*

We are taught to think of history as a series of canal locks, each period neatly compartmentalised from the one before and after. Stone Age, Bronze Age, Iron Age, Romans, Anglo-Saxons, Vikings, Normans and so on. Quite often the locks are defined by the deaths of rulers, famous battles, the arbitrary ticking over of the centuries. And just as the canal waters of history flow obediently from one lock to the next, so they stay within their geographical bounds. It is neat, and, to some extent, necessary. It is also artificial. In reality, history is more like a great untamed river: a flowing entity, shifting and branching, merging again, wild and unpredictable. Its streams do not always have clear beginnings or endings. Nor do they always stay within the geographical boundaries set out for them on a map. And the ordinary humans bumped and bounced along by its currents do not always know where they are, let alone where the river is taking them.

Where, then, to start a history of the Viking Age? With the shock of fiery dragons and lightning in the skies over

Northumberland – or so the *Anglo-Saxon Chronicle* reports for the year 793 – before Scandinavian raiders descended on the monks of Lindisfarne? Or do we head upstream, and trace the churning waters back in time?

Let's head back to the Scandinavian homelands, around two thousand years from the present day, to an unassuming Danish bog. Here, thickly squelching carpets and rounded hummocks of moss shade gradually from lime green to rusty orange. Low-lying lakes are framed by spindly birches and willows. In the warmer months, the mirrored pools are spiked with bright yellow flowers of bog asphodel and bladderwort, dotted with white feathery cotton grass. Snipe wade with their needle-long beaks and creaking-bedsprings call, amorous marsh harriers tumble together through the sky. Then the earth starts to tip away, taking with it the warmth and light. New colours appear: the dusty blues and cherry reds of bilberries and lingonberries, the tawny browns and yellows of mushrooms. And with them, creeping cold and damp. Overcast iron skies arrive, and frost-laced water.

For centuries, bogs such as these were gateways between worlds. Shifting landscapes of wet and dry, hanging mists, bubbling marsh gasses, will-o'-the-wisps. Fitting places to commune with the more-than-human forces of this world. Fitting places for sacrifice. The bogs provided sustenance for humans and livestock, black peat for fuel, lumps of bog iron for weapons and tools. But what is taken must be paid for. Clothes, pots, tools, games, weapons, animals, humans. Gifts to the gods on the other side. They all went into the dark: the airless wet spaces and the saturated soil, pickled by acid, their organic matter preserved long after those who cast them into the water. These bogs were wombs for the dead. Some humans were deliberately sacrificed, others perhaps not, but all were delivered into the safekeeping of the water spirits, who immortalised them with shining bronzed skin and coppered hair.

The particular bog we have come to is called Vimose. It is located on Funen (Fyn), the large Danish island between the peninsula of Jutland (Jylland) in the west and the island of Zealand (Sjælland) in the east. It lies roughly on the same latitude as Hadrian's Wall to the west, and the same longitude as Oslo to the north. *Mose* simply means 'bog'. The origins of *vi* are harder to pinpoint. In the Viking Age, the word *vé* or *ví* referred to a 'pagan sanctuary' or 'pagan shrine'. While it is tempting to make the connection and suggest that Vimose means 'pagan shrine bog', there are more likely, somewhat marshier possibilities: 'willow-bog', 'wood-bog' or 'lapwing-bog'.[1]

Squelching about, our fingers find pottery shards and bones, both human and animal. Ancient tools of metal and wood: hammers and tongs, knives and twist-drills, files and fire steels, even anvils. Gaming pieces and scraps of clothing. We find horse trappings and handle-grips of wood and bone and bronze. Iron shield bosses. Bows and arrows hewn from pine. Axes, swords and spear heads. A complete suit of mail armour, its rings clogged with mud. Out they come from the marshy soil, thousands upon thousands of artefacts, often bound together with cloth or string.

The offerings placed in Vimose started out modestly enough in the last century BCE – a few Iron Age pots, food and animal parts. Around the time when BCE ticked over into CE, the first few weapons arrived: a sword and a dozen spear heads. Over time, more spears, swords, shields and belts drifted down through the water, until thousands of weapons lay submerged with other offerings in the mud. This was no unique phenomenon. Around twenty Danish bogs have been found with Iron Age war gear deposits, reaching a peak in the third and fourth centuries. Often there are traces of ritual destruction – the points of weapons bent – as if they had been neutralised, or perhaps 'killed' would be a better word, so they could pass over to the other side.

3

In this bog, we see hints of what was to come as the centuries marched on towards the Viking Age. These offerings are evidence of the increasing militarisation of northern European societies, and the growth of far-reaching connections, alliances and tensions. In the early centuries CE, wealth, power and territory were becoming concentrated in the hands of a few powerful leaders. An elite military class emerged, capable of raising big armies and controlling resources over long distances. Especially in the case of large-scale sacrifices of war gear, it seems likely that the items belonged to unsuccessful invaders from further afield: other parts of Denmark, north from regions of what are now Norway and Sweden, south from parts of what are now Germany and Poland. Their bodies were stripped by their victorious enemies, their belongings repurposed as gifts to the spirits of the marshy waters.

Alongside Scandinavian-made weapons thrown into the bog were others that came from the Roman Empire. Vimose contains some impressive Roman finery, such as a gilded bronze gryphon head – a mythical beast half-lion, half-eagle – that might once have decorated a parade helmet. Likewise, a sword hilt made from elephant ivory must have travelled a very long way – from Africa or India – before it found its final resting place in this bog. These weapons are a reminder of a culturally fluid, interconnected world. Even though it was never part of the Roman Empire, Scandinavia was a part of this wider network. It lay far to the north of the bristling line of earth banks, ditches, palisades and watchtowers that followed the Rhine and the Danube, running for hundreds of kilometres across the Continent. From the Roman perspective, this defensive line was the hinge between their civilisation and the world of barbarism that lay beyond, in the lands they called Germania.

But the Roman Empire did not – could not – shut itself off from those who lived beyond the frontiers. North of the politically fractious borderlands, they cultivated diplomatic alliances

4

and trade links. Their Germanic enemies would have to watch their backs on two fronts. The tribes of southern Scandinavia – especially those whose territories lay in the lands of Denmark – were among the recipients of this attention. A procession of high-status imports made from materials such as gold, glass and bronze started to head north into southern Scandinavia. Luxury Scandinavian goods such as furs, feathers and amber travelled in the opposite direction, bound for the Roman Empire. In time, they were joined on their southern progress by Scandinavian warriors, looking to sign up to the Roman army as auxiliaries. And when they eventually returned home, they did so with the knowledge, experience and equipment of the most sophisticated military machine of the ancient world.

It was these links between different cultures and places that set many of the wheels in motion for the Viking Age. Alongside the weapons that found their resting places in the bogs of Denmark, other physical objects – often personal possessions that speak intimately of their owners – testify to the cultural influences and ideas about the world that travelled north from the Roman Empire. These too would come to feed into some of the most recognisable cultural features of the Viking Age, from personal hygiene habits to leisure activities, in ways that we will return to throughout this book.

Cast into the dark waters of Vimose were wooden gaming boards scored into grids, together with dice and little round counters made from coloured glass, amber and bones. They are evidence of what the vanquished warriors had got up to in their leisure time. They also tell us something about how board games spread into northern and western Europe from the Roman Empire and found their way north of the frontiers. What began as games of military strategy played by soldiers in their forts and bathhouses snowballed in popularity, until they were adopted and adapted by those whom the Romans sought to subdue. As we will see, by the time of the Viking Age, those who inhabited the Nordic world were enthusiastic – and sometimes boastful – players of such board games, featuring them in their artwork, their poems and their riddles.

Another extraordinary artefact to find its way into Vimose is a comb made from deer antler, thrown into the bog around the year 160, its shaft arched like a cat's back with twenty-five spiky little teeth. Small enough to nestle in its owner's cupped fingers, this comb is a delicate, diminutive object: the physical remains of a highly personal, everyday ritual from almost two thousand years ago. Used to detangle, delouse, decorate, there is a powerful shared intimacy in haircare, from smoothing an infant's first soft fuzz to gently detangling the friable strands of sickness and senescence. But this comb and its owner were not destined to accompany each other into old age. If it was part of war booty thrown into the bog by the winning side, then its owner had probably not survived the encounter.

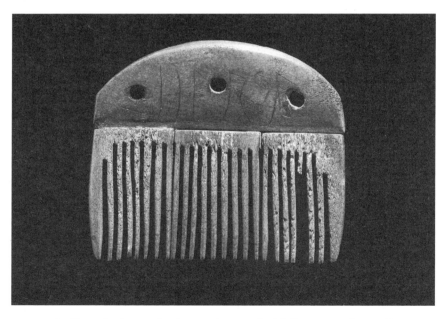

A gift to the bog gods: the comb carved with five runes that spell out the word HARJA. Vimose, Denmark, 2nd century.

The Vikings were famous – even notorious, as we will see – for their meticulous grooming habits and their distinctive hairstyles. Their beautiful combs often surface during archaeological digs, and we will meet several of them in this book. But this is hardly the only comb in the world. It is not even the only comb in this particular Danish bog. What makes it unique are the deliberate scratches across its shaft, spelling out the runic letters ᚺᚨᚱᛃᚨ, or HARJA.[2] If the Vikings are known for their raids and ship burials, they are also known for their runes: that spiky north Germanic alphabet still so familiar today. And on this Vimose comb, from hundreds of years before the word Viking was ever uttered, are the earliest decipherable runes that have ever been found. Their meaning is unclear. Perhaps the runes are a case of something doing exactly what it says on the tin, because it might be that *harja* just means 'comb'.[3] Another possibility is that the runes mean something along the lines of 'warrior', 'war' or 'army', which would be appropriate for the context in which the comb was found. Or else they may have been someone's personal name, or perhaps a military title, or a tribal name.[4]

For such a recognisable, iconic form of ancient writing, no one knows for certain where runes came from, although there are several theories. It's probably no coincidence that many of the oldest runic inscriptions discovered come from a context that shows clear evidence of contact with the Roman Empire and its own writing system. Just looking at the shape of runic letters, we can see definite similarities with many letters of the Latin alphabet, which we still use today, but with an angular shape more suited for carving into materials such as wood and stone. It's likely that knowledge of the Roman writing system travelled north with those returning from service in and contact with the empire: military warbands and craftspeople. This might also explain one possible meaning of the word 'rune' itself: something 'secret' or 'hidden', something originally reserved for a particular segment of society, an elite group.

In addition to the comb found in Vimose were several other items with runes carved on them, including a buckle, part of a scabbard and a spearhead. They were thrown into the bog during the third and fourth centuries, when the sacrifices were at their height. But the time would soon come when no more offerings drifted down through the waters to whatever spirits, powers and worlds lay waiting in the magically time-stopping bogs of the north. Change was on its way.

In the year 406, the bristling Rhine frontier was overrun by a confederation of Germanic tribes. The cities of Gaul burned. By the end of the fifth century, the Western Roman Empire had been dismembered, and new Germanic powers had emerged in its place. This was an age of migration and movement, uprooting and resettling, in which tribes found themselves on the move across Europe. It was an age of political jostling and bloodshed, but, then again, when is it not? And for those north of the former imperial frontier, those who had made diplomatic alliances with Roman governors or travelled south to fight in Roman wars, the world was also moving on.

At this point, we are still several centuries from the dawn of the Viking Age, which we can place in the eighth century. We are even further from the idea of Denmark, Norway and Sweden as three unified, distinct kingdoms. But throughout Scandinavia, the centuries that followed the end of the Western Roman Empire saw territorial units continue to coalesce, ruled by an elite class whose power was based primarily on control of economic resources, political alliances and martial strength. These rulers administered power from what are commonly called central places, where they stamped their supremacy on the landscape itself. They built huge wooden halls, intricately decorated and fabulously furnished, which served as gathering places for communal feasts, large-scale religious rituals and legal proceedings. They gathered together merchants and craftspeople under their protection and control, ensuring their own positions as the fattest spiders at the centre of an expanding web of international trade. And they commissioned burial mounds for themselves and their kin, so that even after their deaths, their presence and power would still loom large in the minds and deeds of the living.

From here, we can start to follow the river downstream again, and see where it leads. For when the fires of the Viking Age began to burn, they fed on kindling that had been laid down at the time of the Roman Empire and in the centuries that followed.

Chapter 1

INTRODUCTION

The Viking Age is a glittering thing. It shines with tales and poems of adventurers, heroes and gods, vivid stories that continue to be reshaped and retold down to the present day. It shimmers with intricate craftwork that adorned bodies in life and death: gemstones and glass beads twinkling between twisted loops of silver and gold. It gleams with once-buried hoards packed with silver bullion, far-travelled coins and looted religious treasures. It sparkles with sunlight on water as oars dip and dig into the waves, propelling longships across deep oceans, icy fjords and shallow bays. And it glints with the sharp edges of weapons in the hands of warriors.

Such a reputation would have delighted many who lived in that time. After all, how one was remembered was vital. On this matter, the one-eyed god Odin is said to to have imparted his wisdom in an Old Norse poem called *Hávamál* ('Sayings of the High One'): 'Cattle die, kin die, the self must also die, but glory never dies for the one who is able to achieve it.'[1] And there is truth in this. This was an extraordinary, transformative period of history, during which many individuals created powerful, complex names for themselves. Their prestige was maintained and embellished in poetry and stories that had deep roots in the

Viking Age itself, flitting from mouth to mouth before eventually coming to rest on the pages of medieval manuscripts. Other facets and colours – many dark and bloody – were added to their fame through the writings of those who encountered them from other cultures. And over the centuries that followed, the many afterlives of the Vikings continued to be constructed by those who looked back and built new reputations for these people of the past. The fame and notoriety of the Vikings, in all their glittering facets, is why books such as this one are written and read.

Even so, most reputations do not last long after death. For the most part, each brief, bright flame of a life flickers, glows, then vanishes into the darkness. But that is not the same as never having lived, and it is certainly not the same as never having mattered. Behind the stars of the Viking Age were the everyday people who inhabited this world, who experienced different, varied existences. These were humans who – like most of us – lived through their own triumphs and tragedies, then disappeared from living memory within a couple of generations. They had deeply felt emotions, loves and losses, frustrations and fears. They had robust – sometimes inappropriate – senses of humour, lustful impulses, medical problems, heartbreaking backstories. They were of different ethnicities, sexualities, classes, ages and abilities. They had names, homes, and loved ones to miss them after they had gone. And yet, at the same time, they occupied a different time and a different place in the great churning river of history. They operated within different social and cultural frameworks. They had different experiences of being in the world and different expectations of life. Familiar in so many ways, perhaps, but not the same.

This isn't a history about the exceptions to the rule: the powerful players and half-historical legends whose lights burned brightly and whose names and deeds of derring-do were commemorated in epic sagas and praise poems. It's a history of the everyday humans who fell between the cracks of history, told through the little bits and pieces that survived the vagaries of time and quirks of fate. At best, some of them might merit a metaphorical footnote in the annals and legends of history. But for the most part this is about those who were never in the stories in the first place. They may have sat round the fire telling and listening to the stories, or caught snatches of these tales as they brought in the food and cleared up afterwards. They may have missed the stories because they were outside answering the call of nature or getting up to indecorous activities under cover of darkness. Or they may have been listening to the distant laughter and chatter from beyond the warm circle of firelight because they were never invited in the first place. In other words, this is a history of the Viking Age with the ordinary humans left in.

Thanks to the geographical and chronological range, this is also a history of humans on an extraordinarily global stage. It is on this stage that people lived, died and left traces of themselves. Sometimes these traces tell us a lot about what their lives were like, at other times they give us only the briefest glimpse. Clothes, toys and gaming pieces, combs, trash and treasure, love notes and obscenities carved into slivers of wood: the sort of intimate ephemera that connect us to the people of the past. These are the 'embers of the hands' of this book title: the glowing remnants that survive when the bright flame of a life has vanished.

The phrase 'embers of the hands' comes from the Viking Age itself. It's a kenning, a little word puzzle that poets – called skalds – tucked up in their fiendishly intricate verses. A kenning describes something familiar in a roundabout, often metaphorical way. In this case, the original meaning of this kenning was 'gold', a precious metal glowing and shimmering like fire on the hand of the one who possesses it. It was part of a verse composed by an eleventh-century Icelander called Thorarin Skeggjason, who was court poet to the Norwegian king Harald harðráði ('hard ruler'), more commonly Anglicised as Hardrada, killed at the Battle of Stamford Bridge in 1066. Harald Hardrada was most definitely one of those powerful players of the Viking Age, whose glittering reputation was preserved and embellished in sagas and poems long after his lifetime. In fact, as we will see, his death is often used as a marker for the end of the Viking Age itself. But the embers that I want to blow back to life in this book are rather different to the ones that kings such as Harald would have recognised and valued. Ours, no less precious, are the personal fragments and everyday detritus that remain of lives long past. They help us to uncover hidden histories and illuminate a world beyond the usual tales of raiders, traders and rulers. By uncovering some of the many and diverse experiences of the Viking Age, by capturing brief moments of past lives, we can build up a fresh understanding of what it meant to live through these times, away from the grand narrative sweep of history.

Such tiny flames, burning in the darkness, also remind us that when we think about this era, indeed any era, the reality for most people is rarely that ordered version of history with clear-cut beginnings and endings. We can fix ourselves in time by thinking of the Viking Age as a period that spanned from roughly 750 to 1100. But the embers of history come from fires that were lit long before any official dates used to define them, and continued to smoulder long afterwards.[2]

Where?

If we interpret the meaning of the 'Viking Age' literally, it starts in the last decade of the eighth century, with the first recorded Scandinavian raids abroad. This is because, at the time, the noun 'Viking' simply meant a raider, usually seaborne. Medieval Scandinavians had their versions of the word (*víkingr* for the raider, *víking* for the raid itself), as did the Anglo-Saxons in England (*wīcing*). Academics sometimes tussle over the origins of the word and where it came from, but no one can quite agree, and the debate tends to go around in circles.[3]

Words change their meanings over time. 'Viking' disappeared for several hundred years, before being reintroduced and polished up in the 1800s. Eventually, it became shorthand for a whole cultural diaspora, a whole historical period and everyone connected to it. That's a lot of heavy lifting for a little word. The danger is that this might colour our perceptions of who these people were too much to be useful. If we referred to Ancient Greece as the 'Hoplite Age', the first thing we might think of is soldiers with round shields, long spears and faceless bronze helmets. Warfare, then, would become the dominant characteristic of the period, probably at the expense of other aspects of Greek history such as philosophy, poetry and pottery. Similarly, if we think of the 'Viking Age' as dominated by macho raiders with big beards and bigger boats, glorying in nicknames such as 'foul-fart', 'troll-burster' and 'ale-lover', then we leave almost everyone out of the picture. All the women, for a start. But at the same time, 'Viking' is a useful catch-all, which helps us define – very broadly – a fascinating cultural group and historical phenomenon.

As an alternative, 'Norse' is a useful, if broad, shorthand for the common cultural sphere of the medieval Nordic world, with its history, languages and literature.[4] It's a helpful word that takes some of the load off 'Viking' as an all-purpose adjective, and some of the historical baggage associated with it. For now, we'll stick to 'Viking', 'Viking Age' and 'Norse' until someone comes up with something better that everyone can agree on. And since, the 'Age Roughly from 750–1100 CE During Which Those Primarily of Scandinavian Origins and Heritage Took Part in Raiding, Trading and Settlement Both Within and Beyond Scandinavia' doesn't have quite the same ring to it, we might be waiting a while.

At its height, the sphere of Viking Age activity and influence stretched north to the spare wastes of the Arctic, and west across the North Atlantic. It extended east across the Baltic to the churning waterways and wide-skied steppes of Eurasia. It ranged south to the glittering splendour of the Byzantine Empire and the sophisticated Abbasid Caliphate. The people who made up the Viking Age story lived different, varied existences. A Greenlandic walrus hunter, an imperial bodyguard in Constantinople, a nomadic reindeer herder crossing the Arctic tundra, an enslaved Briton farming the thin volcanic soils of Iceland: all such individuals might be threads in the densely woven tapestry of the Viking Age.

But the story of the Viking Age begins in the Scandinavian heartlands of Norway, Sweden and Denmark. Geographically speaking, this is an expansive and topographically varied region. Norway's vastly long coastline is deeply indented with glacier-carved fjords and peppered with islands. Inland, huge snow-capped mountains and wide moorland plateaus are broken up by deep lakes and fertile strips of valleys. Trees cluster thickly and agricultural land is scarce. To the east, Sweden too has its share of mountains, and plentiful forests and lakes. It also has gently undulating lowlands and richer agricultural land, especially in the south. Both Norway and Sweden stretch north across the Arctic Circle, where the treeline gives way to the lichens and mosses of the Arctic tundra. Here, midsummer is a riot of bright flowers and peach skies at midnight. Midwinter is a time of deep-blue light at midday, blanketing snow, and colours rippling through the sky. To the south of Norway and Sweden sit the many islands of Denmark, a place of connection by land and water, with marshy tidal flats in the west. Flanked by the North Sea and the Baltic Sea on either side, Denmark is connected to the European continent via the Jutland Peninsula. For the most part, it is a flatter, greener landscape of heaths, bogs and plains, more suited for agriculture than most of Norway or Sweden.

Despite such geographical range and breadth, the concept of this region as a distinct, culturally connected entity can be traced far back in time. In his encyclopedic *Natural History* completed in

77 CE, Pliny the Elder was the first known writer to use the name 'Scatinavia' to describe the Scandinavia Peninsula (an 'n' was added to later manuscripts, giving us the word we know today). The word comes from Proto-Germanic and may mean something like 'dangerous land on the water', the danger perhaps referring to the surrounding seas.[5]

By the time we reach the Gothic historian Jordanes, living in sixth-century Constantinople, there is a strong sense of a geographically distinct region with a social organisation based on tribal divisions. His *Getica*, which he bases largely on the work of earlier classical authors, lists the names of around thirty different peoples who inhabit the region he calls 'Scandza'. In terms of the topography, he describes a vast lake in the east of the region, and immense seas to the west and north. He notes that those living in the far north experience forty days and nights of continual light at midsummer, and the equivalent continual darkness at midwinter, which makes them as joyful in the summer as they are miserable in the winter. Meanwhile, Jordanes reports, the chill is so terrible that wolves cross over the frozen sea and are blinded by the cold, and there are no honeybees in the land.

We have to come forward in time several centuries, into the Viking Age itself, for evidence of the names that we would now recognise as the three Scandinavian countries. One of the most remarkable testimonials is that of an individual we know as Ohthere, a trader and explorer from the far north of Norway. He visited the court of King Alfred in Anglo-Saxon England in the latter part of the ninth century. There, his oral narrative of the far northern lands, resources and peoples of Scandinavia was translated and set down in Old English, the language spoken by the Anglo-Saxons. This is why he is known by the Old English version of his name, Ohthere, whereas his actual name was probably Ottar. Compared to the classical texts that came before, the topographical and ethnographical precision of Ohthere's account is of a different order of magnitude. He provides recognisable descriptions of landmasses and the sailing distances between them, and detailed information about the different peoples who inhabit various regions. In Ohthere's account, we have some of the earliest examples of the names of all three countries that we would recognise: the embryonic realms of *Norðweg* ('Norway'), *Denemearce* ('Denmark') and *Sweoland* ('Sweden'). By the end of the Viking Age, versions of these three countries – not entirely with the same geographical borders as today – were acquiring distinctive identities as nations ruled by single monarchs. But this was a slow and ongoing process, in which Denmark took an early lead, Norway was close behind and Sweden took its time to catch up.

Despite the regional and national distinctions, those who lived at the time were aware that they were part of a cultural network linked through the language we now call Old Norse. Those who spoke the language referred to it as the *dǫnsk tunga* ('Danish tongue') or alternatively *norrœn* ('Norse').[6] As we will see, colonies were established during the Viking Age in locations such as Britain and Ireland, Iceland and Greenland. This is a pattern of migration and expansion that is sometimes referred to as a diaspora, because migrant communities maintained cultural and political contact with their ancestral homelands. Language was among its most important markers.

Ohthere's account is also important because it provides a strong sense of Scandinavia as an interconnected cultural sphere involving other indigenous peoples who inhabited the peninsula. These groups did not necessarily share the same linguistic background or cultural practices as the Norse, and yet they were notable players in the Viking Age story. The most important of these were those known as *Finnar* by their Norse-speaking neighbours. They were the ancestors of Scandinavia's modern-day Sámi population. For the most part, they were nomadic hunters and fishers with ready access to valuable Arctic furs and skins. Their primary territories ranged across the far north of what is now Norway, Sweden, Finland and Russia. Hailing from Arctic Norway, Ohthere himself made much of his wealth through trading with and collecting tribute from his neighbours. But the Norse–Sámi relationship was also characterised by intermarriage and cross-cultural influences. There is also archaeological evidence that the Sámi also operated in southern areas of Scandinavia.

There are many other peoples and cultures who had their parts to play in the history of the Viking Age. To understand when and where they entered the story, we need to return to those great rivers of history for a historical overview.

The Viking Age

The Viking Age, as an especially swampy part of the vast braided waterways of history, is harder to define than many periods. This does not mean that we should ignore the challenge, which can only improve our understanding of the past in all its messiness and complexity. That challenge runs through this book. For now, it will help us to get our bearings if we keep our feet dry and take in the view from a distance.

Through the eighth century the north began to develop rapidly in new ways. Much of this had to do with money. After the economic slump that followed the fall of the Western Roman Empire, a new influx of silver coins spread into northern Europe, lubricating the wheels of trade. Already by the year 700, new trading centres had sprung up on both sides of the English Channel. There was Quentovic, near Boulogne on the French coast; Hamwic, just outside what is now Southampton; Lundenwic, an Anglo-Saxon trading port upriver of the old Roman city of Londinium, where Westminster now stands; and Dorestad near the mouth of the Rhine, in the modern Netherlands. These and similar places formed a network of hubs for seaborne merchants who shuttled between them, exchanging goods and coins that would then penetrate further inland.

People in Scandinavia, on the edge of this slow-motion economic boom, were soon drawn into it. Their homelands, though relatively poor in agricultural land, had much to offer. The far north had the best furs in Europe, hunted and collected in cold climes and shipped south to eager traders who would pay good money for this luxury resource. In eastern Scandinavia, the shores of the Baltic Sea were a major source of amber. Skins, eiderdown and whetstones for sharpening blades would also fetch good prices. Scandinavian merchants would return home with exotic products from the south such as wine, jewellery, and high-quality swords greatly prized by the rising chieftains of the north. A few decades passed, and by the mid-eighth century the first of what would become northern trading hubs had started to appear, reflecting those in the south. These included Ribe and Hedeby in Denmark, Kaupang in Norway, Birka in Sweden, Wolin on the southern coast of the Baltic, and even Staraja Ladoga, a far-flung trading post in what is now north-west Russia. This last settlement was connected by vast waterways to the Islamic world of the Middle East, another lucrative market for northern resources, and in time also to the Byzantine Empire.

In this heady period there were fortunes to be made and power to be had. Two things were crucial: control of resources and control of how those resources changed hands. In Arctic Norway, for example, local chieftains who forced others to give them furs in tribute or taxation would quickly rise to the top of the pile. Meanwhile, Danish rulers who controlled the narrow seaways linking the Baltic to the lucrative markets of the south, or who controlled the trading centres themselves, would likewise gain power and wealth. And traders and craftspeople also brought new ideas and technologies into the lands of the north.

For those leaders who fancied themselves a step or two above the average chieftain, there were ample models of kingship to the south. Britain was home to a patchwork of kingdoms, Ireland to a shifting constellation of quarrelsome petty rulers. On the Continent was the only superpower of western Europe, the Carolingian Empire, which by the year 800 encompassed the modern areas of France, Belgium, the Netherlands, Luxembourg and Switzerland, as well as respectable chunks of Italy, Austria and Germany. As we have seen from the Prologue, northern rulers had long cultivated economic and diplomatic relationships with the south. In the process, they absorbed ideas of what real power could look like, and how they might achieve it. Although historical sources are lacking for this period in Scandinavia, archaeological evidence clearly shows how, in Denmark at least, this had an impact. In 737 work began on a monumental ditch and earth bank topped with a timber palisade that stretched across part of southern Denmark. In later centuries this was expanded into the defensive system known as the *Danevirke*. Scandinavia had never seen a construction on this scale, and it is a vivid sign of an ambitious local ruler with a great deal to protect and the resources to invest in protecting it.

The eighth century saw a steady build-up of wealth, power and ambition within Scandinavia. This also made it ripe for competition and conflict. For every top dog there were others vying for the position, many of whom might devise alternative routes to status and prosperity. As the arteries of trade grew fatter, they attracted the parasitic problem of piracy. And it was only a matter of time before Viking adventurers would burst out into the wider world.

From an Anglo-Saxon perspective, the first acts of violence from seaborne Scandinavian raiders are framed as bolts out of the blue. The *Anglo-Saxon Chronicle* reports that, around the year 787, three ships arrived on the Isle of Portland, off the coast of Dorset: 'There came for the first time three ships of Northmen and then the reeve rode to them and wished to force them to the king's residence, for he did not know what they were; and they slew him. Those were the first ships of Danish men which came to the land of the English.'7

This entry is written retrospectively, with the knowledge that these are only the 'first ships' because worse is to come. And indeed, in the year 793 came the infamous raid on the island monastery of Lindisfarne, just off the coast of Northumberland. It is painted by the scribes of the *Anglo-Saxon Chronicle* as a cataclysmic event where the heavens themselves foretell the horror to come:

> In this year dire portents appeared over Northumbria and sorely frightened the people. They consisted of immense whirlwinds and flashes of lightning, and fiery dragons were seen flying in the air. A great famine immediately followed those signs, and a little after that in the same year, on 8 June, the ravages of the heathen men miserably destroyed God's church on Lindisfarne, with plunder and slaughter.8

More was to follow in the coming years, as a series of alluringly vulnerable and wealthy monasteries from the Hebrides to Ireland and the French coast were brutally attacked. Rulers scrambled to build defences against these unwelcome intruders; clerics lamented the sins that had brought such punishment upon Christian folk and urged repentance. But these raids were just the beginning.

By the 830s, a new generation of Viking raiders was building on the achievements of their parents. Their ambitions were even greater, helped by the descent of the Carolingian Empire into civil war in 830. They began striking less vulnerable targets, and venturing ever farther from their boats. The Carolingian merchant centre at Dorestad – ironically, one of the engines that had helped drive the northern trading boom a century earlier – was so devastated by annual raids from 834 to 837 that it never fully recovered. In 842 Quentovic and Hamwic suffered a similar fate.

Meanwhile, in 836 Viking bands launched inland raids in Somerset and Ireland, while around the same time others began to serve as mercenaries for local rulers in Cornwall, Northumbria and Ireland. From the 840s Viking raiders were feeling confident enough not to return home after each year's expedition, as they had been doing, but to establish winter camps. This gave them the opportunity to strike more rapidly inland when spring arrived. At the same time, the scale and political impact of the raids grew. When a Viking fleet of 120 ships sailed up the Seine and threatened Paris in 845, it was bought off with 7,000 pounds of gold and silver, a fortune vast enough to set up every member of the expedition for life. In 859 another fleet even ventured as far as the Mediterranean and was plundering Carolingian territory in the Rhône valley.

To their victims, the Vikings were a relentless and lamentable plague through the middle decades of the ninth century. Had things stayed like this, the raids would likely have fizzled out as the number of potential targets dwindled and the kingdoms of western Europe strengthened their defences against seaborne attacks. But success breeds success, and by the 860s the grandchildren and great-grandchildren of those first Viking raiders began to nurse ambitions that their forebears scarcely could have imagined. In 865 a large fleet landed in England, with the aim not of hit-and-run raids, but of conquest. Within five years it had demolished the centuries-old Anglo-Saxon kingdoms of East Anglia, Northumbria and Mercia. Only the southern kingdom of Wessex remained. It was from this base that the West Saxon king, Alfred, eventually managed to fight the so-called 'Great Heathen Army' to a stalemate in 878. Thereafter England was divided between English and Scandinavian zones of control. While some of the former invaders decided to try their luck back in Carolingian territory, many chose to remain in eastern and northern England, turning their thoughts from plunder to settlement.

And so, after about a hundred years of raiding and conquering, the temper of the Viking Age began to change. This transition to settling and farming took place simultaneously elsewhere in the Viking sphere of activity. Whereas most of the initial settlers in England appear to have been of Danish extraction, the northern archipelagos of Orkney, Shetland and the Faroes were settled mainly by Norwegians in the late ninth and early tenth centuries. From here sailors ventured ever further into the North Atlantic. From the 870s waves of migrants from Norway and the British Isles put down roots in Iceland, the first permanent settlers on that island of ice and fire. Further south, a Viking called Rollo seized land at the mouth of the Seine before being formally granted it by the Frankish King Robert in 911, thus becoming the first Duke of Normandy. By the end of the tenth century, intrepid settlers had reached Greenland, and archaeological evidence proves that further expeditions even reached continental North America, establishing seasonal camps in what is now Newfoundland around the year 1000.

Meanwhile other adventurous bands of Scandinavians, this time mainly Swedes, were busily exploiting the opportunities to be had to the east of their homeland. As in the west, silver coins were the lubricant of trade. In this case, they were brought north from the Islamic world in the years leading up to around 800. The prospect of wealth drew Swedes to establish trading posts in the region of what is now north-west Russia. From there, they headed down the churning waters of the Rivers Don, Dnieper and Volga, trading highways that linked them to the other two superpowers of their world, the Abbasid Caliphate and the Byzantine Empire.

Again, as in the west, Viking activity blurred between peaceful trading, extortion and outright pillaging. A Viking assault on the Byzantine capital of Constantinople is recorded in 860, followed by another in 907 and a massive raid on the southern coast of the Caspian Sea in 912–13. Their audacity alone indicates that the Vikings of the east – the Rus, as they became known – were no less ambitious than their western counterparts. Indeed, by the late ninth century the Rus had created a powerful state centred on Novgorod in the north and Kyiv in the south. Founded as a Scandinavian dynasty ruling over a predominantly Slavic population, it seems that within a few generations the Rus had adopted largely Slavic linguistic and cultural traditions. Yet Rus princes through the tenth century maintained close political ties to their ancestral homelands. Further south in Constantinople, the heart of the Byzantine Empire, warriors of Scandinavian heritage entered imperial service, some becoming members of the emperor's personal bodyguard. Known as Varangians, they counted among their number King Harald Hardrada, who gained his 'embers of the hands' – that poetic kenning for gold – for services rendered during his time in Constantinople.

It's ironic that we know more about Scandinavians abroad in this period than about what was happening in their homelands. Despite the murky historical sources, however, it is clear that major changes were afoot. In the late tenth century, as Norse settlers were busy building farmsteads in the inlets of Greenland and Varangians were tramping through the imperial palace of Constantinople, Denmark was being forged into a unified kingdom. Under the dynamic and powerful Harald Bluetooth, who succeeded his father as king in 958 or 959, royal power grew to an extent never before seen in Scandinavia. Harald built immense monuments at Jelling to honour his departed parents, extended the *Danevirke* against attacks from the south, ordered the construction of the first and longest bridge known from the entire Viking Age, and peppered his realm with massive circular fortresses. Most significant of all was his decision to convert himself and – according to his own propaganda, at least – the whole Danish nation to the Christian religion.

The unifications of Denmark, Norway and Sweden into embryonic medieval kingdoms was a long and complex process.

But by the year 1000 Scandinavia had emerged from the fog of prehistory and was rapidly integrating itself into the European mainstream. Part of this 'integration' involved more attacks on England. In the 990s, a new wave of large-scale Viking incursions led to heightened prejudice against the Scandinavian minority in England. This minority would have included descendants of the original Viking settlers as well as more recent immigrants, marked out by language and culture as distinct from the Anglo-Saxon population. On 13 November 1002, King Æthelred of England ordered a general uprising against them, in what became known as the St Brice's Day massacre. We will return to this event in the chapter on 'Bodies'.

In 1013, after a turbulent decade of warfare and raiding, the Danish king Svein Forkbeard, son of Harald Bluetooth, invaded England. King Æthelred was ousted, and Svein was crowned king on Christmas Day. Five weeks later he was dead, and Æthelred was back on the throne. But by the end of 1016, Svein's own son, Cnut, was king of England. In this high-stakes game of musical chairs, it was Cnut who was the real winner, and he kept the English throne until his death in 1035. In that time, he also became ruler of Norway and Denmark, establishing what is sometimes called the 'North Sea Empire'. But within a decade of his death, Cnut's nascent empire had dissolved as England and Denmark went their separate dynastic ways.

From an English point of view, at least, the Viking Age is often said to culminate in the dramatic events of 1066. Three contenders for the throne – King Harold of England, King Harald of Norway and Duke William of Normandy – fought a pair of bloody and decisive battles that ended with William's total victory and the beginning of Norman England as a tidily distinctive period of history. As we shall see at the end of this book, the reality was more complicated, especially when we look past the borders of England. The Norwegian king was still fighting for dominion over Scotland and the Western Isles in the thirteenth century, while Orkney and Shetland remained the property of the Norwegian crown until 1472. The settlers of Iceland sustained themselves into the new millennium, although four centuries of effective independence came to an end with their grudging acceptance of Norwegian overlordship in the 1260s. Meanwhile, further west across the North Atlantic, the Norse settlement in Greenland was not destined to survive beyond the Middle Ages. Always remote and marginal, the colonists faced a cooling climate that made their agricultural way of life unsustainable. Communication across the ice-strewn North Atlantic grew ever more sporadic. By about 1500 the last farmsteads had been abandoned, and the last glowing embers of the Viking Age were snuffed out.

Society

Whatever else was happening in the world, people needed to eat. If they were lucky, they had enough to eat; if they were very lucky, they had more than enough. Farming was by far the most important occupation, the foundation upon which everything else – economics, politics, society – rested. This meant that land was the most precious resource of all, the most solid basis of wealth and prosperity, and the most obvious measure of power. It rooted people in the landscape. When Viking invaders in England decided to settle down in 876, they took plots of land in Northumbria and, according to the *Anglo-Saxon Chronicle*, 'proceeded to plough and to support themselves'.[9] Around the same time, the first settlers in Iceland were claiming land: the settlement itself was called the *landnám*, or 'land-taking'.

Where climatic conditions allowed, arable farming was favoured. Crops were the most efficient way of producing nutrients from the earth, and grain could be kept unspoilt for longer than meat. While this was possible in southern parts of

Scandinavia particularly, in many areas it was difficult due to the ground being rockier, the soil thinner and the growing season shorter and colder. These regions were much better suited to expansive pastoral farms of cows, sheep and goats. Pigs could be rather fussy about where they liked to live, especially in colder, more marginal landscapes. A pig rootling around in an autumnal woodland of nuts and berries, or in the muddy outfields of a farm, or in the excitingly squalid streets of a Viking Age town such as York or Dublin, was a plump, happy creature. A pig on a Greenlandic farmstead enduring a long, frozen winter was emphatically less so. Over time, Norse farmers creating new lives out on the islands of the North Atlantic adapted their mix of livestock to the specific conditions in which they found themselves. Goats and sheep emerged as the real winners. Other than keeping farm animals, hunting was common, particularly in more sparsely settled areas such as the Arctic climes of northern Scandinavia and Greenland, where animals were sought not just for meat, but for valuable tradable resources such as fur or walrus ivory. Where it existed – and it was sparse in the North Atlantic – woodland offered the chance to forage for nuts, wild fruit, roots, herbs and even edible leaves and tree bark in times of hardship. For those living near salt or fresh water – and that applied to many Viking Age communities – fish and other marine resources were often an important component of their diet.

Given the importance of food production, it is no surprise that the basic unit of Viking Age society was the farmstead. The people who lived on it tended to be largely self-sufficient. They grew, fished or hunted whatever they could, bartering with neighbours or itinerant merchants for anything else. Other necessities, such as textiles, tools and building materials, were also produced at or near home. Animals were exploited down to the last useful sinew. The majority of the population lived close to subsistence levels much of the time, although fluctuating between scarcity and abundance from season to season and year to year. Life was tough and unrelenting, kept up through physical effort in the face of an uncompromising natural environment. Their material world was one of wood, wool, flax, bone, stone, leather and antler, hand-wrought and fashioned, with metal a precious commodity to be treasured and recycled.

If a farm produced a surplus, it would likely be exchanged for goods or animals in kind, or the services of a specialised craftsperson such as a blacksmith or carpenter. Although coins existed in the Viking world, most people lived outside any sort of monetary economy as we would understand it today. As we saw above, silver coinage was used in the long-distance trade of luxury resources, and large quantities were also acquired through the more nefarious methods of raiding or extortion. It was valued not for its monetary value, but for its intrinsic worth as a precious metal, or bullion, and accumulating it was measure of success and influence. It is no coincidence that the largest concentration of silver hoards discovered anywhere in the Viking world – more than 700 individual hoards to date – is on the island of Gotland in the middle of the Baltic Sea, since it was a turntable for merchants and raiders travelling between Sweden and the east.

Although traders were never more than a minority in the Viking Age, they have left a strong archaeological footprint in the form of their central marketplaces, such as the above-mentioned Ribe and Hedeby in Denmark. They appeared around the year 700, not as fully fledged settlements, but as convenient seasonal meeting places and winter harbours for long-distance traders. After several decades, the trade routes were sufficiently secure and prosperous that some traders, perhaps encouraged by a local chieftain or petty king, chose to build permanent dwellings at specific sites, laid out in regularly spaced plots along the waterfront. These small communities, as well as providing access to regional and international trade networks, themselves became markets for local farmers, blacksmiths, carpenters, textile workers, potters and other craftspeople, and so their populations began to grow. Hedeby, for instance, was quite densely populated at its height between 800 and 1000, with a tidy grid of streets that was home to more than a thousand people, a forest of jetties projecting out into the water.

Such 'proto-urban' trading sites, however, always meant more to the elites than to most of the population. Later in the Viking Age we see a new wave of settlements across Scandinavia, this time deliberate creations by kings and the Christian Church, including Roskilde in Denmark, Sigtuna in Sweden, and Bergen in Norway, that would endure as true urban centres. Beyond Scandinavia there were similarly thriving cities with large Norse populations, such as Dublin, York and Novgorod. Each of these has revealed remarkable evidence to archaeologists, and we shall revisit them later in this book. Nevertheless, urban dwellers were always a minority in an age dominated by scattered rural settlement and subsistence farming.

Of course, our view of farming life so far has been a generalisation, and much depended on time and place. An isolated farming family in the Western Settlement of Greenland, for whom even bread was a rare luxury, would have a very different way of life from their counterparts in the fertile and well-settled hinterland outside the Danish trading town of Hedeby. Even the size and construction methods of houses varied hugely, from the substantial timber longhouses of prosperous chieftains to hobbit-hole Arctic farmhouses with insulating walls several metres thick, while roofs could be made of thatch, shingles or turf. In southern Jutland some farms were clustered together in uniform, carefully laid-out plots that formed what we might call a village; elsewhere in Scandinavia they formed loose hamlets with no attempt at regular organisation. As the centuries came and went, customs of building and laying out the farmstead also shifted. Whereas at the start of the period it was common for the many functions and activities of a farm to be combined in a single longhouse, to the extent that both humans and livestock slept under the same roof, over time there was a trend to separate out the different activities into individual buildings on the same plot.

We find similar variation when we look at households themselves. Generally speaking, larger farms required more labourers, and the wealthier landowners might have more hangers-on, swelling the total size of the household to several dozen. They were a minority, however. The average household was much smaller, centred on a nuclear family, with additions such as older relatives, foster-children and perhaps an enslaved labourer or two. This unit was deeply enmeshed in a wider network of kinship and alliance, formed by ties of blood as well as marriage, concubinage and fosterage, which constituted the primary identity for most people. It was certainly much more important than any identification with a kingdom or nation, which is unsurprising when we consider how weak the power of the state was in this period.

Without a professional police force, the enforcement of laws depended on the wider community itself. Hence personal security came, in the first instance at least, from the support and protection of kin. This is one reason for the prevalence of the inter-family feuds that often liven up the pages of Icelandic sagas. It also helps us understand why exile was such an extreme form of punishment. For many, being torn from the kinship network and thrown out on the mercy of a suspicious and hostile world was a sentence not far removed from death.

Not everybody enjoyed the benefits of a kinship network in the first place. This was no egalitarian society of free peasants; on the contrary, it was based on strict concepts of hierarchy. These are difficult to reconstruct and no doubt varied widely, but some basic points hold true. As we shall see in the chapter 'Unfreedom', an unknown proportion of the population was enslaved, lacking the legal rights and protections enjoyed by the free. Above them was the free bulk of the population, formed of landholders with varying degrees of independence and wealth, and above them a much smaller group of powerful chieftains or kings. Note that both 'chieftains' and 'kings' describe males, and this tells us another truth of the period, namely that women tended to be subordinated to men by the norms of a heavily patriarchal society. Beyond these essential points it is unwise to generalise. For example, even enslaved people were not all equal. Some were enslaved after being taken prisoner in raids or battles. Others were born into the condition or perhaps entered it through financial misfortune. They also had disparate functions in the society and economy, from undertaking the most tedious and undesirable tasks on the farm (herding pigs or goats, spreading manure, digging peat and so on) to working as a household servant, exercising manual skills such as baking, textile-making or carpentry, or even acting in positions of responsibility as estate stewards.

If we consider the position of females in society (as we will throughout this book), things become even more complicated. We can start with the generalisation that women, no matter their status, were more socially constrained than most men and were granted little opportunity to play a formal role in the worlds of law and politics. But beyond that, we are faced with a galaxy of different experiences and realities. A woman could be enslaved, free or noble; she could have a range of craft skills, or none; she might bear and raise children, or not; she could be literate or illiterate. Women may have rarely joined plundering expeditions (except unwillingly en route), but they would have been indispensable both back home in Scandinavia and in the various Norse settlement areas. After all, the next generation of Vikings had to come from somewhere, even though the surviving written sources have very little to say about the topic of childbirth. As we will see in the chapter 'Love', that such a vital feature of society attracted virtually no attention from authors itself tells us something about both the nature of the sources and the contemporary perception of gender roles. It also reminds us what we have to gain from venturing off the beaten historical track into the undergrowth of material evidence.

Religion

Anyone with a passing familiarity with the Viking Age can probably reel off the names and defining features of a few Norse gods. Thor with his hammer, Freyja with her cat-pulled chariot, the one-eyed Odin, the trickster Loki and others are virtually household names. But if we truly want to understand the Viking Age, this pop-culture familiarity might work against us. Over the years, film-makers, novelists and artists have selected, repackaged and made relatable specific bits of a world view that really *ought* to feel uncomfortably weird to a modern audience. Even before we start thinking about the Norse gods, our first task is to acknowledge this strangeness. This was a world in which the concept of 'supernatural forces' itself had no meaning, since gods and spirits were very much embedded in the physical world, as real and obvious as sunshine, wind or gravity. They might be invisible, but their power could be felt; and since they existed, perhaps they could be influenced.

When it comes to understanding the specifics, on the one hand we are very lucky. The Norse world converted to Christianity far later than most of northern Europe. This means we have far more information about their pre-Christian beliefs and practices than, say, those of Anglo-Saxon England before the conversion. But on the other hand, this can lull us into a false sense of security. We need to remember that our written descriptions of Norse pagan practices and beliefs come from outside the system. Texts from the Viking Age itself were written by Christian or Islamic writers from other parts of the medieval world. They tended to be openly repulsed by whatever they deemed 'pagan', and reluctant or unable to understand it on its own terms. Later texts from within the Norse sphere itself were written well after the conversion to Christianity. This makes it difficult to know whether these accounts actually reflect what people did, said or believed centuries earlier. In the case of later Norse texts, the bulk of them came from Iceland. This poses another question: how can we tell if Icelandic traditions were representative of the broader picture? We have so few scraps of scattered evidence that the temptation is to project the vivid and detailed Icelandic sources onto the entire Viking world and beyond, forgetting that there must have been as many differences as similarities across time and space.

Beyond the written sources, other scraps of evidence can help us build a bigger picture of genuine non-Christian beliefs, practices and traditions, even if this picture is still tentative and fragmentary. Archaeology, for instance, provides occasional snapshots that appear to reflect the later written sources, and we will come back to those in the chapter on 'Belief'. Less tangible evidence comes in the form of place names, as we'll also see later on. Finally, occasional written sources from Anglo-Saxon England and Germany refer to gods with similar names to those in Norse mythology. The Old Norse Odin, for example, is etymologically related to the Anglo-Saxon Woden and Old High German Wotan. This suggests that the Germanic-speaking peoples of northern Europe shared, at least to some degree, a centuries-old common heritage of pre-Christian myths and religious traditions.

With that in mind, we can make some important observations about Norse belief. The first is that we are not dealing with a doctrinal religion to compare with Christianity, Islam, Judaism and so on. Such faiths rely on holy books and other texts that define 'true' beliefs and 'correct' behaviour. They portray the universe as an epic moral struggle between good and evil. Pre-Christian Norse religion was different. There were no attempts to record a single 'true' or 'correct' interpretation, and while the mythology was full of good and bad behaviour, most of this came from the wayward gods themselves. Rather than specific doctrines being laid out, stories of gods and other non-human beings were embedded in myths and legends that together formed a tangled, ever-evolving oral tradition. We have no idea how far people believed these myths to be accounts of real events, as opposed to being entertaining tales with occasional moral messages.

The second observation is that certain gods seem to have been associated with certain characteristics. Hence Odin is wise and wily, powerful in magic, the discoverer of runes. He seems to have been the protector of the ruling and warrior classes. Thor, meanwhile, is a god of physical strength and protection. His name can be translated roughly as 'Thunderer', which implies a connection with storms, rain and the weather more generally. In contrast to the high Odin, Thor may have been associated more closely with ordinary farmers, and those embarking on risky sea journeys. Freyja, the most significant of the female deities, has a range of associations from love and pregnancy to war and magic, while her brother Frey is the god of growth and fertility. Then there is Loki, who is portrayed variously as a mischievously unpredictable ally and a treacherous agent of chaos. Besides these gods there were others who play a smaller role in the surviving mythology. Whether or not this means they were less significant generally is a hard question to answer, and we will come back to that again in 'Belief'. It may be the case that most people throughout the Viking world had less to do with the more 'famous' gods, and instead paid more attention to local deities and land spirits, their names now obscure or lost altogether.

Whatever the gods in question, our third observation is that rituals were involved in their worship or invocation. Some of these rituals were public, perhaps involving sacrificial feasts for a whole community, taking place at transitional points of the year or as part of funeral rites. Other rituals were more private in nature, involving the members of a single household or individuals. The fact that animal sacrifices were outlawed explicitly in the early Christian period, along with offerings of other sorts of food and drink, strongly implies that this was a long-established part of Norse culture. Where such rituals took place is equally uncertain. There is convincing evidence for major cultic sites, centres of power used for mass gatherings, such as at Uppsala in Sweden, even if evidence for what actually happened at these places is scarce. They were probably the exception to the rule, with most rituals happening on a smaller scale and in a very different setting. Unlike Christianity, which designated church buildings as proper places of worship, Norse paganism was largely a religion of the open air. Place names and literary evidence suggest the importance of groves, hilltops, outcrops, fields and meadows, springs, lakes and coasts, and artificial structures such as burial mounds.

Drawing the various clues together, we get the impression of a religion that was rooted firmly in the daily realities and anxieties of Viking Age society. A single bad harvest, a bout of livestock disease or a storm at sea could be the difference between life and death. We shouldn't wonder that they used whatever means they had to ensure their own security, including appealing to invisible forces. Placating or influencing gods and spirits offered humans at least some chance of controlling a harsh and fickle natural environment. Beyond this, rituals, myths and traditions had important social functions. They bound communities together by giving them a shared identity. Religious gatherings could also be opportunities to resolve differences or negotiate relationships between individuals or groups, to assert or challenge power structures. Meanwhile, funeral rites were important not only because of whatever beliefs in an afterlife people may have held. They also mattered because they helped the community to express its collective grief and allowed it to redefine its connections, knitting back together a social fabric that had been torn by the death of a friend or family member.

When Christian missionaries started to venture into the Norse homelands, it is doubtful that many of them viewed the indigenous religion with this sort of anthropological mindset. Conversion to Christianity was a long and gradual process, broadly happening between the ninth and eleventh centuries. Norse merchants and mercenaries would have been exposed to the Christian faith already through their travels. After all, most of the southern merchants who visited or settled at trading sites within Scandinavia would have been baptised Christians. Ninth-century Scandinavian kings, while not willing to convert to Christianity themselves, appear to have tolerated the presence of Christians in their midst, and (at least according to Christian accounts) allowed the building of churches at such places as Hedeby and Ribe in Denmark and Birka in Sweden. But it wasn't until the 960s that the powerful king of Denmark, Harald Bluetooth, converted to Catholic Christianity and started to impose the new faith on his kingdom. Meanwhile, in the east, the traditional date for the conversion of the Kyivan Rus to Orthodox Christianity is around 988. In the 990s there were Christian kings on the thrones of Norway and Sweden. Out in the North Atlantic and under pressure from Norway, Iceland and Greenland officially converted around the year 1000.

This simplified account is only part of the picture. The 'unofficial' story of the conversion is much less straightforward. The population of Scandinavia must have included Christians long before kings started to convert. Aside from the above-mentioned merchants, from around 800 Viking raiders were probably bringing enslaved Christians back home with them, although it is unlikely that enslaved people, low status as they were, would have much opportunity to impress the wider population with their religion. There is also evidence that Christians were among the first settlers of Iceland in the 870s, and not only as enslaved people. This isn't terribly surprising, since many of the Norse settlers came not from Norway but from Britain and Ireland, where Christianity was well established. Some of them had married local Christians, or had even converted themselves and become parents to Christian children: A similar pattern can be seen in England from 878 and Normandy in 911: when Viking invaders chose to settle in a Christian country, it did not take them long to change religion. Given that links to their Scandinavian homelands remained strong, they thus provided another possible vector for Christian influence across the North Sea.

Seen in this light, Harald Bluetooth in the 960s is merely one step, albeit a significant one, in a much broader, long-term trend of Christianisation. But it was not one-way. Although there were Christian kings on the thrones of Norway and Sweden in the 990s, they would be followed by pagan rulers in later decades. In the 1080s, there was a particularly nasty conflict between two Swedish kings, the pagan Sacrifice-Svein and the Christian Ingi the Elder, and the country did not officially convert to Christianity until the twelfth century. And meanwhile, away from the monarchy, it turned out that baptising people, persuading them to attend church and teaching them to recite the basic principles of Christianity was often the easy part. Certain behaviours and beliefs were rooted so deeply in culture and community, and fulfilled such basic needs, that they could not be eradicated. Good harvests still had to be secured, animals kept healthy, journeys overseas made safer, childbirths eased. Sometimes these roots stayed hidden under the soil of Christianity, sometimes they evolved over time, adapting through the Middle Ages until they emerge in a much later period to be labelled as 'superstition' or 'folklore'. In 'Belief', we will meet remnants of religious beliefs and practices from across the centuries, all of which tell us as much about continuity as they do about change.

How do we know what we know?

Our sources for the Viking Age lie in the thick parchment pages of manuscripts and buried deep in soil and water. They may take the form of ghostly thoroughfares that still give shape to modern cityscapes and landscapes, or the outlines of buildings traced in the earth. Some sources are cutting-edge and invisible, twisted up in the DNA of modern humans or laid down as particles in ancient ice cores. Others hide in plain sight: Old Norse words in the languages we speak and fossilised in place names. There are stories to be traced in the embossed surfaces of paper-thin coins, or carved with spiky runic letters into stone, wood, metal and bone. Each is a path into Viking Age history, and each has its own twists and turns.

The historical record is capricious, and what survives is largely a matter of chance. Most of the time we do not know how yawning the chasm of lost knowledge might be. At the same time, there is something delightful about the sheer randomness of a thing that has continued to persist in its existence, to come bobbing up to the surface centuries later. The quirks and vagaries of our evidence are part of what makes historical storytelling so compelling and multifaceted.

Manuscript sources from the core of the Viking Age itself – from the eighth century to around 1100 – come in all sorts of languages and scripts, precisely because the Vikings encountered so many peoples and cultures. They are written in Latin, Arabic, Greek or Cyrillic scripts, and in languages that range from Middle Irish to Old English to Old Church Slavonic. They include annals and chronicles, travel narratives, poetry and peace treaties, and the collective picture they paint is bold and colourful. But if these texts are roughly contemporary with the events they describe, then the one language they are not written in will be Old Norse. The sort of literate manuscript culture that gives us many of our written sources for the period only came to the Norse world with its conversion to Christianity.

This is tricky, because it means such sources were written from the perspective of those outside the Norse world, often on the receiving end of their worst behaviour. They were also written by those with different cultural backgrounds, different religious traditions, and the prejudices that these differences brought. In the case of western Europe, such writers were predominantly Christian clerics describing bloody raids by pagans on undefended religious sites or complaining about incoming settlers. And in the case of Arabic writers who encountered various incarnations of the Norse on their travels, we need to allow for their own interpretations of and reactions to unfamiliar customs, make space for misinterpretation and miscommunication. Yet without these texts, we would know very little about what went on during the Viking Age, especially when Scandinavians went out into the world.

Written sources from within the Norse world itself came later, once Christianity had reached the far north. This means that evidence such as Norse laws, mythological texts, genealogies, poems and saga stories only starts to appear in the twelfth century, while most surviving manuscripts are even later than this. The fact that any of this material survives at all is extraordinary and should not be sniffed at. And just because these texts were written down later doesn't mean that they hold no value for the earlier period. Viking Age culture was non-literate but had strong oral traditions. The problem is that oral traditions can be mutable, flexible creatures. Looking at such textual evidence from the distance of almost a thousand years, it is not always clear what facts can be distilled from these parchment pages. In the case of the sagas, for example, these written texts reflect a world view that we would not necessarily share today, in which the appearance of a mountain troll or a reanimated corpse would not be out of place in a historical narrative.

Language too can be a mine of historical information. Modern Icelandic is the closest surviving descendant of Old Norse, followed by Faroese. Old Norse – in its various dialects – is also the main ancestor of modern Norwegian, Swedish and Danish. But other languages, notably English, contain linguistic fossils that tell us about the history of cultural contact and influence, especially when Norse settlers put down roots in England. These Old Norse speakers gifted English with many common words that we still use today. Around 700 such words survive, among them 'scrape', 'skin', 'knife', 'hit', 'skull', 'leg', 'window', 'ill', 'die', 'ugly', 'scare', 'sky', 'law', 'egg', 'take', 'wrong', 'they', 'their', 'them' – even 'glitter', the word that opened this introduction. This tells us that Scandinavian settlers were drawn into a cultural matrix where Old English was the dominant language. Yet at the same time, there were enough settlers, and enough similarities between the two languages, that fundamental elements of Old Norse vocabulary and grammar replaced their Old English equivalents.[10]

Staying with the British Isles, other languages developed that were even more closely related to Old Norse but did not survive down to the present day. Norn, a form of Old Norse, was spoken in the Northern Isles of Orkney and Shetland throughout the Middle Ages and Early Modern period. We will pick up this thread again towards the end of the book, in the final chapter, and see what this language can tell us about Norse influence in this part of the world. But in other places where the Norse settled, such as in what became Normandy and Kyivan Rus, language tells us a different story. Here, the Old Norse language dropped out of the picture relatively early on, certainly compared to the British Isles. Ever the cultural chameleons, the Norse elements within these mixed social groups melted into the dominant French- and Slavic-speaking cultures. In time their language faded away, leaving virtually no trace in modern Russian or French.

Yet where spoken language is lost, place names may still survive. This is a rich source of evidence stamped onto the landscape itself, which can provide clues about who lived where, how they used the land and what they considered to be its most important or useful features. Place names might also hint at religious beliefs and practices, the location of cult sites, a local preference for a particular deity. Taking Yorkshire as an example, we can tell that place names such as Selby, Whitby and Wetherby are of Old Norse origin. Meaning 'Willow Farmstead', White Farmstead' and 'Sheep Farmstead', they can tell us about how the land was used and perceived by Norse settlers. Elsewhere, we glimpse in place names the individuals who lived there at one moment in time. Sticking with northern England, in Grimsby ('Grim's Farmstead'), Ormskirk ('Orm's Church') and Skegness ('Skeggi's Headland'), we likely have the names of three individuals of Norse heritage called Grim, Orm and Skeggi. Turning to the Nordic countries, we can tell that the mountain of Helgafell ('Holy Mountain') in Iceland was considered sacred, as was the island of Helgö ('Holy Island') in Sweden, although in what way is harder to know. We can guess that the island of Frösö ('Frey's Island') in Sweden was connected to the god Frey, and Odense in Denmark was connected to the god Odin ('Odin's Sanctuary'). The picture is often impressionistic, and it is hard to be precise about dates without further evidence. But it allows us to glimpse the land for a moment, through the eyes of its past inhabitants, and grasp something of what they would have seen and thought when they gazed upon it.

Although Viking Age culture was largely non-literate, the chief exception to this was runes, which lie at the intersection between text and object. In the same way that the word 'alphabet' is named after the Greek letters 'alpha' and 'beta', the word 'futhark' is named after the first seven letters of the writing system – ᚠ (f), ᚢ (u), ᚦ (th), ᚨ (a), ᚱ (r), ᚲ (k). Although they're commonly associated with the Nordic world, runes were used by Germanic-speaking peoples across northern Europe. We have already met the earliest decipherable runes in the Prologue, scratched onto the comb from the Vimose bog. This was written in a form of the runic alphabet now called Older Futhark. But in the seventh and eighth centuries, in the run up to the Viking Age, a reduced, somewhat simplified version of the writing system developed, now called Younger Futhark.

Runes are an extraordinary link to those who lived before and during the Viking Age. Over the centuries that followed the Roman Empire, knowledge of how to carve and interpret runes spread. And as we will see, in the centuries leading through and out of the Viking Age, use of runes spanned an ever-broader proportion of society. From the small intimacies of daily life to the grand sweep of history, runes were used to inscribe lives and deaths, preserving people's names, their emotions, their human-ity. Through runes, we come within touching distance of the people of the past: a kaleidoscope of voices, experiences, emotions, relationships and beliefs.

Away from runes, the physical artefacts as source material for the Viking Age range from entire human skeletons laid out as they were buried, to minute slivers of bone, flakes of pottery and fragile textile threads. It is often the case that one Viking's trash is an archaeologist's treasure, because a particularly rich source of evidence are midden heaps full of bones, excrement, fire ash and the broken cast-offs of domestic life. Occasionally, someone will strike it lucky and the treasure is actual treasure: jewellery, coins, buried hoards. Discoveries of this sort of treas-ure tend to make it into newspapers a lot more than a mound of dung, although as we will see in 'Bodies', sometimes a lump of poo can hit the headlines too.

With each generation of scientific techniques and technolo-gies, these old artefacts continue to reveal new secrets. Among the most established (and yet still revelatory) of these techniques is radiocarbon dating, a way of finding out the age of organic material that was first developed in the 1940s. It measures a radioactive form of carbon (carbon-14), which decays at a fairly predictable rate after a plant or animal dies. It's not a perfect tool, and at best results tend to give a rough age range rather than a precise moment in time. Marine-based samples – samples taken from things that live in the sea, or samples taken from things that have eaten things that live in the sea – also tend to show up as being much older than they are, because carbon in the sea is older than carbon on the land. This can prove tricky for archaeologists trying to date Viking Age skeletons, especially when the skeletons belonged to people who lived near the sea and used it as their larder.[11] Nevertheless, radiocarbon dating is an invaluable technique that has revolutionised how accurately we can link organic material to a point in the past. Its precision is increasing as researchers develop ever-more accurate equipment to measure the radiocarbon in their samples, and recalibrate data to allow for changes in the amount of carbon-14 in the earth's atmosphere.[12]

While radiocarbon dating centres on one specific isotope of one particular element, other types of isotope analysis can unlock other clues to the past. For example, by analysing the levels of certain isotopes in tooth enamel, it is sometimes possible to find out where individuals spent their early years. The enamel of adult teeth forms in early childhood, and the particular types of carbon, oxygen and strontium laid down in that enamel depend on factors such as the types of rocks in the area and the composition of rainwater. These isotopes enter humans through what they eat and drink, by moving up through the food chain. There are several examples in this book where isotope analysis has been used to pinpoint where an individual came from, and we will meet the first of these in the next chapter.

Science and technology march on, throwing up new surprises. Even the most unprepossessing archaeological artefact might reveal itself to be the secret star of the show. A recent example comes from L'Anse aux Meadows, the Viking Age site that was found on the tip of Newfoundland. When it was unearthed in the 1960s, this location was a game-changer. It proved for the first time that Norse explorers reached the edge of North America, just as the Icelandic sagas reported. At the time, a few logs of chopped-up fir and juniper wood among the archaeological debris were by no means the most exciting part of this monumental find. But very recently, researchers discovered that three of these wood samples bore the marks of a cosmic storm: a spike of the isotope carbon-14 from a solar event that took place in the year 993. They counted forward from the spike in the tree rings to the bark, which gave them the number of years between the cosmic storm and the tree being cut down. This told them that the trees had been cut down in 1021, giving them the only secure year when we know that the Norse categorically had to be present on the edge of North America.[13]

Other scientific advances continue to open up new paths in the historical landscape. For example, by taking large sample sizes from hundreds of Viking Age skeletons from across the geographical span, researchers have been able to explore everything from international migration patterns down to individual family relationships.[14] In 'Bodies', we will meet two pairs of relatives who have been identified thanks to these extraordinary advances in DNA research. One pair lay beside each other for centuries, and although they were discovered many years ago, it is only now that we know how they were related. The other pair died far away from each other on either side of the North Sea and have now been reunited.

Other evidence for the Viking Age is hidden deep in the ice cores of Greenland, which preserve a unique layered fingerprint of the earth's atmosphere year by year. Ice layers form annually and can be counted and dated just like tree rings. One of these layers contains particles of a volcano that erupted in Iceland, which can be dated to 871, plus or minus two years on either side. Material from this same volcanic eruption has been discovered deep in the Icelandic soil: layers of glossy olive-green basalt, off-white silica and dense, dark tephra. This distinctive volcanic calling card coincides with the first archaeological evidence for humans settling on the island, which tells us that the 870s were an excitingly busy time for Iceland.[15]

This volcano also makes it possible to corroborate elements of the orally derived testimonies that were passed down through generations of Icelanders and recorded in their later medieval texts. In the early twelfth century, an Icelander called Ari the Wise wrote an account of the settlement of Iceland, in a work called *Íslendingabók* ('The Book of Icelanders'). Here, he dates the initial settlement to '870 winters after the birth of Christ', when Viking invaders were devastating England. He cites his sources: Teit his foster-father ('whom I consider the wisest of all men'), Thorkel his uncle ('who had a long memory'), and Thurid the daughter of a chieftain called Snorri ('who was both very wise and not unreliable'). And thanks to a datable volcanic eruption happening at almost precisely the same time, we know that Ari was right to rely on the oral testimony of Teit, Thorkel and Thurid.

As this final example shows, often the most effective way to approach the past (where possible) is to combine different sorts of source material and expertise. This allows the Viking Age to shine as the multifaceted, flawed, glittering gemstone that it is. It also allows us to hold two ideas simultaneously in our minds that may seem contradictory: the idea of a pre-conversion Viking Age defined primarily by raids, voyaging and settlement, and then a longer Norse period where the cultural and political mores of the Vikings still had a great deal of power and significance, but were slowly transformed as they faded away.

Chapter 2

BEGINNINGS

Beginning 1 : Runes on the brain

Three beginnings, each several decades apart. Three artefacts from three moments in time, each reminding us that there is no one opening to any history. The first comes from the western coast of Denmark, in the early 700s. The second looks east from Sweden and across the Baltic Sea, around 750. The third takes us west from Norway and across the North Sea, perhaps in the early decades of the 800s. Each represents a step that takes us towards the Viking Age as we know it, and each tells its own story about those caught up in the flow of history. There are no names, but there are traces of humans through their physical remains, their writing, their possessions, their artwork. And we start with the most intimate artefact of all, a fragment of human skull.

This piece of skull is roughly rectangular shaped, with jagged lines on two sides where the bone plates once met. Measuring 8.2 centimetres by 6 centimetres, it's a touch larger than a standard bank card. It was found in Ribe, the earliest of the Scandinavian trading emporia, on the west side of the Jutland peninsula. And it dates from between 725 and 750, when the first rays of light from the dawn of the Viking Age were just peeping over the horizon. We'll come back to where it was found and why that matters shortly. But for now, we'll home in on the object itself.

A piece of human skull isn't an unexpected find when digging down into the layers of the past. But this one is different. Spiky runes scurry over its surface, and a neat hole has been drilled through the bone. The runes are not easily deciphered, but one possible translation is: 'Ulf and Odin and High-Tyr. Help is brought against the (male) dwarf and the (female) dwarf Bour.'[1]

A human skull may be the ultimate marker of an individual life, but there is little that such a small fragment can tell us about the circumstances of its owner's existence. The runes, however, are more forthcoming. They are witness to the gathering together of several cultural ideas that would come to

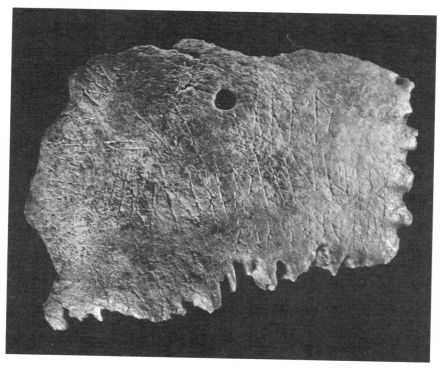

Runes carved into a piece of human skull, apparently asking three supernatural forces – including the god Odin – for help. Found in the trading town of Ribe, Denmark, and dating to the early 8th century.

define the Viking Age. Firstly, they are written in a form of Norse runes somewhere between Older and Younger Futhark, forming a bridge between the Viking Age and the centuries that came before. Secondly, they name-check the sort of supernatural beings that would come to be associated with Viking Age pagan mythology, calling on help from a holy triad of names where the most recognisable is the one-eyed god Odin. Of the other two, the name Ulf can be translated as 'Wolf', although what wolf this might refer to is up for debate. Meanwhile, the Tyr of 'High-Tyr' is indeed the name of another of the gods from the Norse pagan pantheon, and we will return to this shadowy figure later on.

There is no single explanation for the drilled hole. If the intention had been to run a length of string, leather or chain through it and use the piece of skull as a pendant, then this does not seem to have happened, because there were no traces of wear. If the intention had been a form of trepanation, that ancient practice designed to release pressure or malevolent spirits from the head, then it was only symbolic, because the hole was bored from the inside of the skull after death, perhaps with a knife.[2] Either way, from the inscription, it seems that the intention of the skull fragment is to be a protective charm against sickness and/or pain, seemingly caused by supernatural dwarves.

The idea of dwarves and other supernatural beings – such as elves – causing sickness existed in other parts of the North Sea region. For example, on the other side of the water, in what is now Norfolk, a little lead amulet has been found bearing Anglo-Saxon runes that can be transcribed as *dead is dwearg* ('the dwarf is dead'). This brings us to the broader significance of where and when the skull fragment inscribed with runes came from. It was found in the thick dirt and dung of a midden, outside one of the workshops of Ribe. As the oldest international trading centre in the Nordic world, Ribe was a hub for merchants and craftspeople from within and beyond Scandinavia, a melting pot of cultural influences and economic possibilities. From later Anglo-Saxon texts describing the first attacks, Scandinavian raiders seemed to burst violently onto the international stage without warning. As the Anglo-Saxon cleric Alcuin wrote to King Æthelred of Northumbria: 'never before has such terror appeared in Britain as we have now suffered from a pagan race, nor was it thought that such an inroad from the sea could be made.'[3] But when we look for the seeds of the Viking Age, we realise that they were planted long before the raids began. There had been Scandinavians on the stage the whole time. There had always been inroads from the sea.

The skull fragment dates to the first half of the eighth century, just when Ribe was taking its place among the powerful trading emporia of north-west Europe. As we have already seen, southern Scandinavia had been connected to long-distance networks of trade and diplomacy going back at least to the Roman Empire. But Ribe was different. It was a centralised hub for traders and craftspeople, specifically designed to foster international connections. Modelled on and connected to the North Sea emporia of Anglo-Saxon England, Francia and Frisia, Ribe was ideally and deliberately placed at the crossroads between the North Sea and the Baltic Sea, between Scandinavia and the Continent.

Built on the natural sandbank to the north and west of the river, the first town of Ribe sat a few metres above sea level. In around 710, when permanent buildings started to be fixed into the soft earth, they took the form of plots on each side of a main street, running parallel to the riverbank. Each plot was 6 to 8 metres wide, and most were inhabited by traders and craftspeople who left clues to their occupations in the sandy soil. Antler work (for items like combs and gaming pieces) and glass bead manufacture were there from the beginning. Both these crafts were destined to run through the DNA of the Viking Age: it is a rare furnished grave that does not contain at least a bead or a comb. Meanwhile, much of the early glass that found its way to Ribe was recycled from Roman sources, glass tesserae prised from the mosaics that once adorned now-ruined buildings. Over 7,600 such glass tesserae have been found in Ribe alone, showing just how much of this material was making its way north. Some of it had already been melted down in the Frankish kingdom, reshaped into cups and bowls, then brought further north to Denmark and used again. Around the time of the skull fragment, in the early 700s, the glass beads of Ribe were mostly white and blue. Later in that century, they would be transformed into a riot of confetti colours: reds, blues, greens, yellows, turquoises, some monochrome or transparent, others ribboned, swirled, striped and dotted.[4]

Alongside the glass and antler work, the artisans of Ribe were doing exciting new things with other materials such as metal, amber, bone, clay, textiles and wood. Meanwhile traders arrived with materials from across Northern Europe – ceramics, glass, slate, basalt, whalebone – and departed with finished products destined for far-flung buyers. Their presence can be traced in over 200 tiny silver coins – *sceattas* – found scattered in the soils of Ribe. They are very thin, only about a centimetre in diameter and a gram in weight. The most common of these coins is known traditionally as the Wodan/Monster type, on account of the glaring humanoid figure on one side and the twisted loops of a stag on the other. Part of the reason that these little coins are so important is because they have been found elsewhere too, including the emporia of Frisia and Anglo-Saxon England, showing the strong connections that ran between these trading hubs. They also suggest that, from around the time of the skull fragment inscribed with runes, the emporium of Ribe was being controlled by an important central power: a person or persons with the power to issue one set of coins and stop anyone else issuing other coins. Someone was running the show at Ribe and building up their own power and wealth in the process. This would set a precedent for what was to come.

Where Ribe led, other Scandinavian trading emporia followed. Within decades, there would be Birka in Sweden, Kaupang in Norway and Hedeby on the other side of the Jutland Peninsula in Denmark. Such hubs were the exception rather than the rule, and only a few thousand people in total lived in these four towns.[5] Yet their existence represented a major societal shift, a concentration of wealth, power and influence that extended locally, regionally, nationally and internationally. In these crucibles of international trade, craft and power, simmered many of the ingredients that would eventually bubble over into what we know as the Viking Age. And beneath these abstract, overarching ideas of cultural and economic development, networks of international trade and the birth of urbanism, we must remember that Ribe was home to humans getting on with their lives. This is what the fragment of skull reminds us. Firstly, it is a link to the unknown identity of the person it belonged to, the individual whose head was donated not to medical science as we know it, but rather to medical magic. Secondly, the runes and drilled hole remind us that the people of early Ribe experienced pain and sickness, identified a cause, and petitioned hidden forces for their help in controlling the uncontrollable.[*]

In such a beginning, we see the gathering together of many threads that would later be spun into the web of the Viking Age, not least runes and religion, trade and travel. But for now, we'll turn east from Ribe, look past the islands of Denmark, over the southern tip of Sweden, and across the Baltic Sea, where our second beginning is waiting.

---

[*] Or, to put it another way, they weren't sitting around thinking 'how fascinating to be here at the emergence of Scandinavian proto urbanism, sowing the seeds of what will one day be known as the Viking Age'. More likely they were thinking, 'my head hurts, how do I get rid of those bloody dwarves'.

Beginning 2 : Death in the Baltic

Let's try another beginning, still several decades before the first-recorded Viking raids on the edge of western Europe. This one starts with an Agatha-Christie-style murder mystery: a gaming piece in the mouth of a dead man.

The gaming piece is roughly the size of an apricot. It's made from animal bone, with an iron nail through the top that marks it out as the 'king' piece of a Viking Age board game called *hnefatafl*. This was a game of military strategy, where the king piece started in the middle of the board, surrounded by loyal defenders, and had to get to the edge without being captured by enemy pieces. We will return to such games in 'Play'. Placing the king piece between the dead person's teeth was a deliberate act of storytelling in itself. But who put it there and what were they trying to say?

The dead person was buried in a seagoing ship. He was a young man at the time of his death, somewhere between twenty-five and thirty-five years old. His skeleton is witness to his fatal injuries: brutal blade wounds on the bones of his left forearm and his hip. But he was not the only murder victim on board. He was one of thirty-four dead men, piled in rows and buried together on the vessel, their ages ranging from adolescent to mature. The party had been attacked. Their skeletons display the telltale cut-and-slash marks and puncture wounds of violent, brutal deaths. Arrowheads shot by their attackers were embedded in their shields, as well as in the wooden sides of the ship. In death, these round shields covered their bodies, like an articulated shell protecting them from whatever the vagaries of the world could throw at them. But the worst had already happened. Close by, a smaller vessel, more of a boat than a ship, contained seven more murdered men. Three of them still sat at their rowing benches, as if preparing for the voyage into the next world.

There were many gaming pieces on board both vessels – hundreds, in fact – made from whalebone, cow bone and walrus ivory, scattered among the bodies. On the larger ship, one individual had a complete board game set placed on their lap. There were also many other grave goods: dozens of fine swords and other weaponry, bear-tooth pendants, combs made from reindeer and elk antler, and coloured beads of glass, enamel and bone. Animal bones scattered over the ship were probably from the funeral feast: sheep, goats, pigs and cows. Meanwhile other, higher-status animals were sacrificed to join the dead, among them hawks, falcons and dogs.

The discovery of this burial changed the way we look at the start of the Viking Age, not least geographically and chronologically. For one thing, this mass burial itself dates from around 750, several decades before the first recorded Viking activity in the British Isles. For another, it was found on the coastal road that runs through the village of Salme, on the Estonian island of Saaremaa. This island separates the Baltic Sea from the Gulf of Riga. In other words, we are decidedly not in the west of Europe, with its more familiar 'Viking raiders' narrative, but right at the other end of the Continent, in the east.

Males, ships, weapons and violence. It still feels fairly close to the normal 'Viking' stereotype. But this was no raiding party gone wrong. Many of the swords they carried were bejewelled and high-status, not necessarily the gnarled war weapons that would have been taken on a hit-and-run attack over the sea. Hawks were also high-status, high-maintenance creatures that would have served no purpose on a raid. And while a raiding party might take a set or two of gaming pieces to pass the time at sea, they wouldn't need hundreds of them, and certainly not such nice ones. This feels more like a diplomatic mission with warriors attached, a doomed attempt to establish friendly relations and trade links with fine gifts and smooth words. Once again, we see inroads made through the sea, this time east from

Sweden, to forge links of trade and diplomacy with overseas powers.

This would also explain the individual with the 'king' gaming piece in his mouth. Because upon closer examination, the archaeologists discovered that not only did he have the finest grave goods surrounding him, but he had also been born with fused vertebrae in his neck, a painful condition that may well have restricted head movement and perhaps caused neurological difficulties. He may have been the leader of the pack, but it is unlikely that his position was based on his fighting prowess. *Hnefatafl* was a game of military tactics and strategy, and the aim of the game – for whoever had the king piece – was to get the king to the edge of the board flanked by his defending warriors. This time, they had lost.

Where did the dead come from? Isotope levels in their tooth enamel tell us that they came mostly from the region of Sweden around Lake Mälaren (near present-day Stockholm), stretching 120 kilometres from east to west. Others came from the island of Gotland, in the Baltic Sea itself. In other words, they were from eastern Scandinavia. We know that the first raids on Britain and Ireland were carried out by groups from the coastline of western Norway, not least from the pilfered artefacts that accompanied certain individuals to their graves. Here, several decades earlier, so early in fact that we have to reconsider what we mean by 'the dawn of the Viking Age', another group of Scandinavians were setting out in their ships, heavily armed and headed for foreign shores, but with very different goals in mind.

In the larger ship, the dead had been laid out carefully and methodically, rows of bodies stacked on top of each other. In one of these rows were four brothers, all killed and buried together. One of them was laid to rest with a beautiful sword, the blade inlaid with gold wire, the handle made of gilded bronze, its pommel decorated with twenty-five garnet gemstones. Tucked under his upper arm, the head of a dog, sacrificed to join her human companions in death. DNA evidence also tells us that the four brothers had another close relative among the dead, possibly their uncle.[6] What about the families they left at home, waiting to be told the news when the survivors returned? Each dead man was someone's child. Some would have had children themselves, or siblings or spouses. Many of these bones belonged to individuals who were loved, missed and mourned. And like a village war memorial where the same surname appears multiple times, at least one family was hit very hard by the disaster.

We can only guess at who was responsible for their deaths. Perhaps this was a turf war. The Svear (*Sviar*) were the dominant cultural group in what is now central Sweden. Their powerbase included the region where, according to their tooth enamel, most of the Salme dead came from. Further south, the Geats (*Götar*) were another cultural group with their own power base. It is possible that they were the attackers, objecting to Svear attempts to expand their trading networks and cultural connections further east. This would also explain why the survivors had time to bury their dead properly, unmolested by those who had just attacked them, since the Geats would have had no reason to stay behind after the slaughter.

Alternatively, it might have been hostile locals who were responsible. Later saga texts recorded in thirteenth-century Iceland include stories of Estonian raiders attacking Norse ships and killing or enslaving those on board. They also tell tales of skirmishes in the Baltic where the Norse are the aggressors. It is particularly tempting to connect the archaeological story of the Salme ships to the saga story of King Yngvar. He merits a chapter in *Ynglinga saga* ('The Saga of the Ynglings'), about the semi-legendary Swedish dynasty who claimed descent from the god Frey. This saga is the first part of a historical compilation about the lives of Norse rulers called *Heimskringla* ('Circle of the World'), written by the thirteenth-century Icelander Snorri Sturluson (of whom more later). Described as 'a great warrior and often out on warships', Yngvar is king over the realm of the Svear, defending his lands against attackers from the eastern Baltic and Denmark.[7] One summer he goes raiding around Estonia and is defeated by angry locals. A poem is said to have been composed about his death, including the lines:

The host of Estonians
slew the leader,
the light-hued one,
and the eastern sea
sings the lay
of Gymir to cheer
the fallen king.[8]

The giant Gymir is a rather hazy character from Norse mythology, most likely a minor personification of the sea. And before we get too carried away, we need to remember that King Yngvar is, if not mythical, then certainly a semi-legendary figure whose life is traditionally dated to the early seventh century, in other words over a century before the Salme ships. And yet it's not beyond the realms of possibility that the two are connected. History has a way of bending itself out of shape as it makes its way down the centuries.

For over a thousand years, the eastern sea has sung the lay of Gymir to the unnamed fallen men, its music drifting across the waves and onto the ever-expanding shoreline of this Estonian island, which grows thicker with age. The song curls through the slender trees and grass towards the ships and their precious cargo, buried long ago with such care. The cheerful tang of salt on the breeze would have reached them all: the leader with his stiff neck, the four brothers and their uncle, the individuals seated on their rowing benches, the sacrificed hawks and dogs, and the gaming pieces scattered over the bodies, cradled in a lap, placed in a mouth. And then, just at that moment when it feels as though someone is calling out to us from the past, almost close enough to hear them whisper over the sound of rattling waves, they are gone once more, vanished back into the past.

Beginning 3 : Scratched in stone

Our third and last beginning takes us to a place and time that feels more familiar for the typical start of the Viking Age: a coastal monastery on the fringes of Britain, around the time of the early Viking raids. Our object is a piece of slate, roughly the size of an adult hand, found down by the seashore. On it, someone has scratched a series of doodles, faint lines against the grey stone. At some point, the slate has cracked into at least two pieces. But the image is still clear, and extraordinarily expressive. In the centre, a tall, punk-haired, bearded figure wearing what looks like chainmail. He has a scabbard by his side, a long narrow body and spidery legs wrapped in crisscrossed bindings. Slung over his shoulder is what looks like a long, horizontal pole, almost like a fishing rod. There is something on the end, but not a fish. It's a diminutive human figure who seems to be very much alone. He trails behind the wild-haired warrior, half his size. There seems to be a rope around his neck, and perhaps a hood covering his eyes. His arms are stretched out in front, possibly bound together.

This mismatched pair are not the only figures on the stone. Nearby are the lower halves of two companions to the punk-haired figure, also kitted out in links of chainmail and leg-wraps, upper bodies and heads lost where the stone has broken off. On the right-hand side of the slate is a long, narrow ship, with around a dozen oars below and a square sail above. At the very bottom of the slate is what looks like a mast with a flag and perhaps another sail, before the stone breaks off again. The little figure and their captor are heading towards the closest ship.

The slate, commonly known as the 'Hostage Stone', was found on the tiny Scottish island of Inchmarnock. It's just over 3 kilometres long, over the water from the Isle of Bute. Known locally as the place where drunks were sent to dry out in the nineteenth century, its present inhabitants include herring gulls, greylag geese, red deer and grey seals. Once upon a time, it was also home to an early medieval monastery, nestled among the larger islands of the Clyde, a quiet little haven from the literal and metaphorical storms of the world. Our slate was one of many stones found with images scratched onto them: the grids of several dozen gaming boards, five tiny little horses (one with a rider on its back), a face peeping out from behind the arched columns of a church. Scored into other stones are fragments of male and female Gaelic names, and the line from a hymn (*adeptus sanctus premium*, which means 'the holy one obtained the reward').[9] It's a unique window into how monasteries taught their young novices to read and write, and how monks practised their hands before committing words and images to parchment. It's also an insight into the humanity of those who lived here: their imaginations, artistic talents and what they got up to in their spare time.

In the case of the Hostage Stone, a piece of slate is hard to date. But the style of the crosses and letters on the other side of the stone suggests it may be from the late eighth or early ninth century, in other words just when we know that other Viking raids were taking place on the coastal monasteries of Britain and Ireland. There is a long list of such locations devastated by Viking raiders during this period. Many of the attacks are recorded in written sources of the time: chronicles and annals logging events year by year, shocked letters of consolation and victim-blaming written to the affected communities. In north-east England, these communities included the monasteries of Lindisfarne in 793 and Monkwearmouth-Jarrow in 794. Off the east coast of Ireland, the holy community on the island of 'Rechru' (either Lambay near

Dublin, or Rathlin further north up the coast) was attacked in 795, and a shrine torn apart. That same year in the Inner Hebrides, the monastery on Iona suffered the first of four documented raids. Founded in the 560s by the Irish missionary Columba, Iona became the beating heart of Christianity as it spread to the Picts and Scots of Northern Britain. The Irish annals paint a grim picture of the destruction brought to this holy island by Viking raiders. They called Iona the 'Island of Colmcille' after its founder, who is also known as Saint Columba, which is the Latin form of his name: 'The island of Colmcille was burned by heathens' (802); 'The island of Colmcille was invaded by foreigners, and a great multitude of laymen and clergy were killed by them, that is, sixty-eight' (806); 'Martyrdom of Blathmac son of Flann by heathens on the island of Colmcille (825).[10]

There are no written records of an attack on Inchmarnock, which lies around 100 kilometres south-east of Iona as the crow flies. But it is possible that the picture scratched onto this slate is an alternative, personal record, an unofficial visual depiction of what was happening on the peaceful island sanctuaries of Britain and Ireland. Who made the image? Perhaps a young novice in the monastery? Are these scratches the memory of an actual event, witnessed by the artist themself? Do they represent the stories that passed between the monastic island communities – reports of looted sanctuaries, burnt buildings, kidnappings and killings? Or have we completely misunderstood the doodles, and might they be nothing to do with Viking raids at all? (Alternative suggestions have included an anachronistic reimagining of St Patrick's capture or perhaps even a holy procession.)[11]

If we haven't got the wrong end of the stick, so far the picture feels pretty typical for the start of the Viking Age. Tales of longships on the horizon, terror from over the water. But there are other beginnings that we could tease out from those scratches on the stone, other experiences and perspectives. For now, let's zoom in closer and find out what else is in the picture, or just out of it. Who else's stories might the stone be telling? Dangling from the captive's little wrists is an object that looks rather like a handbag. It seems to be attached with a metal chain to a belt on his waist. It's possible that the little 'handbag' is a portable reliquary or shrine, used to house the relics of saints – bones, hair, scraps of clothing – and carry them on holy day processions. To the Christian monks who protected them, these were containers for the precious objects of veneration inside, tangible connections to the holy women and men of the past. To the pagan raiders, the contents were irrelevant – what mattered were the precious metals, the woodwork, the glass and enamel decoration, as well as their conveniently lightweight, portable size. A looted reliquary was a tangible sign of adventures over the seas, deeds accomplished, treasures won. It also made an extremely fine gift for someone back at home.

For most of human history, great women have stood in the shadows of great men (and mediocre men, and bad men). Although there are no women on the Inchmarnock stone, there are certainly women in the story it depicts. To find them, we need to follow the reliquary itself, as it is carried down to the shoreline, taken onto the longship, and transported across the North Sea to Norway. The reliquary depicted on the stone bears a strong resemblance to other reliquaries produced in Britain and Ireland from the seventh to the ninth centuries (in other words, before and up to the early part of the Viking Age), all with distinctive 'house' or 'tomb' shapes, all small enough to be carried easily. Twelve of these reliquaries survive. Three of them ended up in Scandinavia, and all of them are associated with Viking Age women. This is not a coincidence.

Halfway up the Norwegian west coast, a little north of the city of Trondheim, lies Melhus, Overhalla, which is home to at least six burial mounds. The largest is an impressive 22 metres in diameter, perched on a ridge overlooking the River Namsen that rushes past below. Viking Age boats following the river from here reached a network of fjords, rivers and islands that kept them sheltered as they made their way south and west down the Norwegian coast. Finally, they could have crossed the open waters of the North Sea at the shortest and safest point, to the rich pickings that waited on the other side. At the start of the twentieth century, one of these reliquaries was discovered in the largest burial mound. This one is a compact little box that would fit easily into an adult hand, made from yew wood. Covered in bronze sheets with decorative spirals, discs and animal heads, it would have shone like gold as the monks processed it through their church, polished and glowing in the candlelight. Leather carrying straps were fitted to either side of the box, attached with metal fittings covered in red enamel and chequered patterns of coloured glass. No wonder the monks treasured it. No wonder a raider took it. No wonder it ended up accompanying someone into their pagan afterlife.

Inside the mound, no skeletal remains survived, only the objects the bodies were buried with. This is important: there are many difficulties in ascertaining someone's sex or gender – let alone how they perceived themselves or how society perceived them – when there are only grave goods left. But what remains does suggest that two individuals were buried in the mound, in a boat around 9 metres long. The reliquary was found in the middle of the boat, together with other items that suggest that it might have belonged to a woman. Certainly, they were someone of considerable wealth and status, buried with objects including a board made of whalebone (perhaps used to smooth and cut textiles), intricately decorated metal brooches and a necklace made of 137 glass beads and silver wire.

The reliquary found in the topsoil of the burial mound wasn't the only item in the grave that seems to have been the result of looting monasteries over the North Sea. The dead person had also been buried with two ornate pieces of bronze, one like two swirls of cinnamon buns stuck together, the other like a snake eating its own tail with a blob of red enamel in the middle. These were originally mounts of some sort – little decorative nubbins – that had been ripped off something bigger like an ornate gospel book cover, a liturgical vessel or, indeed, a reliquary. Once they had reached their new home, pins were added to the back of the mounts, which could then be used as brooches to fasten a cloak. This seems to be how they accompanied the woman into her burial mound, fastening a cloak around her shoulders.

The dating evidence points to this grave being from the early ninth century. In other words, the reliquary and decorative once-mounts-now-brooches were probably taken on one of the earliest raids over the North Sea. And here we come to the heart of a question that is very difficult to answer: Why? Why did the raids happen at all? And why did they happen where they did and when they did? There is no simple answer. But one piece of the puzzle lies in this burial mound, with the dead woman and her companion.

As we have already seen, in the centuries leading up to the Viking Age, Scandinavian society seems to have become increasingly stratified, with power, status, wealth and land concentrated in the hands of fewer (male) individuals. Alongside this, it has been suggested that these high-status men had access to multiple partners in the shape of wives and concubines, thus taking many of the available women off the table.[12] Adding to this problem, it is possible that there was a social preference for male babies, to the point where unwanted female babies might be abandoned or not equally cared for, thus skewing the sex ratio still further. This meant that young men slightly further down the pecking order (but still with enough capital and social standing to have access to a seagoing vessel, travelling gear, supplies and weapons) needed to accumulate status and wealth if they were going to stand a chance of establishing a household, finding someone willing to marry them and making some babies. A summer raid on an undefended wealthy monastery was a lucrative opportunity to make a reputation and a fortune.

In another part of the Melhus boat burial, a different set of grave goods – two swords, an axe head, a spearhead, a shield boss, a whetstone for sharpening blades – suggests that a further person had been buried in the mound. Since no skeletons survive, it's hard to tease out more concrete information, especially about their ages and the relationship between them. In the absence of evidence to the contrary, archaeologists have tended to assume that a haul of weapons in a grave suggests that the person buried there was male. And if, for the sake of argument, the vanished second body was indeed male, perhaps they were a couple. And if they were a couple, perhaps he was one of the first raiders. Perhaps she was already waiting at home for him. Or perhaps she was sufficiently impressed when he returned that she was prepared to give him a chance. There are too many ifs and perhaps to draw firm conclusions from this one burial, but even if this wasn't their story, it was certainly someone else's. And so, returning to the doodles on the Inchmarnock stone, what we really need to do is to extend it beyond the longships, add some wavy marks to represent the North Sea stretching east beyond Britain, and scratch the figures of women on the other side, waiting for these punk-haired young men to return laden with tall tales and treasures.

There is no trace of a skeleton, let alone a name, for whoever was buried in the Melhus mound. For another Viking Age individual, also with a valuable reliquary in her possession, her name is all that survives. Her reliquary is also made of yew wood, with bronze panels and enamel decoration, and once had carrying straps too. It dates from the eighth or ninth century, so from around the same time as its Melhus sibling. It was never buried, but at some point ended up in a Norwegian church, until it was moved to the Royal Collection in Copenhagen in the seventeenth century. On the bottom of the reliquary are roughly scratched runes that can be translated as 'Rannveig owns this casket.'[13] Rannveig is a female name, and most likely the runes were added in the tenth century, in other words after the initial raiding period and when the reliquary was already quite old. So, what is the biography of this beautiful little box, and the person whose name appears on the bottom? We can never be sure, but it seems to have had many afterlives since it left its original monastic home. Perhaps this was another item looted during the early Viking raids on the British Isles, brought back to Norway and gifted to someone special. Perhaps it was then passed down a few generations (generations that may have existed specifically because a man once returned from a western voyage with notches in his sword, some bling in his bag and a twinkle in his eye). Over a century later, it reached the hands of Rannveig, who inscribed her ownership on the bottom just in case anyone was in doubt.

Of course, not everyone got a whole reliquary when the ships came home. But it's interesting how many times – fifty-two at last count – the little scraps of decorated metal that once adorned reliquaries (mostly bronze, sometimes silver) turn up in Viking Age graves from Norway. Originally from Britain and Ireland, most of these have been refashioned into brooches for clothes and eventually buried with their new owners. Some of these items may have arrived through trade or gift-giving, but many must have been ill-gotten gains. Irish annals report reliquaries broken and plundered as the island monastery of 'Rechru' was burned by heathens in 795, and 'Inis Pádraic' (Patrick's Island) burned by foreigners who also carried off a reliquary in 798. When the great ecclesiastical centre of Bangor in County Down was attacked in 824 (the second time in as many years), the relics of St Comgall were 'shaken from their shrine', presumably so the looters could take the container itself. Other entries in the Irish annals describe reliquaries and humans both carried off by heathen raiders, perhaps just like the little figure on the Inchmarnock stone. The Annals of Ulster entry for 821 notes that 'Étar' (now Howth, a peninsula on the outskirts of Dublin) 'was plundered by the heathens, and they carried off a great number of women into captivity'. Just over a decade later, in 832, Tuathal, son of Ferdach, was taken from the monastery of Donaghmoyne, together with the reliquary of St Adomnán. Tuathal was an abbot of considerable standing, and the annals also record his death in 850, so he seems to have been returned at some point, most likely in exchange for a hefty ransom. Meanwhile in 845, Abbot Forannán of Armagh and his companions were carried off by heathens to their ships, together with their precious holy artefacts.[14]

So, what do we have in terms of human stories? Scraps, yes, but scraps of lives lived in extraordinary times. Some doodles on a piece of stone, discarded on the seashore of a tiny, now-uninhabited Scottish island. An unknown, unnamed monk – a novice perhaps? – from over a thousand years ago, whose casual artistic talents preserve the memory of a horror witnessed, or a horror remembered and recounted. The image of a captive scratched in a few deft lines, perhaps depicting someone who was part of the Inchmarnock community itself, perhaps representing all the Tuathals and Forannáns who were dragged down to the long-ships with their holy treasures. Also scratched into the stone, the captors themselves, young men with wealth and reputations to gain, families and futures to build. And on the other side of the North Sea in Norway, the women who were the keys to these futures, who would be buried one day with their exotic gifts from over the sea, or pass them on to future generations, into the ownership of descendants like Rannveig.

Chapter 3

LOVE

Bergen, Norway c.1200

The air is always sour and heavy with the smell of stockfish and fish oil. Inside the wooden warehouses, headless dried cod are stacked thickly like firewood, split stiffly up to the tail, the colour of yellow-grey parchment. Boats brought them here from hundreds of miles further up the Norwegian coast, beyond the Arctic Circle, where they hung on wooden frames, dried by the cold wind. Destined for sailors' bellies and far-flung cooking pots, these pungent delicacies have been making northerners rich for centuries. Honey, wheat, wine, textiles and glassware arrive in ships and are unloaded. Fish and furs replace them onboard and leave for southern lands. But the smell remains, mingling with the stench of raw sewage and rotting rubbish.

Too often, the world feels wet from top to bottom. The rain clouds envelop the mountains, dripping through the trees and mingling damply with the sea mists below. Down at the quayside, sluggish fjord waters slosh against waterlogged wooden planks, and creaking ships strain at their ropes. It's always noisy by the waterfront. Herring gulls cackle and wail as they fight for rotting scraps of fish guts on the jetty. The humans are no quieter or better behaved: shouting orders, exchanging news and gossip, bartering, arguing, laughing. It's probably raining. It usually is.

Everyone's shoes are sodden. Voices and languages curl around each other, their unfamiliar edges smoothed out by hand gestures and facial expressions. Local Bergen inflections mingle with accents and dialects from across the Nordic world: not only Norwegians, Danes and Swedes, but also Orcadians, Shetlanders, Gotlanders, Icelanders, Faeroe Islanders and Greenlanders. Then there are the travellers from Germany, England and the Low Countries, bringing more languages, more customs, more trade. Everyone knows the important words. *Skreið* for dried fish. *Skinn* and *húð* for furs and hides. *Öl* for something to drink. *Hóra* for someone to spend the night with. In a place like this, there will always be drinking dens down by the water. They will almost certainly be noisy, dark, smoky and smelly. There will probably be what would have been called, once upon a time, wenches. But mostly men. And lots of alcohol.

Inside one of these establishments, someone is getting very drunk. Back at home, someone is getting very cross. Her name is Gyda.

Down in the tavern, the drinkers, like the rain outside, are settling in for the evening. But someone has arrived on Gyda's behalf. A short length of wood is slid across the table

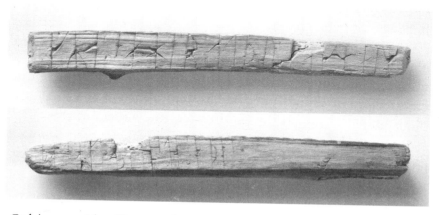

Gyda's rune stick, telling an unknown miscreant to go home. Part of the cache of runic inscriptions found after the Bryggen fire in Bergen, Norway, c.1200.

towards the errant drinker. On it is a message written in runes: ᚠᛆᛁ:ᛌᛏᛅᛁᚱ:ᛅᛏᛒᚿ:ᚠᛁᚠᛆᛏᛁᛦ, or, transliterated into Roman letters, gya : sæhir : at þu : kak hæim.[1] The recipient uncrosses his eyes, and the runes swim into focus: GYDA SAYS THAT YOU SHOULD GO HOME. Blearily, sheepishly, angrily, he takes out his knife to reply on the other side of the wooden stick and starts to carve. But whatever he thinks he's telling Gyda, his inebriated runes make little sense. And he's going to have one hell of a sore head in the morning.

For Gyda and many others like her, their names, deeds and flashes of emotion survive because they carved messages in runes onto scraps of material, most commonly wood – in which case they are called 'rune sticks' – but also bone and stone. These are not the intricately decorated, professionally carved runic inscriptions that we find on memorial runestones, intended to be read and admired by all who passed by. These are ephemera: the scrappy Post-it notes, everyday text messages and crude toilet graffiti of their time. And the biggest haul of these runic inscriptions – nearly 700 at current count – comes from Bryggen, the medieval harbourside at Bergen in Norway. They were found by archaeologists after some of the wooden buildings were destroyed by fire in 1955. The rune stick carved with Gyda's message is one of them.

As we have already seen, runes began life as an arcane, secret, elite form of technology, inspired by southern lands where the tides of empires rose and fell. We met them again in Ribe in the eighth century, scratched onto a human skull to ward off malevolent magic – still a pretty specialised use. But by the time we reach soggy medieval Bergen in around the year 1200, everyone from monarchs at the top of the pile to drunks down the pub seems to have been using runes. Much else has changed in the meantime, too. Norway is officially a Christian kingdom, and a church built in the latest European style looms over the harbour of Bergen. In contrast to earlier trading places like Ribe, this settlement is growing into a true urban centre: a showpiece of royal power in an ever-more connected world, the focus of trade, diplomacy and religion, and home to a diverse population. We've fast-forwarded right the way through the Viking Age, to the end of the period and beyond. Through the runes of Bergen and elsewhere, a cacophony of long-dead voices rises from the ashes to tell us their names, their loves, their losses, their secrets. They call us to connect with them down the ages, invite us to imagine them as recognisable humans with emotions and experiences just like ours.

Or so we'd like to think. But sometimes that's part of the illusion of history, and we need to be careful not to overlay our own inner worlds onto the past. Biologically, humans are very much the same animal that they were a millennium ago, with comparable neurological pathways, hormones and needs. But thoughts and feelings are conditioned by more than just biology, and the cultural frameworks, life experiences and social wiring with which we interpret and express our emotional ranges are very different. At the same time, if we want to get behind the official narratives and stories, we have to get onto our hands and knees and look through the gaps in the floorboards. We have to try to find the people who didn't get to tell the official stories because they were too poor, too enslaved, too young, too old, too female, too queer, too disabled, and so on. Sorrow and mirth, death and birth, all bundled up together, secrets never to be told, hidden in the cracks of history.

Gyda's rune stick dates perhaps to around 1200, when runes were being used widely, for all sorts of purposes, and by all sorts of people. Some of these Bergen runic inscriptions bear the hallmarks of inebriation. One carved into a wooden handle reads 'if only I might come nearer to the mead-house much more often',[2] while a cow bone has been scored with runes that mean 'now there's going to be a fight', followed by an undecipherable reply in another hand (perhaps a couple of drinkers about to witness a noisy punch-up, one too inebriated to carve a coherent sentence?).[3] Other inscriptions tell us that medieval Scandinavians could be as immature as the rest of us: we can almost hear the sniggering across the centuries as someone takes up their knife to carve: 'sit down and interpret the runes, stand up and fart'.[4] And from toilet-based humour it's only ever a hop, skip and a jump to genital-based humour, with a line of alliterative poetry carved onto a length of wood that might be translated as 'the vagina is lovely, may the penis serve it a drink'.*[5] Like all ground-breaking forms of technology, humans will eventually find a way to make it about bums and boobs.

Less racy runic inscriptions provide equally dramatic windows into other corners of human experience, especially those that wouldn't make it into the official records. Runic messages can be deeply subversive, telling us about actions and emotions that would never normally come to light. From Bergen once again, a runic message hidden in a wax tablet dates from perhaps the late 1100s or early 1200s. It urges someone to switch sides in a civil war, and although it's not clear who these people were, the situation was potentially explosive: 'I will ask you this, that you leave your party. Cut runes to the sister of Olaf Hettusvein. She is in the convent at Bergen. Take advice from her and your relatives when you want to come to an agreement. You are surely less pig-headed than the Earl.'[6]

Love and lust

Elsewhere, from Lom stave church north of Bergen, with its dark timbered walls and sloping shingled roofs topped with dragon heads, comes a message carved on a fragment of wood. Dating

---

* Alternatively, thanks to the wonderful ambiguity of the runes, the first part might be translated as 'the vagina is monstrous' or 'the vagina is ugly'.

from around 1300, it seems to be a message from a man called Havard to a woman identified only by the first letter or two of her name, possibly Gudny or Gunnhild. He is proposing marriage, but it seems that he's not her only option, because 'it is my full desire to ask for you' is followed by 'if you don't want to be with Kolbein'.[7] Once again, someone has attempted to conceal this message, this time by scratching out the three names in this potential love triangle and dropping it surreptitiously between the floorboards. Gudny (or Gunnhild) herself is a possible culprit – the wooden stick was found in the area of the church where women sat for mass – but we can't say what emotions were going through her head at the time. Fear of discovery? Confusion? Irritation? Embarrassment? Much of her reaction might have depended on her age, social position and family situation, as well as the general desirability of Havard (and indeed Kolbein). Young women often married for the first time when they were teenagers, and the degree of control they had over their choice of husband varied enormously according to their circumstances. Ultimately, their (male) guardian had the final say. Yet the law did allow them to divorce unsuitable husbands and leave with the property they brought into the marriage, while widows had more control over their destiny.

Other churches held other love secrets, such as the one at Bø in Telemark, around 100 kilometres south-west of Oslo. In the area where the choir sat, an alliterative poem was scratched in runes onto a wooden panel, perhaps around the year 1200. It's the ultimate cryptic crossword clue, where the runes translate as:

> I cannot sleep because of the sickness of the children,
> The worker's torment, the mountain dweller,
> The horse's toil, the wrecker of the hay
> The thrall's misfortune. Interpret that.[8]

To get this far, the reader must be able to read runes. But to grasp what's truly being said, we need to go deeper into their meanings. Each rune had a name that correlated with their sound. In order to interpret the poem, we need to decode each clue and match it to the name of a rune, and then join them all together. So, the rune name for 'ᚴ' ('k') is *kaun*, which means a sore or ulcer (the sickness of the children). The rune name for 'ᚢ' ('u') is *úr*, which means drizzling rain (the worker's torment). The rune name for 'ᚦ' ('th', often anglicized to 'd') is *þurs*, which means a giant (the mountain dweller). The rune name for 'ᚱ' ('r') is *reið*, which means riding (the horse's toil). Then we have the *úr* or 'u' rune again (the wrecker of the hay). Finally, the rune name for 'ᚾ' ('n') is *nauð*, which has a range of meanings including need, distress and bondage (all appropriate ways to describe the lot of an enslaved person). Put these six runes together – ᚴᚢᚦᚱᚢᚾ – and we now realise why the poet-carver can't sleep, because they spell out the name of a woman, Gudrun, which has been hidden in the poem.

Other such inscriptions are rather more straightforward in their messaging. South-east from Bø, over the Jostedal Glacier, lies the famous Urnes stave church. Outside, on its carved wooden doors, sinuous animals curl around whorls of foliage and branches. Inside, a rune stick was found with a short message: 'Arni the Priest wants to have Inga.'[9] Whether this was a confession by Arni himself or a scurrilous rumour started by a member of the congregation, we can't know (although, unless Arni was a particularly foolish individual, perhaps we should err on the side of the latter). But either way, under the sloping shingled roofs of these wooden stave churches, private passions burned.

With both the hidden civil war message and the hidden marriage proposal, it is clear that such runes were intended to be read by women, either directly (Gudny) or indirectly (the unnamed sister of Olaf Hettusvein). In the case of the 'Gyda says go home' message, it is likely to have been written by Gyda herself, in the same way that the marriage proposal starts in the third person ('Havard sends his greetings and his friendship') then moves into the first person ('it is my full desire to ask for you'). It is true that a larger proportion of these scrappy runic inscriptions seem to have been written by men (often for or about women), but others have no indications of gender, and yet others show the women doing the loving and lusting. For instance, on a piece of cow bone found down the coast from Bergen in Oslo, fragmentary runes are scratched that read 'Asa loves St——', where Asa is a woman's name and 'St' likely the beginning of a man's name such as Stein or Stefan. In this case, Asa's feelings don't seem to be much of a secret, because the final runes on the bone spell out the words 'ek uæit', which mean 'I know.'[10]

A multilayered inscription such as the Gudrun poem was one way to express hidden feelings that dared not speak their names. Other sorts of love and lust were much less likely to have been recorded even as riddling runes scratched onto pieces of wood. A substantial range of Old Norse words existed to express non-normative sexualities, identities and practices, such as *argr* ('perverted') and *sorðinn* ('fucked, penetrated'). These words crop up in medieval law codes as serious slanders punishable by fines, outlawry (exile) and death.[11] To insult someone in terms of their sexuality and gender was known as *nið*. The crux of the insult was that the victim was accused of transgressing the bounds of masculinity, performing a 'female' role by being penetrated sexually. In the case of insults directed at men, *rassragr* ('arse-penetrated') and *sannsorðinn* ('truly fucked') were particularly inflammatory terms.[12] It didn't matter if the slanderer was accusing their target of being penetrated by another man (in at least one case, a bishop), an animal, or even a troll. A related slur was to suggest that a man had been impregnated and given birth (to human babies, wolf babies, even troll babies). The real accusation was of acting in a way that would have been considered unmanly, shameful or cowardly. For women, the equivalent was behaving in a way that transgressed social norms, such as wearing trousers, carrying weapons, or being a little *too* keen on being penetrated. Insults aside, other terms occasionally pop up in the law codes that suggest not everyone was performing their prescribed gender roles, not least *fannfluga* (a woman who runs away from a penis) and *fuðflogi* (a man who runs away from a vagina).[13]

Of course, it's one rule for humans and another rule for gods. According to the stories written down in the centuries after the conversion to Christianity – around the same time that many of these rune sticks were also carved – certain pagan Norse gods were colourfully queer and gender-fluid. We'll return to them later on: Loki transforming himself into a mare, luring away a giant's stallion for a bit of sexy time, and later giving birth to the magnificent eight-legged horse Sleipnir. Thor decked out in full bridal regalia and Loki dressed up as his handmaiden, rolling his eyes as Thor complains that people will call him queer (that *argr* word again) if they see him wearing a dress. Whispers that Freyja has slept with gods, elves, dwarves and even her own brother. So perhaps it's telling that the only explicit punishments for homosexual acts (rather than homosexual insults) are found in a Christian context, from no less a figure than the patron saint of Iceland: Bishop Thorlak Thorhallsson. Written in around 1200, the *Icelandic Homily Book* begins with an imaginative list of penances decreed by Bishop Thorlak for acts of homosexuality and bestiality. These included flogging and might last for nine or ten years. Sexual acts between females were looked upon no more favourably than sexual acts between males: 'if women satisfy each other they shall be ordered the same penance as men who perform the most hideous adultery between them or with a quadruped.'[14]

It's a general rule of thumb that if folk are gossiping about it and authorities are prohibiting it, then it's probably going on somewhere.* But finding evidence of it at an individual human level is a different matter. When it comes to casual runic inscriptions, there's only one worth mentioning, and, as might be expected, it seems to be in the form of a crude joke between two carvers. The runes are on a cow rib, and they too have a late date, from around 1200. The bone was found in Oslo's old town district, down the road from the twelfth-century ruins of St Hallvard's Cathedral, St Olav's Monastery and Holy Cross Church. In fact, Holy Cross Church is even mentioned in the runes, although not because anyone involved in the message-writing was doing any praying there. The first hand asks: 'How did that message that you carved in the Church of the Cross go?' The reply comes back: 'Oli is unwiped and fucked in the arse.' The first hand carves again: 'That went well.'¹⁵ Once again, there's so much context that we might be tempted to fill in to make sense of this vulgar and childish exchange, but we can't. Who were the pair carving runes? Who was Oli? How would he have reacted if he ever read the accusations (which, if we're to believe the message written here, were carved more than once)? Would he have felt fear, embarrassment, horror? Or would he have responded with a knowing eye roll and a shoulder shrug? Like the insults prohibited in the law codes and the penances set out by Bishop Thorlak, the carvers are acknowledging a corner of human experience and emotion that must have existed but is often invisible in the historical record.

The runes scratched onto the cow rib are an example of the sort of messy gossip that goes hand in hand with the human condition, but rarely survives for posterity: hints of same-sex acts, affairs, indiscretions and one-night stands. Other inscriptions from various locations in Norway spill other secrets and emotions. One carver tells us: 'The clever woman lets loose for her lover, but folk still think she's a virgin.'¹⁶ Another remembers the good times:

---

* Although not in the case of humans having sex with mountain trolls. Probably.

'Ingibjorg loved me when I was in Stavanger.'[17] Another spills the beans: 'Clumsy-Kari and Vilhjalm's wife are shacked up together.'[18] Then there are people being unhappily friend-zoned: 'I love another man's wife so much that fire seems cold to me, and I am a friend of this woman.'[19] Some are less juicy: fluffy sentiments of the sort that might appear in a packet of Love Hearts: 'Think of me, I think of you! Love me, I love you!'[20]

Norway wasn't the only part of the Nordic world where people used runes to record their emotions, some of which allude to rejection or love affairs gone sour. A square weaving tablet made of bone, from tenth-century Lund (then in Denmark, now in Sweden), provides two out of three names of what appears to be a love triangle: Sigvor (a female name) and Ingimarr (a male name). The unnamed carver of the runes is most likely female because she carved them onto a thin square of animal bone used for tablet-weaving thin textile bands. The runes appear to form a curse, directed particularly at Ingimarr, where the translatable part reads 'Sigvor's Ingimarr will have my weeping!'[21] Another piece of bone, also from Lund, provides a home for another runic curse, this one apparently directed at a woman whose name starts with B. It simply reads: 'May a demon sort out B.'s cunt'.[*22]

As fellow humans, it is very tempting to fill in characters, backstories, emotions and repercussions to these messages. But if we do that, we need to bear in mind that we're likely to be holding up a mirror to our own experiences, our own emotions and the time and place in which we live. Looking at the past is like looking through a glass darkly: we can see shadowy images on the other side, but also our own reflections staring back at us.

* Whoever carved this very unpleasant message was not aware that, an entire millennium after the event, two academics would be writing snarky remarks about their sub-par rune-carving abilities. As Simek and McKinnell note: 'The carver seems to have been as unsuccessful in rune lore as he was in his love affairs, as he produces n for a by putting the correct twig on the wrong side of the stave (right instead of left).' (Simek, *Runes, Magic and Religion*, p. 144.)

Little ones

There are times when love and lust lead to sex. There are times when sex leads to pregnancy, and times when it doesn't. And both outcomes can prompt a range of emotions, from the very good to the very bad. Every single human living in the Viking Age was there because of sex and pregnancy. But it's extraordinarily hard to find evidence of the experience of pregnancy, with all its complex emotions and potential outcomes, in either the written or the material record. Partly, this is a consequence of the fact that, if you had a womb, you probably didn't have much of a voice in the official records, and so that limits the types of evidence available to us. But it's more than that. By its very nature, what would this evidence have even looked like? We're not going to have records of the feelings of delight, fear, excitement, panic, anger or resignation that might have accompanied a missed period. There are no records of the sort of knowledge passed quietly, matter-of-factly, between women: purple spikes of pennyroyal, yellow balls of tansy, and woody green angelica stems gathered to 'put yourself right'. More stories that would never survive because of the nature of who experienced them and who had access to them. We are right at the edge of what we can possibly know about the people of the past.

Neither do we have evidence of the gamut of emotions that might, under different circumstances, have followed the unwelcome arrival of blood, month after month. Prayers to the ancestors. Offerings to the local land spirits. Promises to the *dísir* and the Norns, female protective spirits, supernatural weavers of fates. Sacrifices to the deities Freyja and Frey, divine guardians of peace, prosperity and pleasure. More hidden things. Although, in the case of fertility gods, perhaps we can make a tentative link with a little bronze figure, roughly the height of an adult index finger, discovered in Rällinge, south-east Sweden, dating to around 1000. He sits cross-legged, sporting a big pointy beard, a big pointy helmet, and a big pointy erection. The identification of the statue as the god Frey comes predominantly from a description of the pagan temple at Uppsala in Sweden, written by the German chronicler Adam of Bremen in the 1070s. His account is best known for reports of human and animal sacrifices, which are accompanied by incantations so 'manifold and unseemly; therefore it is better to keep silent about them'.[23] Inside the temple, according to Adam, people worship the statues of three deities. Thor sits on a throne in the middle, presiding over storms, winds, rains and crops. 'Wotan' (i.e. Odin) sits to one side, warlike and furious. 'Fricco' (i.e. Frey) sits on the other side, whose likeness 'they fashion with an immense phallus'.[24] Adam describes how each god has their own personal priest, who offers up sacrifices from the people. If there is a famine or plague, sacrifices are made to Thor. If there is a war, sacrifices are made to Odin. If there is a marriage, sacrifices are made to Frey, presumably to ensure a fertile union.

We need to be careful with what Adam tells us. He came from another culture and country, he was a Christian describing pagan customs in another land and he had never visited Uppsala himself. But it's also true that he was based at the Church of Bremen in northern Germany, which was an important centre for missionary activity in Scandinavia. At one point, he was also a guest at the royal court of King Svein II, who ruled Denmark from 1047–1076. Adam had plenty of connections and opportunities to gather information about life, history and religious practices in the Nordic regions. Some of what he writes can be backed up by other sources. In the case of Uppsala, archaeological digs have revealed large-scale buildings dating back to the Viking Age that tell us that *something* was going on there. In any case, phallic fertility/marriage deities pop up in historical cultures all over the world, not least the lettuce-loving god Min from Ancient Egypt, and the donkey-murdering god Priapus from Ancient Greece. Whether the little figure with the pointy penis depicts Frey or not, fertility – of the land, of animals, of humans – was crucial to ensure the continuation of family lines and society itself.

Perhaps, wanted or unwanted, a pregnancy continued, bringing more complicated, hidden emotions and physical sensations. Among the euphemisms for pregnancy recorded in later medieval Norse texts are *þungað* ('loaded'), *ólétt* ('not light'), *eigi heil* ('not well'), and *óhraust* ('not strong'). It was also said that a pregnant woman *gengr eigi einsama* ('does not walk alone').[25] Always with her, a liminal being growing inside, felt but never seen, its sex and health unknown, hovering with its mother on the cusp between life and death. This creature that hiccupped and stretched under her skin might go on to become the thing she loved most in the world. But in the process of being born it might well also kill her, or die itself, or both. Biologically, the dangers and fears of pregnancy were very real. Emotionally, the desire and the need to control fate and influence outcomes was – is still – deeply instinctive. Superstitions. Rituals. Prayers to whatever gods, ancestors or spirits might be feeling benevolent. Little amulets tucked into clothes, fidgeted with to calm anxious fingers. Perhaps that was the purpose of a little piece of amber, barely the length of an adult's thumb, found in the Danish trading town of Hedeby. It's the figure of a baby, body swaddled with crisscrossed cloth, arms raised above its head, little thumb sticking out as though ready to be plunged into its open mouth. A thick tuft of hair sprouts from its head. It dates from somewhere between the ninth and the eleventh centuries, and it's ridiculously cute. Was it a talisman made to help someone conceive, to protect an expectant mother, or safeguard a newborn baby? Or was it a teething gift designed to give a fractious infant some comfort, the notched incisions of its body designed to be gnawed on by tiny sore gums?

Since runic inscriptions could be used to kick-start a relationship – to flirt, talk dirty, declare love, even propose – it's only fair

A tiny figure made from orange amber, perhaps a swaddled baby with a tuft of hair and arms raised above its head. From the trading town of Hedeby in Denmark, c.9th – 11th century.

that runes might be called on again further down the line, when the time came for any fruits of the relationship to make their way to the exit. *Sigrdrífumál* ('The Lay of Sigrdrifa') is an Old Norse poem that takes the form of a conversation between the Valkyrie Brynhild – most famous of those mythical females who choose slain warriors on the battlefield – and the hero Sigurd. It has a reference to *bjargrúnar* or 'helping runes', to be used 'if you want to assist and release children from women'.[26] These must be cut into the palms of hands and clasped on joints while asking the *dísir* (those protective female spirits) for assistance. Another poem from the same manuscript, *Oddrúnargrátr* ('Odd-run's Lament') describes the main character singing 'sharp spells' for her friend 'overcome with labour pains'.[27] These poems only survive in a single manuscript from medieval Iceland, the *Codex Regius* ('King's Book'), which was produced around 1270, nearly three centuries after the country converted to Christianity. They are about mythological and legendary characters – gods, Valkyries, dragons, heroes, giants – and not much is known about where the poems came from or how long they existed before they made their way into this manuscript. Even so, it's possible that they echo the sorts of beliefs, superstitions and practices that would have been familiar to generations of Nordic women, in one form or another, both in the pagan and Christian era.

So, do any of these 'helping runes' of childbirth survive? One possibility is a little fragment of silver, roughly 2 centimetres square, scratched with runes on both sides. It dates from the eleventh century and was found at Østermarie on the island of Bornholm in the Baltic Sea. The runes are clearly cut in the metal, but their overall meaning is harder to interpret. One suggestion is that among the seeming jumble are several that can be translated as 'Aki carved *bjargrúnar*', those same 'helping runes' as mentioned in that legendary poem.[28] The rest of the runes are tantalisingly fragmentary, but seem to include the name of another individual called 'Sigmod', and possibly a reference to a 'child's mother'.[29] Whatever the runes once said, a hole was punched in the silver square so it could be threaded and worn like a necklace or bracelet. It may well have been used as an amulet, bestowing power and strength upon the individual who wore it. Perhaps it was intended to be worn during childbirth. Perhaps it was meant for another 'helping' purpose entirely, another uncontrollable danger in the world to be counteracted through the power of runes.

The clearest use of runes to help with childbirth also comes from the cache in Bergen, although it doesn't mention the word *bjargrúnar*. This rune stick dates from somewhere between 1100 and 1393, and is written in Latin. Its Christian influences are clear, because it begins 'Mary bore Christ, Elizabeth bore John the Baptist, be absolved in veneration of them.' So far, we have read runic messages addressed to drunkards in the pub, potential civil-war turncoats, and possible future lovers. But it's only in the

second half of this inscription that we realise its intended recipient: an unborn baby. It seems to have overstayed its welcome in
the womb, or the labour might have been a difficult one, because
the message continues: 'Come out, hairless one. The Lord calls
you into the light.'[30]

Pagan gods and protective spirits might have been the first
port of call for labouring women during the pagan era. After the
conversion, they were replaced – or possibly their ranks were
joined – by several Christian saints thought to be particularly
effective in getting a baby out safely. St Margaret was among the
holy figures associated with childbirth. One might wonder why
a famously virginal young woman ended up with this particular

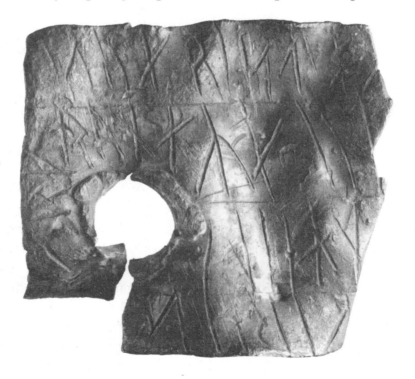

A tiny silver amulet carved with 'helping runes', including the names
Aki and Sigmod, and perhaps a reference to a 'child's mother'. From
Østermarie on the island of Bornholm, Denmark, 11th century.

job title, until we reach the part of her life where she is swallowed by a dragon and rips her way out of its belly. The graphic depiction of this incident in several medieval illustrations bears more than a passing resemblance to the famous 'chest-burster' scene from the film *Alien*, and if you've ever been involved in a birth, you may well find that your sympathies lie firmly with the dragon. In any case, St Margaret was particularly popular in medieval Iceland, where the very manuscripts containing the story of her life were objects of veneration and power. If a copy of *Margrétar saga* ('The Saga of St Margaret') was bound to the thigh of a woman in labour, it was believed that the baby would be safely delivered. Many surviving copies of the saga come in very small sizes, roughly the dimensions of a modern smartphone. This meant they could be held in the palm of a hand or, indeed, strapped to a leg, which is how they were meant to be used during a birth. The point wasn't to read the words – luckily, since that would be a tall order for anyone in labour or assisting with a labour – but rather to have it there as a talisman to protect the mother and her baby.[31]

Some of the manuscripts containing the saga also contain magical formulas, prayers to other saints, and garbled instructions on how to bring a woman safely through labour. Similar parchments and manuscripts were used in other parts of medieval Europe, with prayers to the saints for safe delivery, invocations against evil, and holy images. One of these, an English scroll from *c*.1500, was found to have traces of human proteins associated with vaginal fluids, as well as honey, cereals, milk and legumes (all used as historical treatments during pregnancy and childbirth).[32] It seems likely, then, that this parchment at least was used for its intended purpose. No similar tests have been done on the medieval Icelandic manuscripts containing *Margrétar saga*, but the number of copies that still exist and their diminutive sizes suggests that at least some of them would have seen action in the field.

It's extraordinary to think that so little survives of the very process that enables societies, cultures and histories to continue at all. Throughout human history, women – from the highest to the lowest social standing, under all sorts of circumstances, in all sorts of locations – have been pregnant and given birth, often in mind-boggling amounts of pain, always with the very real possibility of death or serious injury hanging over them. Yet so little remains that might serve as a witness to that experience. And so many who fell between the cracks of history are not only the

The opening page from *Margrétar saga* ('The Saga of Saint Margaret'), traditionally used to protect medieval Nordic women during childbirth. Events seem to have developed quickly in this illustration, because although the dragon is still gnawing on a fold of St Margaret's clothing, the saint has already reemerged up top. This version comes from the Icelandic manuscript AM 431 12mo, which dates to 1540–1560.

ones who were physically pregnant and gave birth, but also the many others who helped them get through labour, helped raise the children, helped pass on the knowledge and the stories and the values that would be transmitted to the next generation. The people, in other words, who were responsible for the fact that there is any history to talk about in the first place.

All the talismans, runes and prayers in the world couldn't save every mother and baby. Many women died in childbirth, and rates of infant mortality were very high. But it's hard to translate statistics into human emotions, to gauge how individuals and families would have reacted to these deaths. On the island of Rousay, north-east of the Orkney mainland, a young woman and a full-term infant were buried together at Westness, around 850–900. There is a good chance – although we don't know for sure – that both had died together, during or shortly after birth. They were buried with many beautiful and valuable grave goods, including a multicoloured necklace with several dozen beads made from glass, paste, bone and stone, and two bronze oval brooches, all probably of Scandinavian origin. Nordic settlers first arrived in Orkney in the first flush of the Viking Age, perhaps during the late eighth or early ninth century, so there's the question of how these beautiful items got there. Were they imported from Scandinavia, brought over as personal possessions, or passed down the generations? Other items in the grave – a weaving sword (used to pack threads together on the loom), a sickle, shears and a comb – were linked to the sort of domestic textile production practised by most women in the Viking Age. Still others seem to have been precious heirlooms, including an intricate silver brooch-pin decorated with gold, glass and amber. A fusion of styles and techniques from across Britain and Ireland, it may have already been a century old by the time it was placed with the woman and her baby in the grave. By this time, it had already lost some of its most delicate ornamentation, but it was still a precious treasure. Another item found in the grave might provide more evidence of what happened to some of the artefacts looted from Christian sites on Viking raids. It's a gilt bronze figure of a lion or wolf, leaping as if to pounce with its jaws wide open and tongue springing out, and it may well have come from a gospel book plate or a reliquary somewhere in the British Isles. After it found its way into less pious hands, it was cut into a little rectangle, a pin was added, and it was repurposed as a brooch. And here it found its final resting place, in the grave of a mother and her baby.[33]

We can tentatively reconstruct something of the biographies of these physical items: where they came from, when they were made, how they ended up in Orkney. But it is harder – impossible, in fact – to reconstruct the biographies of the emotions that accompanied this burial, and the relationships between the individuals involved, both living and dead. Among the fragments of bone, wood and metal that remain, the human stories have vanished. But the important thing is that they existed in the first place. For over a thousand years, the woman and the baby have nestled together in their grave on the headland overlooking the Bay of Swandro, sheltered by the even smaller island of Eynhallow just over the water. As in life, so in death. They were not alone.

What of the children themselves? For the most part, they're there as a low hum in the archaeological background of everyday life. A toddler's wooden highchair and a little suckle cup, both from eleventh-century Lund in Sweden. Evidence of some of the basic needs that a baby enters the world with, the cluster of reflexes that drives them to seek sustenance and physical comfort. But none of this tells us much about the experiences of individual children living in the world. Because most history is about grown-ups: big people doing big deeds. The voices, experiences and opinions of children don't survive very often, and the further back in time we go, the fewer children we hear from. To get a sense of a child with personality, imagination and agency,

A gilt bronze mount featuring a lion or wolf, found in the Orcadian
grave of a woman and baby. Made in the 8th or 9th century, it
probably once decorated a Gospel book, but was looted by Vikings,
who refashioned it as a brooch. Rousay, Orkney, *c.*850 – 900.

we have to transport ourselves to the faintest afterglow of the
Viking Age, to a place where Scandinavians had once settled and
ruled, but where other languages and customs and cultures had
come to dominate.

Novgorod lies around 160 kilometres south-east of St Peters-
burg in Russia, and around 900 kilometres north of Kyiv in
Ukraine. It sits on the northern shores of Lake Ilmen, from
where water flows north up the River Volkhov to Lake Ladoga,
and then west into the Baltic Sea. The Norse called it *Holmgarðr*,
which essentially means 'island fortification'. According to later
written sources, the first Nordic ruler of Novgorod was Rurik,
who set up his powerbase there in 862 and founded a multi-
ethnic state now known as Kyivan Rus (because the seat of power
shifted to Kyiv in the following decades). This was a melting pot

of east Slavic, Baltic, Finnic and Scandinavian cultural groups. A consciously Scandinavian cultural presence persisted for several centuries afterwards, in some parts of the region more than others. This can be traced through identity markers such as the names that people gave their children, the material evidence that survives from burials and urban sites, the use of runic inscriptions, and the connections that were maintained between the ruling families of Scandinavia and Kyivan Rus.

Novgorod was a swampy place with thick clay soil, surrounded by dense undergrowth and birch forests. As it turned out, this was lucky for everyone concerned. For the medieval inhabitants of Novgorod, birch bark made excellent writing material. For modern archaeologists, dense, waterlogged soil makes excellent preservation conditions for organic matter. Over a thousand birch bark documents have been found in the claggy mud of Novgorod, dating from around the eleventh to fifteenth centuries. Just like the runic inscriptions of Bergen, these tell us all sorts of things about the lives of ordinary humans: invitations, arrests, proposals, requests for shirts and trousers. They were written in the Cyrillic script, and in a form of the Old East Slavic language that was spoken in the region. Of the several hundred personal names recorded in the birch bark letters of Novgorod, a handful are Old Norse names, echoes of the melting pot of languages and cultures – both Slavic and Scandinavian – that had once come together to form Novgorod. The oldest of these names is Asgut, mentioned in a letter dating to the 1080s. Others date to as late as the second half of the fourteenth century, including Vigar, Sten and Jakun. But everything else about these letters tells us that these residents were fully Novgorodian, with no other markers of Norse heritage or cultural traditions.[34] For now, it's the middle of the thirteenth century, and we're in Novgorod to meet someone called Onfim. He was a mighty warrior on horseback. He was a diligent scholar. He was a wild beast that breathed fire. He was also a little child.

Over a dozen of these pieces of birch bark were the hand-iwork of Onfim. Some of these seem to be schoolwork: practising the alphabet, writing out psalms. But more of them are pictures and captions that invite us into Onfim's imaginative life, a tangible link to how he saw the world, himself, his friends and the adults around him. They hum with drama and – intentionally or not – humour, the sort of drawings that a proud parent might stick up on the fridge if their child brought them home from school. In these strips of birch bark, we meet Onfim as a curly-tailed stick-figure monster with something fiery or feathery coming out his mouth. We know it's him, because he has written, 'I am a beast', and 'a bow from Onfim to Danilo', so perhaps the drawing is a present for the friend he greets so courteously.[35] On another strip, Onfim has started to copy out the alphabet, lost concentration, and ended up with a self-portrait of himself as a stick-figure knight on a stick-figure horse, eyebrows stern as he skewers his trampled enemy with a spear.[36] Elsewhere, under two lines of carefully written religious scripture, Onfim's attention has wandered again. This time the result seems to be a portrait of his classmates, sat in a row in front of their teacher, all with the same stiff garden-rake arms (Onfim's artistic leitmotif).[37] No prizes for guessing what occupies much of Onfim's imaginative world, because he has drawn several other battle scenes, many with warriors on horseback, some rather grisly. One individual looks boggle-eyed with worry as someone advances from behind, arms raised menacingly. Even more evocative are a pair of warriors, one very short and one very tall, perhaps a stick-figure Onfim with his stick-figure father? They stand together, the mini-me warrior wearing an identical helmet, holding identical weapons, and contorting his face into an identical expression of bloodthirsty delight.[38]

But the most poignant of all Onfim's drawings is another small figure, nowhere near as dramatic as a fire-breathing monster or a warrior on horseback. They are holding out their little garden-rake arm towards someone else and smiling at them. The piece of bark has been broken off, and all that remains of the other person is a larger arm, their hand stretched towards the smaller one. I like to think that it's his mummy or daddy.[39] We don't know what happened to Onfim. Maybe he grew up to be a warrior on horseback. Maybe he grew up to be a scholar. Maybe he didn't grow up at all. But through a handful of bark scraps, stripped from a birch forest nine centuries ago, a child reaches out to us across time and space to share his world.

Sketches showing two examples of Onfim's birch bark artwork. Onfim the mini-me warrior (perhaps with his father) is on the left. Onfim the fire-breathing beast is on the right. Novgorord, 13th century.

Chapter 4

TRAVEL

The outline of a right foot, scored across two planks of wood. Five neat little toes, the smallest protruding at a jaunty angle. Five tiny toenails added in, meticulous half-moons. It's a petite foot, around 22 centimetres long. Today, we might expect to see a foot that size on an average ten-year-old. Even by the smaller standards of humans who lived in the past, it's likely that the owner of this foot wasn't fully grown, perhaps a young teenager. And, like many teenagers today, this one was bored. The big difference is that this teenager was a crew member on a ninth-century Viking longship.

This wasn't just any longship. This was the Gokstad ship, now an iconic image of the Viking Age. When Norwegians decided to build and sail a Viking vessel all the way from Bergen to Chicago, for the World's Columbian Exposition in 1893, it was the Gokstad ship they replicated. It's a sleek and supple vessel, with a bulbous hull made from overlapping oak planks, the 'clinker built' style so characteristic of early Nordic ship-building. Long, narrow and flat-bottomed, such a ship could ride the open waves and still slide safely into shallow sandy bays. It was built at the end of the ninth century, at the pinnacle of Viking expansion, an all-purpose vessel perfect for trading, raiding, even invading. On board, there were no built-in seats, so the crew probably sat on wooden chests containing their kit, clothes and keepsakes. On each side of the ship were sixteen holes for the oar ports and the remains of thirty-two shields, alternately coloured yellow and black, overlapping like half-moons. A woollen tent or sail with red-and-white stripes completed the excitingly flamboyant picture. But even for crew members sitting in one of the finest ships of the Viking Age, sailing across the ocean in search of adventure, fame and glory, travel could be pretty tedious. There was a lot of sitting around. And for one young crew member, it seems, plenty of time to do their nails.

The Gokstad ship had seen many voyages. This is clear from the oar ports, which had been worn down by the oar shafts that slid every time the blades cut through the water. But around a decade after it was built, somewhere between 895 and 903, it was sent on a very different journey, from over the sea to under the earth. A warrior's journey to the next world, which began inside a burial mound. The individual buried in the Gokstad ship was precisely the sort of person we might expect to find there. A 6-foot-tall male, violently killed, with battle blows to both legs that cut through to his bones. He was powerfully built, and in his forties when he died. Together with the ship, the other items he was buried with suggest that he was an important, wealthy figure with international connections: a gaming board, fishing and riding gear, shields, multiple beds and boats, a sledge and a menagerie of peacocks, goshawks, dogs and horses. For almost a millennium, the ship was buried beneath the ground, encased in blue clay and peat. Then, over the winter of 1879–1880, the frozen earth above it was split and broken by the two bored teenagers who lived on what was now a farm, ferreting around in the hope of discovering something interesting. Every historical era has its bored teenagers. Sometimes they deface priceless ships. Sometimes they break into burial mounds.

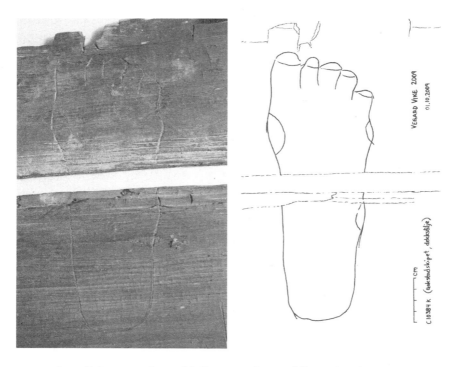

A small foot complete with five toenails, carefully outlined on two wooden boards of the Gokstad ship. Gokstad, Norway, 9th century.

The Viking Age world was extraordinarily wide: a web of connections that spanned cultures, countries and continents. This meant a lot of travel, in many different forms. Initially from their Scandinavian homelands of Norway, Denmark and Sweden, people set out bound for distant lands, and from these new lands the journeys continued. Their travels took them west to Greenland and the edge of North America and north beyond the Arctic Circle. Others travelled east down the tangle of Eurasian waterways that flow all the way to the Black Sea and the Caspian Sea, and to the powerful empires of Byzantium and the Abbasid Caliphate. For others, their destinations lay south, in the Mediterranean and the Holy Land. In those few sentences, centuries of cross-cultural connections, colonisation, warfare and cultural assimilation have been snarled and matted together. It's possible to fill an entire book with the history of Norse travels beyond the northlands. In reality, we're talking about people from different backgrounds, different centuries and different parts of the Nordic world, with different connections, motivations and purposes for travelling.

Travel wasn't a new thing, of course: thanks to the rune-carved comb in a Danish bog, we have already witnessed the long-distance movement of those living in northern lands during the era of the Roman Empire, and the connections and cultural influences they brought back home with them. But one of the defining features of the Viking Age is precisely the large-scale raiding, trading, exploration, colonisation, conquest and cultural assimilation that started to ramp up in the eighth century and continued to escalate in the centuries that followed. Most of these activities required ships, and so it is no surprise that when we think of travel in the Viking Age, the first image that springs to mind is probably ocean-going vessels: the sort of 'Plato's perfect form of the Viking ship' typified by the Gokstad ship. It probably isn't traders bumping over the desert sands on camel-back, destined for the markets of Baghdad. It probably doesn't involve boats riding the fearsome white-water rapids of the River Dnieper, which flows to the Black Sea through what is now Russia, Belarus and Ukraine, or less dramatic forms of transport like skis, horses and wagons. But these are all vital pieces of the puzzle: all part of the living network of Viking Age connections that stretched from the edge of North America to the steppes of Eurasia. So how to find the ordinary people in these extraordinary situations, and access their experiences of travelling through the world, its landscapes, climates and weathers? How to find the human tracks across the Arctic snows and desert sands, their paths over glaciers and mountains?

On water

First, down to the sea again. Because there's a reason that Vikings are so strongly associated with their ships. Waterborne travel was enormously important in the Norse cultural sphere. This is hardly surprising, given that it included the vast coastlines of Scandinavia, the colonised lands of the North Atlantic, the ribbons of rivers that took them far inland to raid and trade with other countries. Their ship technology and navigational abilities were second to none. These magnificently crafted vessels were rightly admired by the Norse themselves, many of whom seemed to have sea travel on their minds even in idle moments. For instance, among the slim rune sticks from Bergen, there's a chunkier branch of split juniper wood, dating from the second half of the thirteenth century. On one side it is carved with a fleet of forty-eight longships, some with long-eared dragon heads, some with weathervanes, all with beautifully curved prows and overlapping planks. On the other side of the branch is another ship, even more detailed and magnificent than the fleet that accompanies it, and a concise little line of runes that translate as: 'here goes the sea-brave'.[1]

Other examples of Norse ship graffiti are detailed and lively – testament to the imaginative and practical importance of seaborne travel to this cultural group. These include several longships scratched into the walls of Hagia Sophia, in the city of what is now Istanbul and was then Constantinople. During the Viking Age, Hagia Sophia was the greatest Christian cathedral in the Byzantine world. It was visited by Norse travellers who came to make their fortunes and reputations (sometimes through gainful employment, sometimes not so much). But clearly not all of them treated this great cultural and religious icon with the respect it deserved. The finest of the graffitied ships has a dragonhead on the prow. It rocks a pair of perkily upright ears, a raised mast and an enthusiastic but not entirely successful attempt at overlapping shields: thin lines that capture the spirit – if not quite the letter – of a longship from far-away northern homelands.[2]

Three thousand kilometres north-west of Hagia Sophia, on a piece of wooden plank discovered at Christchurch Place in Dublin, another vessel has been carved with a central mast, rigging ropes and furled sail. Perched on top, a human figure, who appears to be in the process of mending something. On another wooden plank, found just around the corner in Wine-tavern Street, the sketch of another rigged ship, this time with a weathervane on the top of the mast. And from the same street, a carved wooden longboat, only around 37 centimetres long, most likely a children's toy. Dating from the twelfth century, this beautifully proportioned vessel once had a tiny mast, sail and rudder, proof that you're never too young to start learning how to sail a ship.[3] Following the route from Christchurch Place to Wine-tavern Street, the road leads straight down to the River Liffey. Once upon a time, this river was the main artery through the

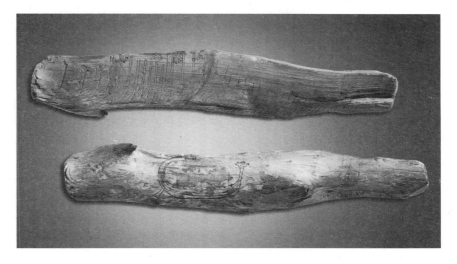

Juniper wood carved with a fleet of forty-eight ships on one side, and a more detailed ship on the other side together with runes that read 'here goes the sea-brave'. Bergen, Norway, 13th century.

town and further inland, a major thoroughfare for longships. The two planks with their ship-themed graffiti and the little wooden boat are a reminder of how ingrained such a form of transport was in the imaginations of those who lived and worked down by the riverside in Dublin, during the Viking Age and in the centuries that followed.

Just as ships and boats were built on different scales, so waterborne travel in the Viking Age encompassed everything from the local to the global. There were smaller rowing boats to scoot up fjords and down rivers, sturdy fishing vessels for sheltered coastal waters and choppier open seas, large warships for transporting invading forces and their weapons, and substantial cargo boats capable of crossing deep stormy oceans, carrying multigenerational families to settle new lands. When ships and boats survive down to the present day, it's normally because they were used for high-status burials (as in the case of the Gokstad ship) or because they had reached the end of their useful life and had been deliberately sunk to make sea defences (as in the case of the six ships that ended up in the Roskilde fjord in Denmark, with boulders piled on top to stop enemy fleets getting into the harbour). This can tell us an awful lot about ship technology. But it doesn't tell us so much about the individual human experience

Wooden plank with graffiti of a Viking ship complete with weathervane, found at Winetavern Street close to the River Liffey. Dublin, Ireland, 11th–12th century.

of what it was like to travel on a ship: the sheer physical effort, the hardships and danger, the camaraderie and exhilaration, the irritation and boredom, the homesickness and seasickness. Open vessels meant being drenched to the skin with saltwater and rain or getting sunburnt and parched. Storms and shipwrecks were a constant threat, as were the dangers of getting ill and dying at sea. While the Bergen runes that read 'here goes the sea-brave' probably refer to the magnificent ship carved into the same side of the wood, really they should refer to all the hardy humans on board. And yet – except for the image of the boat with furled sails, found in Christchurch Place in Dublin – most images of Viking vessels rarely include people.

If we turn to written evidence, few sources conjure up the sheer physicality of sea travel better than skaldic verses. Full of dense imagery and complex allusions, these knotty poems evoke the exhaustion, the danger, the excitement and the frequent bad weather: 'pebbles and the foul storm gnaw at the sturdy spike', as one poet puts it.[4] Rowing is hard work, the oars tearing free of the water's grasp as they rise, before violently pressing back down into the waves. We can almost feel the strain in our back muscles, the fire in our legs. We need to remember, of course, that this poetry is highly romanticised, likely composed during the Viking Age but only written down centuries later, mostly in medieval Iceland. An even bigger problem is that skaldic poetry is a high-status art form, largely composed for the powerful rulers at the top of the pile. As has been pointed out, this means that the elite often seem to be doing everything themselves in these verses: not only the owning of the ship, but also the steering, the sailing, the fighting, even the building of the thing.[5] It's the poetic equivalent of the Gokstad burial, where the key human presence in the tableau is the high-status leader.

And yet, through a foot traced on the wooden floorboards, a very junior member of the crew reminds us that the leader wasn't alone and wouldn't have got very far without everyone else pitching in too. Let's just hope that this same leader didn't catch them defacing their fabulously expensive, extremely high-tech ship with a sharp blade.

Leading stars and loose verses

When it comes to the real-life practicalities of sea travel, we can move from poetry to other textual sources, archaeological inferences and the experiences of those who sail on modern reconstructed Viking ships. From these we can learn an extraordinary amount. What seafarers ate and drank (mostly dried, salted and pickled fish and meat that would last for weeks, along with hard unleavened bread; beer, sour milk and rainwater). How they slept (when in coastal waters they might have had the luxury of tents to cover them, when on open seas they probably just hunkered down as best they could). How they went to the loo (in a bucket or straight off the side with a shipmate holding on to them for dear life to stop them falling overboard if the sea was calm enough). Then there's the question of navigation without the luxury of timepieces and magnetic compasses. Much depended on personal experience and inherited information passed down the generations. When they were in sight of land, familiar landmarks would have been crucial: headlands, islands, fjords, inlets, skerries. Out on the ocean, on a clear night, Polaris, known to the Vikings as the *leiðarstjarna* – 'leading star' – would have been very useful, likewise the position and quality of the sun during the day. Winds coming from different directions had different characters, different temperatures, even different smells. There would be hints that land wasn't too far away: the flight paths of foraging and migrating birds, the barnacle-backed acrobatics of whales, clouds piled above mountains that lay over the horizon, driftwood on the water, the scent of grass, trees and ice. Then there was the colour and texture of the sea, the swirling and ebbing of the waves, and countless other minute details that an experienced sailor would be gauging constantly, calibrating consciously and unconsciously. But it wasn't an exact science; open seas were treacherous and unpredictable, and many ships and lives were lost.

When ships were used for raiding and trading, the crews were predominantly male. Not necessarily the cargo, though, at least when it comprised captives being taken to the slave markets and bartered down the rivers towards the Abbasid Caliphate. But even when we're thinking about the sort of characteristic 'Viking' activities that colour our perceptions of this era, we need to think about the real humans behind the cartoon travel stereotypes. Not just the ones on the ships, but the ones left at home, or waiting on the other side of the water.

There's a *lausavísa*, literally a 'loose verse', preserved in *Egils saga* ('The Saga of Egil'), written down in thirteenth-century Iceland but based on older oral tales and murky historical origins. The verse is attributed to the star of the saga, Egil, a cantankerous and violent anti-hero who also feels his emotions deeply, loves his family fiercely, and composes poetry brilliantly. In fact, if we are to believe the saga (never an entirely wise thing to do, but in this case not beyond the realms of possibility), this verse was composed by Egil when he was six years old:

My mother said
I would be bought
a boat with fine oars,
set off with Vikings,
Stand up on the prow,
command the precious craft,
then enter port,
kill a man and another.[6]

This verse is full of the stereotypical activities and imagery that we might associate with the word 'Viking'. But the most interesting line is the first one. The possibility that this verse might have been composed by a six-year-old child, and the fact that it opens with the words 'my mother said', reminds us that sea travel in the Norse world was about far more than the stereotype of adult male aggressors in longships. Even when this was indeed what was going on, their actions were part of a web of familial and cultural connections, often with women and children at the centre, that transmitted cultural values down the generations through stories and songs, through children's toys, through images carved into wood and scrawled onto walls.

For longer-distance travel, for example in the case of exploration and settlement, women, children, older people and animals all had their places on board. Not all ships made it to where they were going, but it's hard to gauge just how many were lost at sea. When Erik the Red set out with his family and followers in 985 to build new lives in Greenland, it was said that twenty-five ships left Iceland. According to *Landnámabók* ('The Book of Settlement'), written in thirteenth-century Iceland, almost half the ships that set out didn't make it to their destination: 'According to learned men, about twenty-five ships set out for Greenland that summer from Breidafjord and Borgarfjord, but only fourteen completed the voyage. Some of them were driven back, and others were lost at sea.'[7]

This is a brutal attrition rate, and each vanished ship represented dozens of human lives lost, hopes and fortunes dashed, and families shattered. But for the most part there's no way we can access their stories. And even when the ships did make it to the other side safely, not all those on board did. In one wooden coffin found in the Norse graveyard of Herjolfsnes, close to the southernmost tip of Greenland, there was no body, only a wooden stick carved with runes. They read: 'This woman, who was called Gudveig, was laid overboard in the Greenland Sea.'[8]

Having died on the voyage, it seems, this was as close to a burial as her fellow travellers could give her.

Even if individuals made it to the other side of a vast open ocean, as in the case of the crossing to Greenland, there might be harder, more dangerous travels waiting for them and their descendants. The Norse Greenlanders lived in two main settlements located on the west coast of the country. The larger one was called the 'Eastern Settlement', close to the southern tip of Greenland. This includes Herjolfsnes graveyard with Gudveig's rune stick, and this will not be the last time we visit it. The smaller settlement was called the 'Western Settlement', around 500 kilometres further up the coast (in the fjords around the modern-day capital city of Nuuk). It was in these settlements that the Norse Greenlanders built their farmsteads and lived their lives. But the real riches that Greenland had to offer came from further up the coast, beyond the Arctic Circle. The frozen icy fjords of the 'Northern Hunting Grounds', as the Norse referred to them, in the area now called Disko Bay, were home to walrus colonies with their immensely valuable ivory tusks. Greenlandic walrus ivory was the white gold of the Viking Age, and has been found in places as far away as Kyiv and Novgorod.[9] If it got as far as what is now Ukraine and Russia, there is a good chance that it was also being traded further afield, to centres of culture and wealth like Byzantium and Baghdad, where Arabic writers referred to it as 'fish teeth'. Walrus ivory was used to create extraordinarily intricate pieces of art in the workshops

A rune stick from Norse Greenland found in an empty grave, with runes that read 'This woman, who was called Gudveig, was laid overboard in the Greenland Sea.' Herjolfsnes, Greenland, c.1300.

of Dublin, Trondheim, Bergen and further afield. These were high-status artefacts bound for ecclesiastical institutions, monarchs and other wealthy individuals. Walrus hide also made incredibly strong rope, which was perfect for seagoing ships. But someone much further down the pecking order had to go and get the raw materials in the first place. And it was a long, dangerous journey, which, if the hunters were lucky, finished with an attack on a formidably aggressive, be-tusked and be-whiskered sea mammal that could reach 3 metres in length and 2 tons in weight.

As time went on, it seems that the Norse Greenlanders overextended themselves and wiped out too much of the walrus population.[10] This means that they had to travel further afield into ever-more dangerous Arctic regions to find their prey. Perhaps this explains one of the most extraordinary runic inscriptions ever discovered, almost 500 kilometres *further* north than Disko Bay, on the uninhabited rocky island of Kingittorsuaq. On the highest point of the island are three cairns arranged in an equilateral triangle, traditionally built as way-markers for travellers. In one of the cairns was a triangular slab of grey stone,

Runes carved by Erling, Bjarni and Eindridi, who found themselves on the rocky island of Kingittorsuaq, far to the north of the Norse Greenlandic settlements. Greenland, c.12th–14th century.

carved with runes that can be translated as: 'Erling Sighvatsson and Bjarni Thordarson and Eindridi Oddsson built these cairns the Saturday before Rogation Day.'[11] Several undecipherable, cryptic rune marks follow. This was the first runic inscription to be found in Greenland, back in 1821. It is hard to date and might have been carved anywhere from the mid-twelfth to the mid-fourteenth century. But this does fit with the possibility that those on the hunt for walrus were having to go further and further up the coast as their supplies dwindled, and the fact that they were so high up in the Arctic in April (which is when Rogation Day falls in the liturgical calendar) suggests they had been there all winter. We don't know the fate of these Arctic hunters, whether they made it back to the settlements or whether they were lost to the icy whiteness. But we have three names, a location, and a moment in time, that reminds us of the individual human stories that came together to spin a web of international trade and travel, spanning thousands of kilometres from Arctic Greenland to Byzantium, Baghdad and beyond.

On land

For most people living in the Viking Age and the centuries that followed, their experience of travel was most often a case of local practicality. There were family and friends to be visited and assemblies to be attended. Livestock had to be transported from lower-lying farms to high summer pastures. Fuel and fodder had to be gathered, fish had to be caught and wild animals hunted. Goods had to be transported to be sold, bought and bartered.

Different regions and landscapes presented different physical challenges and advantages: the glaciers and rocky lava fields of Iceland with their sharp black rocks and fuzzy green moss, the deep fjords and jagged mountains of the Norwegian coastline, the low-lying bogs and marshes of Denmark, the wide lakes and deep forests of Sweden. Snow, ice, rivers and mud all had to be navigated. In fact, land travel could be even more challenging than sea travel. Depending on the terrain and time of year, it required a combination of sturdy boots and walking sticks, horses, wagons and sledges, rowing boats and wooden skis. When these items survive in the archaeological record, they can tell us more about the technology of travel. But to understand more about the experience of those travelling overland, to try to find the human stories behind the artefacts, we need to leave the open seas and sheltered fjords and lift up our eyes to a lost mountain pass, frozen in time.

Thousands of lumps of damp horse dung, scattered across the dirty brown ice and rocky ground. When they arrived, the glacial archaeologists had to watch where they put their feet. After all, this was ancient and venerable excrement, dating back to the Viking Age, and some even older. Once upon a time, sturdy little horses came over this mountain pass, pulling loaded sledges, carrying humans of various shapes and sizes, stamping down the snow to lead other farm animals to and from the high summer pastures. They left their poo, frozen in the ice, where it remained for over a thousand years. And sometimes they left their bodies too, when injury or exhaustion stopped them in their tracks. Also left behind were personal items that tell us about the human travellers who crossed this high mountain pass. A ninth-century mitten, woven and patched together from different textiles, its snug little thumb gusset revealing that it belonged on someone's left hand. A stout shoe made from animal hide, with long laces to secure it in place. Dating from the eleventh century, the animal hairs were left on the outside of the leather, to give its owner some forward traction when they were walking, and prevent them slipping on the snow. And, from around 1000, a wooden walking stick. If we are in any doubt as to who it belonged to, there are runes carved on the shaft that seem to read 'Ivar owns this.'[12]

All these items – and many hundreds more besides – come from the Lendbreen ice patch, high up in the mountains that run like a spine through central Norway. As climate change bites and the world continues to warm up, they appear with the meltwater on the bare, black rock. These organic scraps of the past have been miraculously preserved through the centuries. But now time is unfrozen, and the decomposition process restarts. Glacial archaeology is a race against the clock: a bittersweet celebration of what has been found because of what is being lost.[13]

The mountain pass running through the ice patch was part of an ancient highway. It wound through the deep valley of Skjåk, nestled between craggy peaks on both sides, cut through with the looping glacial waters of the River Otta. From there, the trail led upwards to a craggy mountain pass, which made its steady way through the mountains and summer farms towards the coastal fjords. This was a route mostly used through late winter, spring and early summer, when the blanketing snow and smooth ice made it easier to travel with sledges and skis, transporting goods over long distances. More than 100 stone cairns mark the way across the pass and its immediate vicinity, together with a stone shelter for when conditions became too treacherous. This was a major travel artery, a local track for farming families heading up to and down from their summer pastures, and a longer-distance road for traders and travellers bound for other parts of the country and across the sea. Also suspended in the ice were other items that paint a picture of what was being taken back and forth from the summer farms. There was leaf fodder – birch twigs – to keep the animals going over winter, a bit made of juniper wood (to stop young animals suckling their mothers and using up all the milk), a birch bark container full of raw wool, a scythe for cutting grass, a whisk perhaps for cooking or making butter, and a distaff for spinning wool. When we think of Viking Age travellers, this was the reality for most people. Not cutting-edge ships sailing the high seas, but extended family groups travelling shorter distances between their farmsteads and pastures, as they had done for many generations, dealing with everything from misplaced mittens and lost farm produce to injured animals and treacherous mountain storms.[14]

The mountain pass was used by travellers long before the Viking Age. One of the most extraordinary early discoveries was a complete woollen tunic, well worn, mended and patched up, dating from the third or fourth century.[15] An even older find testifies to humans moving through these snowy mountains as early as the Late Bronze Age, around 650 BCE. A wooden object roughly a metre long and 20 centimetres wide was found in four pieces, which appeared as the ice melted over several years. Originally, it was probably lined with fur underneath to provide traction, and likely to have been used as a ski or a snowshoe.[16] The pass continued to be travelled throughout the Middle Ages before it was gradually forgotten, possibly going out of regular usage during the social rupture of the Black Death. But it was during the Viking Age – especially around 1000 CE – that the transport route was used most heavily, in an age of increased mobility and centralisation.

There were other passes through the mountains, some still known about and some doubtless forgotten. As the ice disappears, other discoveries continue to appear in the meltwater. Around 30 kilometres north of Lendbreen, as the crow flies, is the mountain Digervarden. Here, two wooden skis from the run-up to the Viking Age – the early eighth century – were found, with twisted birch bindings to support the wearer's toes, and leather straps to secure their heels.[17] Journeys through the snow and ice were a fundamental part of life for those living in these mountainous northern climes, and a crucial part of travel not only in the Viking Age but in the many centuries before and after. Skiing was a vital way to get around and also to hunt in a wintry, snowbound landscape. Spooling forward in time over 500 years from the point at which the Digervarden skis were in use,

Archaeologist Runar Hole holding a wooden ski from the
dawn of the Viking Age, found in the Digervarden ice patch
in Reinheimen National Park. Norway, 8th century.

a Norwegian text called *Konungs skuggsjá* ('The King's Mirror')
has plenty to say about the marvels of travelling by ski:

> It would seem a greater marvel to hear about men who are
> able to tame trees and boards, so that by fastening boards
> seven or eight ells long under his feet, a man, who is no fleeter
> than other men when he is barefooted or shod merely with
> shoes, is made able to pass the bird on the wing, or the fleet-
> est greyhound that runs in the race, or the reindeer which
> leaps twice as fast as the hart. For there is a large number
> of men who run so well on skis that they can strike down
> nine reindeer with a spear, or even more, in a single run . . .
> We, however, have sure information and, when snow lies in
> winter, have opportunity to see men in plenty who are expert
> in this art.[18]

Frozen faeces: ancient horse dung found at the top of
the Lendbreen mountain pass in Norway.

Heading in the other chronological direction back into prehistory, some of the oldest rock carvings found in Norway depict little figures on skis. Despite the chronological distance that separates these images from the skis discovered in the melting glacier, they can add to our picture of how skis were used. Four hundred kilometres north of the Arctic Circle, some 6,000 petroglyphs have been discovered at sites dotted around the coastline at Alta. One of these is a beautifully animated little human with their legs apart and their footwear – either skis or snowshoes – pointing in different directions. They have been captured in a moment of decisive action, with a bow raised in one hand and the other arm flung backwards, as if to fire an arrow. To understand what they are doing, we just have to follow the direction in which the bow is pointing, to where an elk stands motionless, staring at their swift attacker.

Another animated landscape of prehistoric petroglyphs comes from further south, on the rocks above the Bøla river. This time the figure on skis is unmistakable and enormous, almost 1.5 metres in length. There are zigzag patterns on the inside of their skis, which may represent the leather bindings that hold their shoes in place. In their hands they hold a single pole for balance and propulsion. And once again, there is the suggestion that the skiing is done within the context of hunting, since behind them are the outlines of what might be bears or elks.

In one final case of a prehistoric petroglyphic skier, the images survived the passage of several thousand years unscathed before meeting a horrible fate in 2016. Perhaps there should be a support group for ancient artefacts injured by teenagers with too much time on their hands, because, like the planks of the

Prehistoric rock carving from Alta in Arctic Norway, featuring a human figure on skis or snowshoes, apparently hunting an elk. Thousands of these petroglyphs were created close to what was once the seashore, and the oldest date back to around 5000 BCE.

Gokstad ship, this petroglyph found itself on the receiving end of a pointy sharp object wielded by an adolescent. The incident took place on the island of Rødøya. The victim appeared to be a humanoid figure on skis. 'Humanoid' because there seemed to be two horns rising from the top of its head, but otherwise the image could well be that of a skier side-on: slight bend at the waist, bum sticking out, arms held out in front with a pole, and two long, fluid lines at the bottom conjuring the distinctive curve of the skis. Another possibility is that the figure is in a boat on the water: their stance is also like that of a modern-day paddle boarder. Unfortunately, the sharp white scratches that the teenagers made all but wiped out the original image.[19]

The sea and the land were equally important for the Vikings, being separate but closely interconnected environments. We see hints of that in the mythological stories of the pagan gods: the uneasy marriage of Skadi, the giantess deity of skiing and hunting, to Njord, god of the sea. They try their best, alternating nine nights by the sea with nine nights in the mountains. But their marriage is doomed, for, as the sea god complains: 'I hate mountains – not long was I there, just nine nights: wolves' howling I thought ugly compared with the swans' song.'[20]

Meanwhile, his mountain-dwelling, bow-wielding, skiing spouse has the opposite problem: 'I could not sleep on the sea's bed for the birds' screaming; he wakes me who comes from out at sea every morning, that gull.'[21]

We don't know how old these verses are or where they originally came from. They are preserved in a thirteenth-century Icelandic text now known as the *Prose Edda*, written by the politician and poet Snorri Sturluson. It's one of the most valuable collections of pagan mythological stories and explanations that we have, and we will come back to it in the next chapter. But it was written over two centuries after Iceland officially converted to Christianity, and we can't be certain about what Snorri put in or left out, or how he shaped the material according to his own world view. Yet the likelihood of a pre-Christian deity linked to skiing, hunting and the snowy mountains, and another deity connected to the wide sea, tells us something about what was important in the Norse cultural mentality. And in the surviving tales about the pagan gods and other mythological beings, travel is a constant theme. So perhaps it shouldn't come as a surprise that another important topic that crops up in the mythological texts is that of hospitality to travellers.

Together with Snorri's *Prose Edda*, the other major source of pagan mythology from thirteenth-century Iceland is a collection of poems called the *Poetic Edda* (the name can be confusing, since this collection is nothing to do with Snorri, and is preserved in a single manuscript from around fifty years after Snorri was writing). We already met one of the poems from this manuscript in the Introduction. *Hávamál* ('Sayings of the High One') is the poem that purports to be advice from Odin, the rascally one-eyed god of wisdom and war. Many of his most useful vignettes concern travel and travellers: 'never hold up to scorn or mockery a guest or a wanderer';[22] 'on mountain or fjord should you feel like travelling, make sure you've enough food along';[23] 'from his weapons on open land no man should step one pace away';[24] and 'no better burden one bears on the road than a store of common sense'.[25] Odin was the itinerant, far-roaming god, and so it's no wonder that a poem connected with him has so much to say about traveller hospitality:

> Fire is needful for someone who's come in
> and who's chilled to the knee;
> food and clothing are necessary for the one
> who's journeyed over the mountains.[26]

If travel on sea was inherently dangerous, travel on land brought hazards of its own, and those who made it to a friendly hearth were often the lucky ones. Travellers might be betrayed by the swiftly changing weather, by hostile humans, or by a simple slip of the foot. One such unlucky voyager set out on her last journey in the middle of the tenth century, travelling on the old path between Seyðisfjörður on the coast and Egilsstaðir further inland in eastern Iceland, a wind-whipped range of bare rock and ice 700 metres above sea level. We know that she was in her twenties, wore a coat of sheep wool, was not Icelandic by birth, and possessed an unusually large collection of more than 500 beads. We also know that she did not survive her journey across this inhospitable expanse. Her last act was to hunker down beneath a small overhang above an icy mountain stream, finding what little protection she could against the merciless elements and the

One of the picture stones from Viking Age Gotland (Lilbjärs III) showing a warrior on horseback being greeted by a female figure offering a drinking horn. Below, two cloaked figures sail in a ship with tightly curled prow and stern.

deadly effects of hypothermia. Quite probably, given the small-
ness of her shelter, she was alone. Her unfound body froze and
thawed countless times as the years rolled by, was picked apart,
eroded, dismembered; her bones dispersed, her pearls scattered
on the rocks and in the stream below. There she stayed until
2004, and a chance find by locals, who christened her *Fjallkonan*:
the Mountain Woman.[27]

After eleven hundred years of silence, she offers us a cold
reminder that in these often-harsh northern climes, the hospitality travellers received at farmsteads along the way could mean
the difference between life and death. Whether you were the
hornkerling (corner hag) who occupied the chilliest spot in the
hall, or the guest of honour warming your toes by the fire, the
most important thing was that you were safe. You had food in
your belly and a roof over your head. According to *Grágás* ('Grey
Goose'), the collection of law codes from medieval Iceland, even
those sentenced to three years of temporary outlawry (known as
'lesser outlawry') were allowed to specify three safe farmsteads
where they couldn't be attacked, and nor could they be attacked
on the roads connecting them. To be out in the cold, whether
socially or legally, often meant that an individual would be out in
the cold quite literally. Given her strange adornments of pearls
and her origins outside Iceland, was the Mountain Woman one
such unfortunate? We must wonder why she died alone on an
isolated pass, miles from the nearest farmstead. What was her
place in tenth-century Iceland?

Onwards

After death, pagan bodies destined for the afterlife still had travelling to do. In the case of the warrior buried in the Gokstad ship,
presumably he was expected to sail to the next world, together
with the planks adorned with the casual graffito of a bored,

barefoot youth. Other high-status individuals – both men and women – were accompanied not only by boats and ships, but also sledges, wagons and horses. Viking Age picture stones from the Swedish island of Gotland show warriors arriving in the afterlife on horseback. Ships often feature prominently in these images too, sometimes with only one or two figures on board rather than an entire crew. Those who died in battle were said to be destined for one of two sought-after afterlives: Valhalla, ruled by Odin, or Folkvang, ruled by Freyja:

> Folkvang is the ninth, and there Freyja fixes
> allocation of seats in the hall;
> half the slain she chooses every day,
> and half Odin owns.[28]

Even for those who hadn't died in battle, there were other after-lives to travel to. The Oseberg ship burial from 834 contained the bodies of two women, and among their grave goods are forms of transport including a highly decorated wooden cart, three beautifully ornate sleighs, another more everyday sleigh, fifteen horses, and of course the ship itself with the remains of the oars, rigging, anchor and sail. Carved directly into the back panel of the magnificent wooden cart are the faces of several cats, while a pair of cat heads rise up from the front corners of one of the sleighs. Since the cat was sacred to Freyja – her chariot was pulled by two of them – perhaps these women were expected to travel to her halls and enjoy an afterlife in her company.

On the other hand, another little travel-related detail from the Oseberg ship burial suggests a different destination. Among the grave goods were also several iron spikes fastened directly into the horses' hooves, designed to stop them from slipping on the snow and ice. This wouldn't be unusual, except that the burial took place in late summer or early autumn: the grave also contained a bucket made of yew wood, with a handful of wild apples – still red – inside. This wasn't the time of year to be worrying about travelling on an icy road. Except if the travellers were heading for another world, and one that lay in the far, cold north.[29] Perhaps this is also the explanation for two pairs of crampons that were found in a high-status double grave from the island of Birka in Sweden, where the dead man was found seated in a chair and the dead woman was sitting on his lap.[30]

Most inhabitants of the Viking Age were not destined for a glorious afterlife in Valhalla or Folkvang. If they drowned, it was said that they belonged to Ran, sinister wife of the sea god Ægir, who tangled unlucky seafarers in her net and dragged them down into the depths. If they died of sickness or old age, then they were destined for Hel, that Norse underworld with parallels across the pagan Germanic world. The etymology of this word tells us that this was a place that was covered and concealed, not the more familiar idea of a realm where souls are subjected to eternal punishment, but simply the underworld where the dead reside. The mythological and legendary poems preserved in the thirteenth-century *Poetic Edda* include several characters who travel the road to Hel. Their mode of transport is usually horses, but in the poem *Helreið Brynhildar* ('Brynhild's Ride to Hel'), the character of Brynhild – she who was later to enjoy another successful afterlife as an operatic sensation courtesy of Wagner's *Ring* cycle – arrives in the wagon in which she was burnt on her funeral pyre. Whoever recorded this poem in its one surviving manuscript (*Codex Regius*, that Icelandic manuscript from around 1270) opens with a short prose description: 'After Brynhild's death two pyres were made, one was for Sigurd, and that was kindled first, and Brynhild was burnt on the second one, and she was in a wagon draped with costly woven tapestries. It is said that Brynhild drove the wagon along the road to hell.'[31]

In our other main source for pagan Norse mythology and legendary material, Snorri Sturluson's thirteenth-century *Prose Edda*, the road to Hel is said to lie 'downwards and northwards'.

The remains of the Oseberg ship burial in situ,
during archaeological excavations in 1904.

Although Snorri was writing in a Christian context, this information is the clue that suggests why there might have been spiked
winter horseshoes in the Oseberg ship burial. If the women were
bound for Hel with the horses, sleighs and wagon that accompanied them into the mound, then the journey northwards and
downwards might well prove icy, and the horses would be grateful for their spiked shoes.

Those not sent into the afterlife accompanied by means of
transport – in other words, most people – would have to rely
on their own feet to take them northwards and downwards. For
some of them at least, it is possible that they were equipped
with shoes suitable for the task. One of the Old Norse-Icelandic
sagas – *Gísla saga* ('The Saga of Gisli') – includes an episode at a
funeral, where 'Hel-shoes' are tied to the feet of the dead man

('and when he had done this, he said, "If these come loose then I don't know how to bind Hel-shoes"').[32] In this case, the afterlife they hope he will be travelling to is Valhalla, as befits his status as a young male. And yet the clue to where most people were heading is in the name of these shoes: Hel. This saga was probably recorded in the thirteenth century, and nothing survives from the earlier archaeological record to back up the possibility that such shoes existed. In any case, if the idea was to provide traction against the slippery, icy road, then there wouldn't be much obvious to see: perhaps a thicker shoe to guard against the cold, or lined with fur on the bottom to keep the walker moving in the right direction.

In our end is our beginning. This chapter began with the Gokstad ship, hidden under the earth, bound for a glorious afterlife, carrying a dead warrior. But someone else had snuck on board for the journey into eternity, or, rather, their ghostly foot, carefully outlined on the wooden planks, together with the outlines of five neat little toenails. And toenails, it seems, may have had a surprisingly important part to play when it came to travelling between this life and the next. Whether you arrived in the afterlife in a wagon, a warship, or on foot, hopefully your nails had been trimmed. Otherwise, they might end up contributing to the onset of Ragnarok, the end of the world according to pagan mythology.

Once again, we have Snorri Sturluson to thank for this information. He writes of a ship called Naglfar, made of the nails of dead people: 'and it is worth taking care lest anyone die with untrimmed nails, since such a person contributes much material to the ship Naglfar which gods and men wish would take a long time to finish.'[33] Captained by a giant called Hrym, or possibly Loki himself, the vast ship sails to the field of battle and the final showdown begins.

Chapter 5

BELIEF

Iceland, c.900

First came the trembling earth. Swarms of juddering earthquakes shaking the hillsides, spooking the dogs and horses, making the cows and sheep twitchy. After the earthquakes came the floods of glacial meltwater, rushing down from the mountains. Rivers of ice were followed by rivers of fire. Inky clouds of ash surged into the sky, billowing over glowing, crimson horizons, lit up by sparks of lightning. The molten earth began to spatter and dance out of fissures in the ground. Lava fountained, pouring down from the highlands and across the heath, bubbling and boiling and hissing, rattling and popping like broken glass, scorching the moss, consuming everything in its path. A pungent, eggy sourness hung thickly in the air, mingling with the grey grit and smoke. Over many months, the earth burned under black skies.

For the new settlers, still jockeying for land, building up farms and lives out in the middle of the North Atlantic, this was something shockingly new. For many, it may have felt like the end of the world. For some, perhaps it was. Most of the settlers came from Norway and the British Isles, where the land was old and steady. True, they already knew that this was an island of elemental forces. In the middle of the ninth century, it had been named 'Snow Land' by the first Norse sailors known to have landed here, accidentally blown off course on their way from Norway to the Faroe Islands. Later, it was renamed 'Ice Land' by a man called Floki, nicknamed Raven-Floki because he was said to have brought three ravens to help him navigate the as-yet-unknown route. It is said that Floki, his family and companions only stayed for one bitterly cold winter, during which all their livestock died, before returning to Norway. According to later stories recorded about the settlement of Iceland – the *landnám* or 'land-taking' as they called it – the first permanent settler was Ingolf. Tradition has it that Ingolf arrived in 874 and settled in Reykjavik, named for the steam that rose from the hot springs in the region (*reykr* means 'smoke', *vík* means 'bay').[1]

So the new settlers already knew about the ice. They already knew about the smoke. But only now were they finding out about the fire.

Religious belief is never truly a static thing. It morphs, evolves and adapts to a changing world. Such awe-inspiring phenomena as the settlers witnessed in Iceland had to be explained somehow, and they did so by seeking out invisible, sentient forces. They had already brought their own gods and beliefs with them across the sea. For those who arrived from Scandinavian lands, these were mostly the red-blooded, larger-than-life gods of the Norse pagan pantheon, such as Odin, Thor, Freyja and Frey. Others, particularly those of Celtic extraction, arrived accompanied by the god sometimes known to Vikings as the 'White Christ'. As we saw in the Introduction, over time the Christian religion would seep into, spread across and eventually conquer the Norse world. For now, at least in Iceland, it was a minority faith.

Whether Christian or pagan, the first settlers of Iceland found new forces and new land spirits waiting for them in this elemental terrain. A land where fire can spill from the ground, its fumes blotting out the sun for months on end. A land where steam rises from hot pools with a warm, sulphurous tang. A land of black sands and eerie, humanoid rock formations. In such a land, stories and beliefs spring easily from the ground. Stories to explain the inexplicable. Beliefs to control the uncontrollable. Hidden folk on the hillsides, trolls perched on the cliff tops, giants lurking underground in the hollowed-out lava caves. The settlers learned to be respectful of the unseen forces in here and out there. To sing them songs, leave them offerings. Keep them onside.

But how to find solid evidence of these everyday beliefs? And what would they even look like? After all, in the archaeological record, a saucer of milk left out for the fairies will look much the same as a saucer of milk left out for the cat. But we might find an answer if we are prepared to look beneath the surface.

Light from light

The first settlers to make Iceland their permanent home arrived just after a major volcanic eruption, in around 870. We might remember from the Introduction that, over much of the island, the earliest archaeological evidence for human settlement sits on a layer of volcanic ash. This makes it remarkably straight-forward to work out when the settlement began: literally a year or two after the ash fell. But it wasn't until several decades later that the earth ruptured again and the fires returned. To the west of the country, perhaps around the year 900, a massive eruption split the ice of Langjökull ('long glacier'), around 100 kilometres north-east of Reykjavik. This was likely the first major eruption that the settlers would have witnessed after arriving in Iceland. We have no way of telling what effects it had on those living in the area, how many people and animals might have died during the eruption itself or in the years afterwards from poisoning or famine. But by comparison, following the cataclysmic

Laki eruption of 1783, perhaps a sixth of the Icelandic population perished from exposure to toxic elements thrown up by the explosion, or in the famines that followed, known as *Móðuharðin-din* ('The Mist Hardships').[2]

Back around 900, the lava continued to flow from the mountains for months, possibly even years. It swallowed vast swathes of prime farming and grazing land – around 185 square kilometres – and perhaps several farmsteads. The steaming lava folded over itself in thick, smooth waves, many metres deep. New passages and caves were hollowed out, far under the new ground, snaking through the massive lava field of Hallmundarhraun. Even now, a thousand years later, little more than a green-white fuzz of moss and lichen covers much of the hard black crust. But for the early generations of Icelanders, the more pressing question was not what might live on top of the hardened lava, but what might lurk underneath. And one lava cave seems to have become a magnet for strange stories and even stranger rituals in the decades following the eruption.

The lava cave Surtshellir is named for the notorious figure of Surt, fire giant and destroyer of worlds. His name means 'the Black', the colour of burning mountains, solidified lava, inky sands and scorched earth. According to the Norse myths preserved in thirteenth-century Icelandic manuscripts, at the end of the gods' world – Ragnarok – Surt travels from the south enveloped in burning fire, brandishing a flaming sword that shines brighter than the sun. He will slaughter Frey, the god of growth and fertility. The flames that swallow the world are called 'Surt's fire', a fittingly apocalyptic vision for a society that sprang up on an island formed by the meeting of a continental rift and a magma plume.[3] We simply don't know whether the settlers brought the legend of Surt with them to Iceland, or whether he was invented in response to their fiery new home. Either way, a cave deep under the ground, formed from a terrifying volcanic eruption, would seem to be the perfect place to encounter such a being. The earliest written mention of Surtshellir is in *Land-námabók* ('The Book of Settlement'), recorded in several versions in the thirteenth century. The story goes that a man called Thorvald Hollow-Throat travelled to the cave 'and declaimed a poem there that he'd composed about the giant living in the cave'.[4] But songs and poems sung in the darkness leave no trace. If we want to find more, we need to descend deeper into the black.

At that time, the route to Surtshellir would have been a journey in pitch-black darkness, down deep tunnels that snake for several kilometres through the lava crust. So far, so strange. But stranger still is what was built inside, almost 300 metres from the entrance. First, a vast drystone wall, blocking the passageway, around 10.5 metres across and perhaps once 4.5 metres high. A considerable building project in itself. Beyond the wall, further into the darkness where two side caves branch off from the main tunnel, the remains of seven large piles of unburned animal bones in a line stretching 120 metres through the cave. The largest of these heaps of unburned bones was originally around 3 metres wide, 4 metres long, and at least 80 centimetres high. It was heaped next to the entrance of a stone structure constructed on the floor of the cave, shaped with long sides and tapering ends. Perhaps this was intended to be the outline of a ship: the shape is very similar to the stone ship settings found as a burial custom across Scandinavia and into the Baltic, roughly from 1000 BCE to 1000 CE. On each of the long sides was a narrow opening: one to enter from the 'human side' of the lava tunnels, one leading further into the darkness. Inside the stone ship outline, a thin layer of crushed basalt rock and shards of burned animal bones. Also on the lava floor, dozens of glass beads coloured yellow, green and blue. Fragments of red, yellow,

---

* He came from a long line of individuals with excellent nicknames, being the grandchild of Bjorn Butter-Box, the great-grandchild Hroald Spine, the great-great-grandchild of Bjorn Ironside, and the great-great-great-grandchild of Ragnar Hairy-Breeches.

brown and green jasper and grey chalcedony, used during the Viking Age to spark fires, brought to the cave from distances of at least 50 to 70 kilometres away. A dozen shining shards of mustard-yellow orpiment – arsenic sulphide – a mineral formed in volcanic vents and hydrothermal hot springs, but, strangely enough, not naturally ocurring in Iceland. Used as the bright-yellow pigment in sumptuous medieval illuminated manuscripts from Ireland, Anglo-Saxon England and the Carolingian Empire, orpiment was a rare and precious mineral. Its main source at this time was in what is now Hakkari, the mountainous region that straddles Turkey, Iran and Iraq. While the origins of the Surt-shellir fragments haven't been established definitively, their most likely origin points to high-status, long-distance trade routes that stretched all the way from the Middle East through Europe and across the North Atlantic to Iceland.[5]

Orpiment, basalt, glass, charred bone: offerings all formed in heat and flames. Fitting gifts to placate a fire giant. For almost one hundred years, for much of the tenth century and into the new millennium, Surtshellir was visited from time to time. Fires were lit, animal bones were cracked and piled in large heaps, other animal bones were burnt inside the stones, and tiny glass beads and mineral fragments were left on the ground. A meeting place between worlds.

What accompanying rituals may have been performed deep under the ground, we don't know. In any case, this is very new evidence, and the picture may change as archaeologists continue to investigate the cave.[6] But as we've already seen from *Landnámabók*, there may be echoes of these beliefs and rituals in the texts later recorded in thirteenth- and fourteenth-century Iceland, many of which were rooted in the oral stories passed down the generations. Thorvald's song of praise does not survive, so we may never know how best to flatter a lava-dwelling giant. But another poem does survive, as part of a short tale about two men who get lost on their way to mass during a winter snowstorm, and find a certain cave to shelter in. They are already nervous about what might be lurking inside, so they trace a Christian cross with a knife point, and perch gingerly on two stones close to the entrance. At the back of the cave, they hear something moving and then two glowing eyes appear, the size of full moons. The owner of the two enormous eyes is a mountain giant. It starts to recite a poem, rich in mythological allusions and volcanic imagery. This is the second of twelve verses:

Dark flames drive the spit,
split the mountain ridge,
harshly rumble round
the swarthy treasure-strewer.
Embers shoot, I say,
rushing, black, straight upward.
Round Hrungnir's hall is heard
the roaring of the spark-storm,
the roaring of the spark-storm.[7]

According to Norse mythology, Hrungnir is a giant made of stone, and his hall is the mountains. There seems to be a volcano brewing, with the splitting ridge, embers shooting up into the sky, and a roaring, sparking storm. But as the poem continues, we realise that this is no geological event, but the ending of the world:

Dim cliffs break; the flame-tongues
blaze at faster paces.
From the ground begins
a strange new clay to flow.
The heavens crack and split;
giants come to life.
Twilight comes from torrents,

till the world's extinguished,
till the world's extinguished.

Peak to peak I stride
between first light and sunset.
Northwards I go farthest,
down along the Hel-road.
I'll fight any giant.
Let him fear my coming,
the swarthy mountain-warden,
in Elivagar's waters,
in Elivagar's waters.

As the poem builds towards its climax, the allusions to mythological stories grow, and so do the parallels with what was found
in the cave of Surtshellir, far under the lava field. The 'clay-folk' –
giants – gather together in caves for safety, plunged into a 'world
of darkness'. Another giant is introduced, named Aurnir, who is
sent an iron-braced boat made from stone. We have already met
one boat outlined in stone in the darkness of Surtshellir, and this
one is more elaborate:

And I sent to Aurnir
a sturdy boat of stone.
Iron-braced it was,
with ornamented bowsprit,
with ornamented bowsprit.

And finally, Thor appears, the hammer-wielding, red-bearded
pagan god, scourge of the giant race. He seems to have killed
the 'glacier-kindler' – in other words, the one who sets fire to
the ice on the mountaintops and triggers the volcanic eruption.
The speaker turns 'earth-inward', to where Surt's fires burn
ferociously:

Harm is done by Thor,
a warning often heard is:
vex him, you regret it.
The glacier-kindler's killed.
Fewer are the rock-folk.
My spirits sink – with reason –
On my way earth-inward
to black Surt's conflagration,
to black Surt's conflagration.

Despite the reference to Surt in the poem, there is no sense that the story takes place near Surtshellir itself. Nor do we know whether a specific eruption is being described, or a more general evocation of volcanicity. The date of the tale and the poem it contains are also unclear. It survives in a fragmentary manuscript from the end of the fourteenth century, and the prose part of the story is clearly Christian in context. On the other hand, the giant's poem sits oddly in this context, being full of purely pagan myth and legendary figures, with no hint of Christianity. It may be that the poem was around for a very long time independently before it was incorporated into the tale and written down.[8] Indeed, this might be the point. Remember that the humans are on their way to mass. They scratch a cross for protection. This is now a Christian land, and the creatures of the pagan past must huddle together in the darkness, out on the margins of the mind. Perhaps, amid the prophecies of fire and the slaughter of giants, there's another kind of apocalypse being referenced here: the end of one belief system and the rise of another.

Eventually, like the poetic giant with the glowing moonlike eyes, Christianity also caught up with Surt the fire giant. Inside the lava field, inside the cave, inside the stone boat. A final gift, or perhaps a warning, placed on top of the thin layer of fiery offerings. Four lead weights, one in the shape of a cross, little more than a centimetre long, put there twenty or thirty years after Iceland's official conversion to Christianity in around 1000. And then, nothing. A farewell to the fire giant, left alone to smoulder in the darkness.

In the beginning was the void

This was not the end of the story for pre-Christian religion. In Iceland the irony is that it was Christians who preserved much of what we know (or think we know) about the older Viking myths and gods. So let's spool back again, to a time before the coming of Christianity, before the final conflagration, before the destruction of the gods. To an incomprehensibly vast, cosmic ash tree, showered with shining soil. Yggdrasil. Home to a gossipy squirrel that runs up and down its immeasurably long trunk, taking snide messages between the imperious eagle that perches in the highest branches, and the disgruntled dragon that gnaws at its roots. World-encompassing. Nine-worlds-encompassing, in fact.

In the beginning was Muspelheim, a world of flames and broiling heat. In the beginning was Niflheim, a world of primordial ice and mist, source of poisonous rivers called Elivagar ('frozen waves'). These two worlds of ice and fire met in Ginnungagap, the yawning void, the windless nothingness, the endless abyss. And where the toxic icy vapours of Niflheim encountered the sparks and glowing embers of Muspelheim, life was born, in the form of the primordial ice giant Ymir. From Ymir, the world was fashioned: his flesh the earth, his blood the sea, his bones the rocks, his teeth the stones, his skull the sky, his brains the clouds.

To the worlds of Muspelheim and Niflheim, we can add Asgard, home of the gods, and Midgard, home of the humans. Other worlds are populated by giants, elves and dwarves. Then there's the realm of the dead, Hel, presided over by the gloomy ruler that shares its name, half blue corpse, half living flesh. Upon this stage of cosmological ash wood, a troop of gods and giants behaving badly, elves and dwarves lurking in the wings, Norns and *dísir* spinning fates – all colourful, larger-than-life characters playing out their soap opera lives for us storytelling mortals.

There's the one about that rascally Loki, transforming himself into a sexy mare and luring a giant's horse off into the woods for a quickie. The one about Sleipnir, the magnificent eight-legged offspring of that union, Odin's beloved steed. The one about Loki's other children, this time with a giantess: the half-corpse Hel, the monstrous wolf Fenrir and the Midgard Serpent that encircles the earth. The one about Thor and Loki dressing up as Freyja and her maid, setting off to rescue Thor's hammer from the giants. The one about Idunn and her golden apples of youth, spirited away by a giant so that the gods start to age and wither. The one about Loki – him again – losing a bet with the dwarves and having his mouth sewn shut. The one where Thor and the Midgard Serpent kill each other, where Odin rides out to battle and is devoured by Fenrir. The one where fire splits the sky and the world turns black.

It's a neat picture. Too neat, of course. Much of our evidence for Norse mythology and cosmology comes from two texts, which we have already met. One is the poet's handbook now called the *Prose Edda*, authored by the Icelandic politician and writer Snorri Sturluson. The other is the anonymous collection of mythological and legendary poems now called the *Poetic Edda*. Both were written in thirteenth-century Iceland, over two centuries after the country had officially converted to Christianity. Both are extraordinarily consistent in the details and stories they give us, especially given that they are independent sources, both describing an apparently defunct mythological system. Snorri's work in particular is enormously multilayered and complex, but – to quibble pedantically and ungratefully over this wonderfully rich resource for a moment – it's also true that he creates a rather too-systematic picture of the whole thing, heavy on the description and explication. The closer we get to the material he provides, the more the stories start to blur around the edges and the inconsistencies appear. Given the geographical and cultural sweep of the Viking Age world and the many centuries it encompassed, we need to be particularly wary of viewing these thirteenth-century sources as pre-Christian religious dogma. We can't be sure of how stable the characters of these myths were, how universal their stories, how unchanging the rituals and superstitions associated with them. We can't be sure of how representative these stories were of what ordinary people believed on the ground, at any given time period or in any given location.

To give one example, the pagan Norse god Tyr plays a fairly minor role in the Icelandic textual sources. He is best known as the brave god of war who stuck his hand in Fenrir's mouth as an act of faith, only for the wolf to bite it off when the gods betrayed him and broke their promise (no one comes off well in this story). But back in the mists of time, before the dawn of the Viking Age, it is possible that Tyr was the most important deity in the pantheon, the ultimate, supreme being. His name may stem from the Proto-Germanic *Tiwaz,* which would put it in the same etymological family as the names of the gods Zeus and Jupiter: the shining father-gods of the sky.[9] From this, it's a fair bet that Tyr was once held in similar regard to Zeus and Jupiter but slipped down the pecking order over the centuries. Indeed, he is the only god from the Old Norse pantheon to give his name to one of the runes, Tiwaz (ᛏ).

We could point the finger of responsibility at Snorri: his account of Norse mythology certainly seems to have been informed by his own Christian framework, and this might affect the prominence and characteristics he gives to certain gods

---

* Proto-Germanic is the reconstructed ancestral language from which Germanic languages – including English, German and the Nordic languages – ultimately descend. The asterisk indicates that this is a word that doesn't exist in writing anywhere, but it's as close as linguists can get to working out what words were spoken in the distant past.

(Odin, for example, he describes as the 'All Father', while Loki is said to have an 'evil disposition'). But it's also true that Tyr doesn't really appear on images from the Viking Age, which suggests that his demotion came earlier. To find a convincing image, we have to go back to the Nordic gold medallions – known as bracteates – that were produced in the fifth and sixth centuries. One of these comes from Trollhättan, a little north of Gothenburg in Sweden. It's a tiny thing, not even 3 centimetres across, but the image is wonderfully detailed: a little figure with luxurious long locks, with one hand lodged firmly in the jaws of a wolflike creature. Tyr, perhaps once *the* powerful god of the north, now standing on the sidelines while a supernatural wolf uses his hand as a chew toy. This is where he will remain, watching his fellow deities land their own epic opera cycles and blockbuster Hollywood films.

As Tyr reminds us, the tales that were once the lifeblood of a rich storytelling culture and belief system may fade, but they do not disappear easily. Other, earlier sources can help us to join some of the dots. Place names that still exist today hint that the cults of various gods were popular in different regions. For example, from the many place names containing his name, Frey seems to have been particularly worshipped in some parts of Sweden, but less so in Denmark. Place names with 'Thor' and 'Odin' elements are more widespread, suggesting that they were relatively popular in many parts of Scandinavia. Tyr has no surviving place names in Sweden, but the many Tyr-related place names in Denmark suggest that his cult was a bigger deal here. In western Norway, according to the place names, Tyr was also popular, as was the sea god Njord (unsurprisingly). Other gods, such as Loki, never appear in place names, suggesting that no cult of worship had come together around them. In the case of Loki that's probably for good reason: if you're looking for a god you can trust to take care of you, he really shouldn't be your first port of call.[10]

Place names aside, what other evidence helps us to connect the dots? Back to our old friends, the runes. Not scrappy little sticks this time, but a picture stone from the Swedish island of Gotland, in the Baltic Sea. The Tjängvide picture stone stands proudly nearly 2 metres high and over 1 metre wide. The runes state that it was raised by one brother to another, and it can be roughly dated to 700–900. The bottom half depicts a vast long-ship with an intricately patterned sail and a raised prow and stern curled tightly like snail shells. Armed warriors stand on the deck. The top half contains several characters: a figure mounted on the back of a horse, and a woman standing in front of them holding out two horns. In the background, two figures appear to be fighting. Another lies prostrate, perhaps dead, below something large and curved. Off to one side something canine lurks.

How to connect these images from Viking Age Gotland with the texts from thirteenth-century Iceland? Let's start with the horse. If Loki had given birth to any old equine offspring, it would be hard to tell it apart from any other of the species. Luckily, an eight-legged horse is considerably rarer, and so our first association is likely to be Sleipnir, or, at a push, one of his relatives. And yet even here, it has been argued that this might not be Sleipnir at all, just a representation of a horse moving quickly.[11] The rest of the picture stone, like many of them, is more of the mythological equivalent of a Rorschach inkblot test: subjective at best. Perhaps it's Odin arriving at Valhalla, being greeted with mead horns, watching his chosen warriors enjoying their daily battles before the nightly feast begins. Perhaps it's a warrior arriving for the first time, having borrowed Sleipnir for the journey, his dog waiting to be reunited in death inside the hall. Or perhaps it's Ragnarok kicking off: the ship of human corpse nails with its ghastly crew sailing towards the final reckoning, Thor battling with the Midgard Serpent and losing, Odin arriving on Sleipnir to fight not a dog, but the slinking, ravenous wolf Fenrir.

Other picture stones suggest that other mythical stories recorded in the later Icelandic texts do indeed have much older origins. One of the best known of these is the tale of Thor's fishing expedition, where he ends up hooking the Midgard Serpent – that terrible creature that was said to encircle the world – on the end of his fishing line. Versions of this myth are preserved in several skaldic verses, including a poem from the *Poetic Edda* called *Hymiskviða* ('Hymir's Poem', named after the giant Hymir, with whom Thor goes fishing). Another version is found in a passage from Snorri Sturluson's *Prose Edda*.[12] In the last of these accounts, Snorri includes a telling detail, in which Thor heaves on his fishing line so hard that his feet burst through the bottom of the boat:

> The Midgard Serpent stretched its mouth round the ox-head and the hook stuck into the roof of the serpent's mouth. And when the serpent felt this, it jerked away so hard that both Thor's fists banged down on the gunwale. Then Thor got angry and summoned up his god strength, pushed down so hard that he forced both feet through the boat and braced them against the sea-bed, and then hauled the serpent up to the gunwale.[13]

Several picture stones from across the Norse world, including Denmark, Sweden, Gotland and England, may depict versions of this story. On two of them, a little foot pokes out from underneath the boat, which seems to tally neatly with Snorri's version of the myth. The first of these picture stones comes from Hørdum, on Denmark's Jutland peninsula. This one has two figures in a boat, perhaps Thor and the giant Hymir, facing sideways on. Part of the image has sheared off the stone, but it is still possible to make out a beautifully carved boat, a straight fishing line descending far below, and the double curve of a giant creature in the depths. The foot is a tiny but unmistakable detail, sticking out jauntily beneath the hull. The other image comes from Altuna in Uppland, Sweden. It depicts a single cartoonish figure facing straight ahead, hammer raised, fishing line dropped over the side to where a knotted, snaky beast writhes and twists. Between the boat and the beast is another telltale foot. Both of these images are likely to be pre-Christian, and so pre-date Snorri's account.[14] But what would we make of them if there had never been any *Prose Edda* to tell us what we should be seeing? And is there any way of telling what beliefs – if any – lay behind such a colourful story? When the Vikings put out to sea, did they keep a wary eye on the horizon in case the Midgard Serpent uncoiled itself from the depths and put in an unwelcome appearance? Or did they know that such a creature was only likely to be conjured from the imaginations of storytellers?

Then there's the Snaptun Stone, from around the year 1000. It was found on a beach in Denmark, but is made from soapstone and likely comes originally from either Norway or southern Sweden. It's a hearthstone with a hole running through it, designed to protect bellows from the heat. The point is to stick the nozzle in the hole, which means that air can be puffed into the fire without scorching either the bellows or the person doing the puffing. Above the hole is a face, with curling eyebrows and an extremely dapper handlebar moustache. Under the moustache is a horizontal mouth with little vertical lines protruding up and down. It's Loki, having bet his head in a wager with a dwarf. When he lost the bet, the dwarves came to collect their prize. Loki told them that they could only have his head as long as they didn't touch his neck, which wasn't included in the deal, so the dwarves were forced to leave his head. But before they went, they took an awl and a leather cord, pierced his lips, and sewed his mouth shut.

Why put Loki's face on a hearthstone? True, sometimes he is mislabelled as a fire god. Certainly Wagner didn't help with that, reincarnating the Norse trickster as Loge, god of fire, in his operatic *Ring* cycle. And to be fair to Wagner, it's an easy mistake to make, since there's only one letter between them, and a similar-sounding letter at that. In the Old Norse language, the word *logi* means flame or fire. According to Norse mythology, there is a giant called Logi, who is the personification of wildfire. But that's certainly not Loki, and in one of the stories Loki inadvertently gets into an eating contest with Logi, which he can't win because the voracious Logi consumes everything: the food, the dishes, even the table. The etymology of the name 'Loki' is rather twistier, as befits the character himself. It may relate to the older Germanic root **luk*, which is to do with things that are knotted and tangled, shaped like hooks and loops.[15] It has been suggested that in the later, post-medieval Nordic world, Loki also took the form of a *vätte* or 'domestic spirit' who lived under the fireplace. In parts of Norway and Sweden in the early modern period and into the twentieth century, tradition had it that if a fire started to crackle or whistle, it was Loki spanking his children or blowing on the fire ashes.[16] If these associations also existed in earlier centuries, then this might explain something about the Snaptun Stone. Every time someone took a pair of bellows to the hearth they would be reminded of this link between Loki and fire: a mirroring of wild, unpredictable, destructive forces, and a warning to keep them under control.[17] This is a reminder that the divine beings of the Norse world were not necessarily stable beings with a single identity. They might mean different things to different people, even exist in the world alongside them.

Of all that is seen and unseen

Beyond Iceland, it's highly likely that the rest of the pagan Nordic world was just as busily populated with more-than-human inhabitants. And much of the time, it wasn't about who might be up in the sky, or who could be conjured in stories around the fire. It was about who – or what – was sharing the familiar land-scapes of everyday life, living in the fields and woods around the farmsteads, glimpsed by the rivers and forests. It was about the uncanny beings that lurked in burial mounds: trolls, elves, land spirits that could be as tiny as a pebble or as vast as a forest.

It wasn't about 'religion' as such, a word that didn't really have an everyday equivalent in the Viking Age. It was about *siðr*: a custom or habit, a way of being, a way of life. Not separated, not institutionalised, not universalised. Different regions, house-holds and individuals would have different affinities, practices and traditions. Different gods and spirits might be called on for different purposes. Thor for good weather at sea. Freyja for good pregnancies and births. Frey for good harvests. Odin and Tyr for

A hearthstone featuring the face of Loki, his lips sewn up having lost a wager with the dwarves. Snaptun, Denmark, c.1000.

good battles. Much of this we can only guess from later textual sources – skaldic verses, the Old Norse-Icelandic sagas, the *Prose Edda*, the *Poetic Edda* – and from the hints we pick up from little surviving artefacts, such as protective amulets (more of those later).

This doesn't mean that there was no consistency, no underlying sets of beliefs and ideas. But it was perhaps a more fluid, dynamic, evolving system of meanings, rooted in the local environments, with dominant cultural tropes and local variation. Perhaps we can compare it to the traditions associated with Father Christmas in Western Christian culture, at least before everything got more homogenised with the advent of global media. The green- or scarlet-robed Father Christmas of Tudor England is a very different beast from the version incorporated into Alpine folklore, with his monstrous horned companion Krampus. Likewise, the Joulupukki of Finnish tradition may now sport red robes and a white beard, but his name translates as 'Yule Goat', and he seems to have had darker, more caprine origins than many of his Christmas counterparts. The overall idea has coalesced into a related set of meanings and traditions, even if their precise forms change through time and space.

How to find traces of these individual beliefs and practices? We're back with that saucer of milk again: was it meant for the cat or the elves? The situation is slightly easier when it comes to large-scale communal activities, often led by those at the top of the social pecking order. We've already looked at Adam of Bremen's description of Uppsala in Sweden in the 1070s, with the human and animal sacrifices and the 'complex and shameful songs' of the worshippers. We know that something big was going on (other than Frey's genitalia), but it's hard to match up Adam's lurid description with the archaeological evidence on the ground. And it's not the only one. Hundreds of kilometres to the south, just to the west of Copenhagen in Denmark, lies Lejre. It's a sleepy place now, but through the Iron Age and

Viking Age it was the centre of a powerful ruling dynasty. Sixty years before Adam was writing about Uppsala, another chronicler was describing what had been going on in Lejre. His name was Thietmar of Merseburg, and he was not afraid to pass on a good bit of gossip:

> Because I have heard marvellous things about their ancient sacrifices, I will not allow these to pass by unmentioned. In those parts, the centre of the kingdom is a place called Leire, in the region of Seeland. Every nine years, in the month of January, after the day on which we celebrate the appearance of the Lord [6 January], they all convene here and offer their gods a burnt offering of ninety-nine human beings and as many horses, along with dogs and cocks – the latter being used in place of hawks. As I have said, they were convinced that these would do service for them with those who dwell beneath the earth and ensure their forgiveness for any misdeeds. [18]

As with Uppsala, the archaeology does confirm that there was something significant going on here. There is evidence of a series of vast halls built for powerful leaders, the biggest perhaps 60 metres long, and a cemetery that included enormous stone ship burials (at least one of them more than a dozen times longer than the stone ship outline in the lava cave of Surtshellir). As with Uppsala, there is no evidence of sacrifice, either human or animal. But one exquisite little object was discovered inside the main area of the largest hall, likely dating to around 900–950 (which is also the time that Thietmar is looking back to in his description). It's a tiny silver figurine less than 2 centimetres in height and width, with a person sitting on an ornately carved chair. They are wearing what look like strings of beads, and a long, decorated tunic. Two large birds perch on each arm of the chair, and two animals stand behind, their jaws mid-bite. The biggest clue as to who this person is, is that while one of their eyes is clearly defined, the other has been scored through with a blade. A one-eyed figure wearing clothing of an ambiguous gender – could this be Odin? In which case, are the birds his ravens Huginn and Munnin ('thought' and 'memory') who fly through the world gathering information for their master? And are the animals with the open jaws Geri and Freki ('ravenous' and 'greedy'), Odin's pet wolves?

While Uppsala and Lejre have no archaeological evidence of the attention-grabbing gory sacrifices that Adam and Thietmar describe – at least, not yet – other sites tell us that such things did happen. Take Frösö, an island in central Sweden. The clue to its pagan significance is in its name, which simply means 'Frey's Island'. Close to the island are several other places that contain name elements related to other Norse gods – Odin, Njord, Ull – as well as other places whose names connect them to pagan cult sites (Vi, from *vé* meaning 'shrine' or 'sacred enclosure' and Hov from *hof* meaning a sanctuary, shrine or building used for religious rituals). During excavations under the island's church, archaeologists found the stump and roots of a birch tree, scattered with the bones of wild and domesticated animals. They had been placed there when the tree was still standing, most likely in the decades between 980 and 1030, and the bones showed signs of weathering, as if they had been displayed after death. Piglets and brown bears seemed to be the top choice for sacrifices on Frösö, which took place particularly in late autumn, early spring and perhaps the summer solstice. The piglets in particular chime with what later written sources tell us: Frey's sacred animal was said to be the boar, and his chariot was pulled by the magnificently flashy Gullinbursti, a boar with golden mane and bristles that glowed in the dark. Also found close to the birch tree and dating to the same period as the animals were the bones of several humans: one infant, one child and two adults. Unlike the animal bones, the human bones showed little sign of weathering, and it's not clear whether these were human sacrifices or burials that had been disturbed when the church was built later. But certainly something was going on, and had indeed been going on since the seventh century, judging from the age of the burned bones of sheep or goats that were also found in a nearby pit.[19]

Another site, this time in Iceland, is at Hofstaðir in the north-east of the island. Once again, the place name is the first clue that something was going on here: *hof* is that same word as above, *hov* ('sanctuary', 'shrine'), while *staðir* means 'places'. Once again, there was an unusually large hall here, this time around 38 metres long, which seems to have been a centre of communal religious activity. And once again, archaeologists have unearthed evidence of animal sacrifice, in the remains of at least twenty-three cattle skulls that were found in and around the large hall. The cattle had been in the prime of their lives, killed by a powerful blow between the eyes followed by decapitation. Their skulls were weathered, which suggests that they had been mounted on the outside of the hall. The activities at Hofstaðir peaked in the tenth century. The site was shut down in the middle of the eleventh century, a time when, it has been noted, a Christian church was being built only 140 metres away. This, too, is a pattern we see repeated: at both Uppsala and Frösö, the Christian church was built in the same location as the pagan temple. For missionaries this served a dual purpose. Firstly, it eased the transition by allowing converts to come to their traditional place of worship, even if the worship itself had changed. Secondly, they could make sure the weeds of paganism didn't start springing up there again.[20]

In the cases of Uppsala, Lejre, Frösö and Hofstaðir, whatever was happening seems to have been as much about community, politics, power and drama as it was about belief in a particular deity or ritual. These were large-scale, communal activities, likely led by those at the top of the social ladder. It is no coincidence that an Icelandic chieftain was called a *goði*, which comes from the same root as 'god': these were social and political leaders who were also responsible for pagan rituals and communal feasts. The same word occasionally appears on commemorative runestones from mainland Scandinavia. The Glavendrup stone in Denmark dates from the early tenth century. The enormous runestone was placed at the end of a stone ship setting, itself a massive 60 metres long. Carved into it is the longest runestone inscription in Denmark, which shows how blurred the edges were between political and religious office. The question marks in the translation indicate that it's not entirely straightforward to interpret, but certainly there is plenty of information to go on:

> Ragnhild put up this stone in memory of Alli the Pale, *goði* [priest] of the sanctuary, honoured *þegn* [military leader] of the troop. Alli's sons made this memorial in memory of their father, and his wife did so in memory of her man. And Soti carved these runes in memory of his lord. May Thor bless these runes. He who damages (?) this stone or moves it to stand in memory of another, be accursed (?).[21]

These were influential, rich people. In fact, Ragnhild commissioned Soti to carve another runestone for *another* husband, Gunnulf. It too had a similar curse, and it too was placed in a stone ship setting. When it comes to communal religious rituals, there were also other high-status figures who played prominent roles but wouldn't necessarily have been memorialised on stones. Seeresses, for example, with links to the spirits that existed beyond the human world. They might appear in a community for a few nights and perform the necessary songs of protection and rituals to ward off famine and disease. Such a character is described in intricate detail in *Eiríks saga rauða* ('The Saga of Erik the Red'), recorded, like most sagas, in medieval Iceland, but its plot centred on the Norse colonies in Greenland. Her name is Thorbjorg *lítilvölva* ('little seeress') and she is invited by an important local farmer in the district when the community falls on hard times. Her physical appearance alone is enough to set her apart and indicate her special talents:

> She was wearing a black mantle with a strap, which was adorned with precious stones right down to the hem. About her neck she wore a string of glass beads and on her head a hood of black lambskin lined with white catskin. She bore a staff with a knob at the top, adorned with brass set with stones on top. About her she had a linked charm belt with a large purse. In it she kept the charms which she needed for her predictions.[22]

This description comes from an Icelandic saga that was recorded centuries after both Iceland and Greenland officially converted to Christianity. But several dozen Viking Age burials from across the Nordic region perhaps hint at the underlying truth of what is indicated in the story. These are all high-status women, buried with precious and often exotic grave goods, accompanied by mysterious metal staffs, amulets and figurines, and the remnants of mind-altering plants (such as cannabis or henbane seeds). One or both women from the Oseberg ship burial are possible candidates for such a position, not least because a little pouch with cannabis seeds was found among their possessions (perhaps for communing with the divine, perhaps for pain relief, perhaps both). Such an identification is strengthened by the fact that the wagon is decorated with cats, the sacred animal of Freyja, and there are tapestries apparently decorated with scenes of hanging (sacrificed?) bodies.[23]

Exalted guests aside, most members of the community would have been the ones in the crowd, or on the edge of the action, observing the same communal rituals as they came round year after year. Some of these, as we have seen, were dramatic events on the largest farmsteads, the kind that might leave traces in the archaeological record. Others were private affairs performed behind closed doors, perhaps the equivalent of a spectacular public firework extravaganza versus its back garden equivalent. Whether big or small, later written records have a name for such sacrificial rituals: *blót*. Some of these were seasonal, associated with the start of the winter nights, the winter solstice and the summer solstice. Others were performed to worship particular beings: sacrifices to gods, elves, protective spirits, land spirits.

One skaldic poem, *Austrfaravísur* ('Verses on an Eastern Journey'), tells us that private rituals were going on even if we're not allowed to know what they were. The author was Sigvat Thordarson, an Icelander who became court poet to several Scandinavian kings. Born in around 995, barely five years before Iceland officially converted to the new religion, he was a Christian. Skaldic poetry of the sort composed by Sigvat generally survives because it was included in later sagas. The main source for these verses is the saga of King Olaf Haraldsson, the king who sent him on the mission, *Óláfs saga helga* ('The Saga of Saint Olaf', written by Snorri Sturluson as part of his collection of sagas about Nordic kings, called *Heimskringla*). But it is thought likely that Sigvat did indeed compose at least some of these verses on the journey itself, perhaps to entertain the king's retainers. What this tells us about the reliability of what he claims to have witnessed, it is hard to say. But unlike foreign writers such as Adam of Bremen and Thietmar of Merseburg, here we have a witness from within the Norse world itself, with his boots on the ground. And unlike the later thirteenth-century saga accounts of pagan activity and belief, there is a good chance that these verses date to the start of the eleventh century.[24]

The story goes that one year, at the start of winter, Sigvat was sent by the Norwegian king as part of a diplomatic mission to Sweden. Journeying through the forest that runs close to the Norwegian–Swedish border, he reached a farmstead called Hof (and perhaps that name is ringing some bells). Having found the door locked firmly shut, he stuck his nose in and was met with the following response:

> 'Do not come any further, wretched fellow,' said the woman; 'I fear the wrath of Odin; we are heathen.' The disagreeable female, who drove me away like a wolf without hesitation, said they were holding a sacrifice to the elves inside her farmhouse.[25]

Just like Sigvat Thordarson, we find ourselves on the outside of a door closed firmly in our faces. What is going on inside? And even if we were able to be a fly on the wall, we might be able to see traces of rituals, but that wouldn't necessarily tell us much about the beliefs that lay behind them. In any case, the most important beliefs and rituals aren't necessarily the ones that take place at particular points in the year. They're the everyday

A Thor's hammer made from bronze, carved with runes that helpfully read 'this is a hammer'. Lolland, Denmark, 10th century.

superstitions and actions designed to make life that bit more controllable: little protections against illnesses, bad harvests, property theft and dangerous travel. Most of these have long since vanished into thin air: herbs tied to a sickbed or a baby's cot, prayers and chants uttered to departed relatives or hidden folk. Others – especially if they were made of stone or metal – had a better chance of surviving the centuries.

Indeed, what better example of a statement of identity, of belief, than the iconic symbol of Thor's hammer? Around a thousand have been found in Viking Age sites across the Nordic world, the British Isles, the Baltic and beyond. These include a little tenth-century bronze hammer from Lolland in Denmark, with runes on the back that simply read 'this is a hammer'. Given how tricky it can be to identify artefacts from the past, it's a nice change to have something that tells us exactly what it is.

Not all requests for the thunder god's protection took the form of a hammer itself, let alone one as thoughtfully labelled as the example from Lolland. We have already seen one case of Thor being asked for his blessing, in the runestone commissioned by Ragnhild for her husband Alli the Pale. Similar requests for Thor's protection are found on other runestones, as well as other items. An early eleventh-century copper pendant from Kvinneby in Sweden contains a long – and not entirely clear; this is one interpretation of it but there are others – runic inscription that runs over two sides, asking for protection and healing for someone called Bofi:

> I cower in here (in the ashes of the hearth?) under the god of soot; I, Bofi, carry a festering sore (scar?) in my skin – it is known to you (the god of soot?) where the glistening one (the demon) is – keep evil from Bofi! May Thor guard him with the hammer with which he strikes Ámr (a giant = the demon). May you have the affliction Ámr! Be gone, evil being! The affliction leaves Bofi, the gods are below him and above him.[26]

In this inscription, the voice of the individual who is suffering seems to come through the runes clearly. There is also a strong sense of non-human beings other than the one familiar name in the inscription (Thor): gods and their antagonists battling it out above and below the suffering Bofi. We will meet more of these runic amulets in the next chapter. In *Hávamál* ('Sayings of the High One'), one of the mythological poems preserved in the thirteenth-century Icelandic manuscript *Codex Regius*, Odin sacrifices himself on Yggdrasil – that sacred ash tree – for nine whole days and nights, to gain the hidden runes of power. He asks:

> Do you know how to carve, do you know how to interpret,
> do you know how to colour, do you know how to question,
> do you know how to ask, do you know how to sacrifice,
> do you know how to dispatch, do you know how to slaughter?[27]

The verse begins by asking whether the unknown person being questioned can carve, read and colour runes, but it ends by asking them if they can sacrifice, dispatch and slaughter. If this does indeed tell us anything about older beliefs and practices, then it tells us that powerful forces were thought to run through runes themselves, just as they ran through sacrifices to the gods – and an individual who could harness one source of magic might also harness the other.

The earliest surviving Thor's hammer pendants date from the early ninth century in what was, at the time, the hazy borderlands between the pagan Danes and their southern neighbours, the aggressively Christian Carolingians, whose empire included much of north-west continental Europe. The hammers gradually gained popularity, flooding through the rest of Denmark and into southern Sweden by the tenth century, before petering out in the eleventh.[28] It's likely no coincidence that this timeline matches the onset of Carolingian missionary activity and Christian conversion. Pendants were as much about identity as belief,

Copper pendant with runes asking Thor to protect Bofi from the evil beings
who have given him a festering sore. Kvinneby, Sweden, 11th century.

although the two concepts are closely interlinked. When everyone around you is pagan, you don't really have to think about it:
the beliefs and practices are woven through everyday life, public
and private, shared and individual. But when another religion
appears – especially one backed by a foreign empire – suddenly
you have to think harder about who you are, what you believe,
and how you signal that. Perhaps you do it in a way that actually
mirrors Christianity, consciously or otherwise. After all, a Thor's
hammer sits as neatly on one's chest as a crucifix.

Humans being humans, however, things are not always so
simple. A case in point is a woman buried in the first half of
the tenth century at Thumby-Bienebeck, 25 kilometres (as the
longship sails) east of Hedeby. She was laid to rest in a large
wood-lined chamber, her body placed within a wagon that had
had its wheels removed. Accompanying her were some modest
valuables: a small wooden casket; a necklace made from beads

of clay, glass, silver and gold; a knife and needles. Most precious of all, though, was the silver crucifix that hung around her neck. This seems like a clear and unambiguous expression of Christian faith, and it may well have been that. However, the picture is muddied somewhat by several Thor's hammers that hung from rings on the sides of the wagon.[29] How should we interpret this? It's an archaeological truism that dead people don't bury themselves, so does it mean that those who put her in the ground were hedging their bets, giving her the best chance of passing into the afterlife? Or did the crucifix and Thor's hammers mean something else to them entirely? Is this perhaps a similar situation to one described in *Landnámabók*, where a settler called Helgi the Lean was said to have a faith that was 'very much mixed', believing in Christ but praying to Thor 'when it came to voyages and difficult times'?[30]

The burial from Thumby-Bienebeck is not the only example of the symbols of Christian and pagan belief being brought together. Thor's hammers also appear on several coins, including an early tenth-century piece struck in the Viking Age kingdom of York. One side features a Christian cross. The other side bears

Two sides of a coin from the Viking Age kingdom of York, featuring an upside-down Thor's hammer on one side and a Christian cross on the other side. York, England, 10th century.

the legend 'SCI PETRI MO', an abbreviation of the Latin 'Sancti Petri Moneta' or 'Saint Peter's Money', after the patron saint of York's cathedral. But at the bottom of the coin, in the letters beneath the sword, the 'I' of 'Petri' has been turned into an upside-down Thor's hammer. Saint Peter himself might not have approved, but the traders of Viking Age York, it seems, belonged to a broad church. This attitude is reflected most starkly in two soapstone moulds, used for casting metal pendants, found at the Viking Age sites at Hedeby (in modern Germany) and Trengården (Denmark) and dated to the time around the conversion in the tenth century. Their enterprising owners seem to have taken advantage of the mixed religious communities they operated in, because the same moulds include both crosses and hammers. This is pragmatism on the ground, a recognition

Thorvald's Cross, depicting a figure – most likely Odin at Ragnarok – with one foot in the mouth of a wolf, and a bird perched on his shoulder. Isle of Man, 10th century.

by the pendant makers that people are going to believe different things and identify in different ways, but that silver has no religion.

A more extreme form of religious syncretism – that mixing of belief systems or incorporating elements of one into another – can also be observed in the images carved on two stones, both from the British Isles and from regions where the Norse settled extensively. One is the Gosforth Cross from Cumbria, carved in the first half of the tenth century, towering 4.4 metres high in the churchyard of St Mary's. The other is Thorvald's Cross from the Isle of Man, made perhaps several decades later and located in St Andrew's Church at the northern end of the island. The two crosses lie almost directly across the Irish Sea from each other, barely 60 kilometres apart. It's obvious just from the names that both are Christian, because they're crosses and they include carved images of Christ's crucifixion. But the Gosforth Cross also has carved stories that we might remember from Norse mythology, including Loki bound and tortured with snake poison for his crimes, and a figure with its foot in the mouth of a monstrous fanged beast, perhaps Odin fighting the wolf Fenrir at Ragnarok.

Thorvald's Cross – so named because it includes runes that state 'Thorvald raised this cross' – is badly damaged in comparison to the Gosforth Cross, yet it too seems to depict Odin's final battle against Fenrir. The figure's foot is once again in the beast's mouth, and this time there is a bird perched on his shoulder, perhaps one of Odin's ravens. Also carved into the stone is a large cross. It's not clear whether this is about two sets of beliefs coalescing, about Christ being incorporated into the Norse pantheon as another one of the gods. Alternatively, the stories of one mythological system (Norse paganism) may be being used to explain those of another increasingly dominant religion (Christianity).

One holy Church

Different parts of the Viking Age world have different stories about how and when the official conversion to Christianity happened. It was, unsurprisingly perhaps, uneven and patchy, with a fair amount of toing and froing, political messiness and inevitable bloodshed. The official stories are inevitably top down, involving charismatic and powerful rulers asserting considerable pressure and nastiness. Official conversion narratives are often written by those who have skin in the game: a Christian monk in a scriptorium, for example, is likely to *care* that his team emerges from the scrum of history looking like winners. Likewise, for a powerful pagan king who had Christian powers hovering menacingly over the border, it might have been an excellent decision to jump before they were pushed, and make sure that everyone knew who was responsible for converting their country (i.e. *them*, rather than a dominant foreign power). But on the ground, for everyday people getting on with their lives, there might often have been space for a certain amount of flexibility and pragmatism. For some, genuine belief might, of course, follow a conversion that was originally about the swift or gradual changing of allegiances from one power to another. But for others, as long as the stories were worth telling, as long as they were still allowed to leave out offerings for the elves and mark the seasons with communal celebrations, perhaps the result was simply a compromise between the old ways and the new. After all, if there were plenty of gods at the party, adding another wasn't necessarily such a big deal. It was the Christian missionaries, on the other hand, who were so keen on defining their relationship and making it exclusive.

If we are looking for evidence for just this sort of pragmatism, Iceland's official conversion narrative is particularly interesting. In the decades leading up to the year 1000, missionaries began to arrive on the island, each with a fairly muscular notion of conversion. The first was an Icelander who went abroad, converted to Christianity, and returned home with a Saxon bishop. The duo's attempts to convert locals to Christianity went extremely badly, resulting in the composition of scurrilous verses and then killings (it doesn't get more Viking than that). The second was another Icelander, this time sent by the Christian King Olaf Tryggvason of Norway. He was even more badly behaved than his predecessors, smashing up pagan sanctuaries and images of the gods. The third was a missionary from the court of King Olaf himself, described in one saga as 'a very violent man and a fighter, but a good cleric and a valiant man'.[31] It goes without saying that this didn't end well either. Eventually, the Icelanders took the matter into their own hands.

The traditional story of how the conversion came about is recounted in *Kristni saga* ('The Saga of Christianity'). By the time everyone reached the national assembly (the *Alþingi*), trouble was brewing. The pagans were armed and spoiling for a fight. The Christians were burning strong incense, which could be smelled both upwind and downwind. Then the two sides declared that they would be ruled by separate laws. As tensions continued to ratchet up, someone arrived with the news that a volcano had erupted, and lava was about to engulf the farmstead of one of the chieftains. The pagans decided this was a sign that Odin and his posse were furious about what was going on ('It is no wonder that the gods are enraged at such talk').[32] The Christians pointed out that volcanoes had been erupting in Iceland since before there were any humans living there ('What were the gods enraged by when the lava we are standing on here and now was burning?').[33] Eventually, a pagan chieftain called Thorgeir was called in to sort things out. He lay down with a cloak over his head and stayed there for twenty-four hours to think things through. By the time he emerged, the whole thing was getting very ugly.

Thorgeir's decision was based on pragmatism: everyone should follow the same religion because 'if we tear apart the law, we will also tear apart the peace'.[34] At the same time, however, he decided that the old customs should remain: people could continue to eat horse meat, practise infanticide and make sacrifices to the pagan gods (as long as they did it secretly and no one caught them). And this is where private belief and public religious practices diverged, at least for a time. Eventually, a few decades after the conversion, the fire giant Surt was left alone in the darkness of his lava cave, a Christian cross placed inside the stone boat. Around the same time, in the north of the country, the sacrificial rituals at Hofstaðir petered out, the hall was closed, and a church was erected instead.

Yet the need to control the uncontrollable was just as great as it had ever been. There were still hidden beings and unseen forces everywhere in the world. Echoes of older beliefs and superstitions endured. Sometimes, Thor's protection was replaced by that of the saints: there are Bergen rune sticks where Michael or Mary are called upon instead, but the other words are the same. At least one Bergen rune stick, dated to the late twelfth century (nearly 200 years after Norway's official conversion to Christianity) still calls upon the old gods for their assistance: 'May you be healthy and in good thoughts. May Thor accept you, may Odin have you.'[35] An even younger Bergen rune stick, from the late fourteenth century, calls on Odin to recover their lost property, but at the same time refers to the old god as the 'greatest of fiends':

I exhort you, Odin, with heathendom, greatest of fiends; assent to this: tell me the name of the man who stole; for Christendom; tell me now your misdeed. One I revile, the second I revile; tell me, Odin! Now is conjured up and lots of devilish messengers (?) with all heathendom. Now you shall get for me the name of he who stole. A(men).[36]

Even as Odin is reviled, he is called upon for help. What to make of such a rune stick, and one carved so late in the day? Is there any wisp of belief left here, or is it simply the remnants of a good story?

Either way, good stories are hard to kill. So are the worlds inside people's heads. The Norse pagan gods are still with us. In fact, in 2015 construction began on a new pagan *hof* in downtown Reykjavik. And the Icelandic lava fields are still hotbeds (sorry) of activity, seen and unseen. When protesters came together in 2013 to stop a road being built through Gálgahraun lava field, just north of Reykjavik, it is true that they were concerned about the environmental impact of the new highway. But some of them were also there to protect a 70-tonne rock they believed to be an elf church. When the road was finally built, the rock was moved safely to another location, just in case. Perhaps, for a modern world where environmental concerns grow ever more pressing, this is one of the less weird aspects of the Viking Age. Because belief in hidden forces and unseen beings is also belief in the more-than-human natural world; belief that its power, fragility and sanctity are all inextricably linked to our own.

Chapter 6

BODIES

A good comb

A smooth length of curved, polished bone – most likely antler – from Viking Age Lincoln, in the heart of the Danelaw. Bookended by triangular plates and secured with bronze rivets, it's an easy fit in the hand of an average-sized adult. A neat line of runes runs from one end to the other, presumably written by the person who made it. In Old Norse, they can be read as '*Kamb góðan gerði Þorfastr*', which means 'Thorfast made a good comb.'[1] But we'll have to take Thorfast's word for it, because this is only the protective case made to house the comb, and the comb itself has long since vanished. So too has the hair it once groomed, keeping the tangles and lice at bay. The comb case is all that survives to remind us that, at some point in the tenth or eleventh century, there lived a human whose body needed upkeep and maintenance, as all bodies do, regardless of the larger historical narratives unfolding around them.

Lincoln, where the comb was found, was part of the region of England settled by Scandinavians from the late-ninth century onwards. The area was sometimes known as the 'Five Boroughs' for its five main towns: Lincoln, Derby, Leicester, Nottingham and Stamford. Today, we know the area better as the Danelaw, although the first recorded use of that term comes later, in an

Anglo-Saxon law code from 1008. In Old English texts 'Danish' doesn't necessarily and exclusively mean someone from Denmark, and indeed settlers came to Britain and Ireland from various parts of the Nordic world. Thorfast the comb-maker is a case in point; we don't know that he was Danish, but he was probably of Nordic extraction. His name is decidedly Scandinavian, made up of the elements *Þórr* (the hammer-hefting pagan god) and *fastr* (meaning 'firm' or 'faithful'). He was also writing in Younger Futhark – i.e. Viking Age – runes and in the Old Norse language. What is harder to tell is whether he lived in the Danelaw himself and/or how many generations of his family might have lived in the Danelaw before him. Alternatively, his handiwork could have been brought over to England from Scandinavia by a settler or visitor, meaning that perhaps Thorfast never travelled west across the North Sea himself. In either case, it reveals the intimate connections between the Danelaw and the Norse homelands.

How did events develop from the early smash-and-grab raids on the British Isles that we have already seen to permanent settlement, where Scandinavian laws were recognised officially, and the work of a proud Nordic comb-maker ended up in Lincoln? The story of how Scandinavians came to put down roots in England, and what they got up to when they arrived, is a rather shadowy one, especially when it comes to the lives of ordinary people. What we do know is that by the 850s, lightning raids on

The runes tell us that 'Thorfast made a good comb', but only the comb case survives, so we'll have to take his word for it. Lincoln, England, 10th or 11th century.

coastal parts of Britain and Ireland were being replaced by over-wintering camps and longer summer campaigns that penetrated further inland. In 865, the *Anglo-Saxon Chronicle* reported the arrival of pagan forces from overseas, which one version of the chronicle described as a *micel hæðen here* ('great heathen army').[2] By 871 the leader of the combined Nordic forces was Guthrum, who promptly set about toppling the Anglo-Saxon kings of East Anglia, Mercia and Northumbria before setting his sights on the last remaining kingdom: Wessex. At the start of 878, following a surprise midwinter attack, King Alfred ('the Great', as he later became known) and his followers were forced to retreat to the woods and the moors, hiding out in the swamps and marshes of Somerset. Later that year, they regrouped and defeated Guthrum and his army at the Battle of Edington.

Following this defeat, Guthrum converted to Christianity with Alfred as his sponsor, became king of East Anglia, and started parcelling out land to his followers. A peace treaty drawn up between Alfred and Guthrum secured the territorial claims and legal rights of both Anglo-Saxons and Scandinavians. According to this agreement, the boundary between the two kingdoms ran up the River Thames, up the River Lea, to Bedford, then up the River Ouse to Watling Street, which in modern-day terms takes us from London to somewhere north-west of Birmingham. It's not entirely clear how stable this arrangement was, or how defined the boundaries were on the ground. Even so, the sheer volume of Old Norse place names that survive north of the boundary line suggest that this area was heavily influenced by Scandinavian incomers.

Power ebbed and flowed between Anglo-Saxon and Norse rulers over the next few generations. In 947, a new character moved centre stage: Erik Bloodaxe, who was already king of Norway when he set his sights on an English crown. He ruled as king of Northumbria from 947 to 948, and again from 952 to 954. His death is a complicated and murky affair, but he was essentially driven out of York and murdered by a political rival, possibly in the lonely wilds of Stainmore in the Pennines. A skaldic poem called *Eiríksmál* ('Words about Erik') describes his arrival in the halls of Valhalla. He is welcomed by Odin who tells his Valkyries and *einherjar* (his chosen warriors, literally 'those who fight alone') to rinse the beer kegs, prepare the feasting benches and carry in wine for this glorious newcomer. The god declares: 'What kind of dream is this, that I thought that a little before daybreak I was preparing Valhalla for a slain army? I awakened the *einherjar*, I asked them to get up to strew the benches, to rinse the drinking cups, [I asked] Valkyries to bring wine, as if a leader should come.'[3]

After Erik's death the story passes on through the generations until we reach Cnut, who became king of England in 1016 and later created a North Sea empire with Norway and Denmark that would last until his death in 1035. By this time, we are a little more than three decades from the Norman Conquest in 1066, and a whole new cast of historical protagonists are waiting for their cues.

This is a whistle-stop tour centred around the famous rulers and war leaders who ended up in contemporary chronicles and later history books. It is a narrative mostly built from the *Anglo-Saxon Chronicle* and other written sources, texts that had limited interest in the ordinary human lives bumping along underneath. These ordinary lives included those who had migrated from Scandinavia and settled new lands, and the generations that followed them. They also included those for whom these lands were old rather than new. In this fluid, shifting new world, people from different cultural backgrounds rubbed alongside each other, sometimes getting on well and sometimes not.

So, what about the ordinary people in this part of the world, whose lives and deaths – unlike Erik Bloodaxe's – didn't merit warriors scrubbing beer kegs and Valkyries pouring glasses of wine in the afterlife? What about Thorfast the comb-maker, who was unlikely to find himself feasting in the halls of Valhalla, but whose talents were probably more appreciated by his clients than the political jostling and bloodshed that made its way into the chronicles? Haircare was important. Grooming regimes mattered. There's a reason that Thorfast was so proud of his work. Let's swing the spotlight from centre stage to the wings again.

Good hair, do care

Haircare isn't the first thing that springs to mind when we picture those who lived during the Viking Age, but it's a far more accurate representation of the culture than horned helmets and drinking skulls (neither historically accurate). Combs turn up in archaeological excavations of the period, often delicately crafted and intricately decorated, an intimate link to their individual owners. In the two Salme ship burials from around 750, a dozen combs were found, made from reindeer and elk antler. One of these belonged to the leader of the expedition, the body found with the 'king' gaming piece in its mouth. Far from the muddy dirt of archaeological investigations, in the dry parchments of saga manuscripts, a later, better-known leader of the Viking Age is the semi-legendary king of Norway, Harald 'Fairhair'. But he took a while to earn his flattering nickname. Prior to that, sagas tell us that he vowed not to comb his tresses until he had managed to bring the whole country under his command, earning himself the less salubrious nickname 'Tanglehair'.

Even the pagan gods and their immortal companions cared about good hair. Norse mythology tells how the golden-haired Sif, wife of the hammer-wielding god Thor, had her hair cut off by the mischievous prankster Loki. To atone for his horrible trick (and to prevent Thor from killing him) Loki commissioned dwarves to make even nicer hair for Sif, fashioned from strands of gold. Meanwhile, back in the human realm, a tiny silver-gilded figurine was found in the village of Hårby, on the island of Funen in Denmark. Only 3.4 centimetres tall and dated to around 800, it depicts a female figure. She holds a sword raised in one hand, and a shield in the other. Her hair is pulled into a twisted knot at the back of her head and falls straight down her back. We can't say for certain that she is a Valkyrie, but it certainly seems likely. Indeed, on the Tjängvide picture stone on the island of Gotland (which we met in the last chapter), the rider on his eight-legged steed is greeted by a woman holding a drinking horn, again, most likely a Valkyrie. Her hair is identical to that of the figurine's: a twisted knot at the nape of her neck and a long ponytail down the length of her back.

One might think that such good hair would be appreciated by everyone, but there's always a critic. From very early on, Scandinavians enjoyed a reputation abroad as snappy dressers with excellent tresses. Following the notorious Viking attack on Lindisfarne in 793, Alcuin, an Anglo-Saxon scholar living at the court of King Charlemagne, wrote to King Æthelred of Northumbria. He complained that the Northumbrians were styling their hair and dressing like the very people who were attacking them: 'Consider the dress, the way of wearing the hair, the luxurious habits of the princes and people. Look at your trimming of beard and hair, in which you have wished to resemble the pagans. Are you not menaced by terror of them whose fashion you wished to follow?'[4]

This wasn't the last time that Anglo-Saxons would attempt to emulate the grooming regimes and hairstyles of Nordic incomers. Nor was it the last time that others would be irritated by those whom they considered to be disloyal fashion victims. Around the turn of the first millennium, Abbot Ælfric of Eynsham sent a letter to a man named Edward, whom he addressed as 'brother' (whether this means that Edward was his actual sibling or a fellow man of the cloth isn't clear). The abbot was particularly cross at copycat English fashion victims such as

Edward, who dressed like the Danes and cut their hair the Scandi-chic way, 'with bared necks and blinded eyes' (i.e. short and shaved at the back, long and shaggy at the front).

> I also say to you, brother Edward, now that you have asked me for this, that you do wrong in that you abandon the English customs which your fathers observed and love the customs of the heathen people who did not give life to you and by doing so you reveal that you despise your kindred and your ances-tors by such evil customs when you dress in insult to them in Danish fashion, with bared necks and blinded eyes.[5]

Ælfric goes on to remind Edward that people shouldn't be eating while on the privy ('I often heard it said, and it is an evil truth, that country women will often drink and even eat foully on their privies at their beer parties').[6] This comes almost as an afterthought, after the apparently more despicable business of dressing like a Dane. But who can blame Edward for his love of a sharp cut? And whether or not Edward gave in to the sinful temptation of Scandi chic, it seems from Ælfric's letter that male Norse settlers and visitors would have been distinguishable from Anglo-Saxons on account of their 'bare neck and blinded eyes' hairstyles.

In 1066, only a few decades after Abbot Ælfric made his snide remarks about Edward's tonsorial proclivities, a new wave of immigrants arrived in England, led by William the Conqueror. Although they spoke French, they were only a few generations removed from their Scandinavian roots, the clue being in their name, 'Norman' or 'Northmen'. Yet while the Normans were Northmen only in name, some clues as to their older cultural heritage remained. And one of these is the identifying hairstyle they sport on the Bayeux Tapestry: shaved at the back and long at the front just like the Danish settlers who so incensed Ælfric.

Almost two centuries later, the reputation of the Norse

settlers as well-groomed smoothies persisted. Writing in around 1220, John of Wallingford described these Scandinavian males as sexy heartbreakers who went to unthinkable extremes of personal hygiene:

> They brought many hardships to the people of the land, for – according to the custom of their country – they combed their hair every day and bathed every Saturday. They also changed their clothes often and groomed their bodies with many such frivolities. Hence, they assailed the chastity even of married women, and persuaded the daughters of nobles to become their lovers.[7]

There is, however, a dark side to this story. Behind these complaints about the seductive powers of these new inhabitants were serious tensions, which often boiled over into violence. John of Wallingford's description comes in the middle of a description of the massacre of Scandinavian settlers that took place on 13 November 1002 – St Brice's Day – on the orders of the Anglo-Saxon king Æthelred. The *Anglo-Saxon Chronicle* has a brief description of what happened: 'And in that year the king ordered to be slain all the Danish men who were in England – this was done on St Brice's day – because the king had been informed that they would treacherously deprive him, and then all his councillors, of life, and possess this kingdom afterwards.'[8]

The fullest contemporary account is one of King Æthelred's royal charters, written two years after the event. It describes the rebuilding of St Frideswide's Church in Oxford (now part of Christ Church Cathedral), and the reason for this makes for grim reading:

> For it is fully agreed that to all dwelling in this country it will be well known that, since a decree was sent out by me with the counsel of my leading men and magnates, to the effect

that all the Danes who had sprung up in this land, sprouting like cockle amongst the wheat, were to be destroyed by a most just extermination, and this decree was to be put into effect even as far as death, those Danes who dwelt in the aforementioned town, striving to escape death, entered this sanctuary of Christ, having broken by force the doors and bolts, and resolved to make a refuge and defence for themselves therein against the people of the town and suburbs; but when all the people in pursuit strove, forced by necessity, to drive them out, and could not, they set fire to the planks and burnt, as it seems, this church with its ornaments and its books. Afterwards, with God's aid, it was renewed by me and my subjects.[9]

Both the chronicle and the law code summarise events from an Anglo-Saxon perspective, while leaving out the human cost. The Scandinavians are like 'cockle amongst the wheat', weeds to be removed by a 'most just extermination'. As far as Æthelred is concerned, the main victim is the church in Oxford, which must now be rebuilt. So where are the real-life victims of this massacre? The best candidate is a mass grave found in the grounds of St John's College in Oxford, with at least thirty-five Viking Age bodies that had been dumped on top of an old Neolithic earthwork. Apart from two skeletons that were too young for their sex to be determined, all of them were young males, most between the ages of sixteen and twenty-five. The trauma on their skeletons showed that they had been killed violently with a variety of weapons. Many of their injuries were on their backs, which suggests they had been trying to escape when they were cut down. Some bones showed signs of charring, which fits with the description of the church burning as people hid inside.

But other evidence from this mass grave doesn't quite fit with the picture of the St Brice's Day massacre. The dating of the bones suggests that they may have lived a few decades earlier. Their bones also indicate that they had a diet higher in marine protein than those living in the area, which would mean that they weren't local settlers. This fits perfectly well with the *Anglo-Saxon Chronicle*'s brief account (which states only that 'Danish men' were killed), but less well with Æthelred's law code, which claims that the victims were settled Scandinavians living in Oxford. It also fits less well with other later (albeit less reliable) sources, which claim that the victims were women and children as well as men. The bodies in the grave were males, mostly young, many with healed weapon injuries on their bones, as if they had seen battles before.[10] So perhaps this was a Scandinavian warband or raiding party that ran out of luck. Of more certain victims of the St Brice's Day massacre – and we don't know how many there were, or where else the violence took place other than Oxford – no bodily remains have been found.

There is, however, a coda to this story. It reminds us that while the bodies of the dead might not fit the neat historical narratives that we have laid out for them, they may have other, more intriguing stories to tell. When the DNA of one of the men in the Oxford mass grave – who died in his twenties with multiple weapon wounds to his head and back – was sequenced by researchers, they found that it was a close match with another body in their database of 442 humans. These had been selected from archaeological sites across the Viking world. The other body belonged to a man in his fifties with a healed wound on a neck bone that also suggested some violence in his past. He had died from a stab wound to his hip, perhaps from a sword, and this time it hadn't healed. Extraordinarily, the two men were second-degree relatives, which meant they might be half-brothers, uncle and nephew, or grandfather and grandson. But while one had been found in a mass grave in Oxford, the other had been discovered all the way across the North Sea, on the island of Funen in Denmark. Coincidentally, they had been discovered by archaeologists just three years apart. Their bodies can't be dated precisely enough to know when each of them died. Perhaps they raided

The skeletons of two relatives brought back together at the National Museum of Denmark in 2021 after a millennium spent on either side of the North Sea.

together as contemporaries, or perhaps the younger one grew up listening to the older one's tales of travel and derring-do, and in time set off to emulate him. But together, their bodies tell a story of family ties, far-off travel, brutal lives and brutal deaths. Today, their story continues, and in 2021 the two men were reunited in Denmark, for an exhibition at the National Museum of Denmark called *Togtet* ('The Raid').[11]

Bath time

In John of Wallingford's account of the St Brice's Day massacre he includes a fascinating nugget of information. Having already noted that the Norse settlers combed their hair every day and bathed every Saturday, he goes on to describe how the king and his advisors decided the date when the coordinated attacks should take place: 'They fixed the day on which they would rise up against them, that is, on a Saturday, when, as has been mentioned, they were accustomed to bathe.'[12] The thirteenth of November 1002 was indeed a Saturday. There are no sources other than John of Wallingford that include this piece of information, which makes it impossible to know if this really was a consideration when the attacks were planned. Even so, the importance of Saturday for bathing and washing is preserved in its Old Norse name, *Laugardagr*, which means 'bath day'. It's still there in the word for Saturday in all the languages of the Nordic world: Icelandic, Faroese, Norwegian, Swedish, Danish, even borrowed into Finnish. The same element *laug* – which could mean bath, pool or hot spring – was also a popular element of Viking Age names, especially for women who might be called Áslaug (god-bath), Þórlaug (Thor-bath), Sigrlaug (victory-bath) or Snælaug (snow-bath).

Open-air bathing was – and still is – a particularly enjoyable activity in volcanic Iceland, blessed with its natural hot springs. It was said that when the country officially converted to Christianity around 1000, many at the national assembly insisted on being baptised on the way home, so they could do so in the warm springs of Reykjalaug (which means 'Smoky Pool') in Laugardalr ('Valley of Baths/Pools'). Two centuries later, Snorri Sturluson – the author and politician whose writing preserves so much Viking Age mythology and history – enjoyed his own outdoor hot tub at his home in Reykholt ('Smoky Ridge'). The pool can still be seen today, a work of impressive engineering with an underground passage that connected it to the farmhouse, with a conduit that brought water down from the hot spring. But the pool itself dates back before Snorri's time. In fact, the hot springs at Reykholt are mentioned in *Landnámabók* ('The Book of Settlement') as a place where one early settler kept his sheep sheds, and where he fled to avoid marital tensions between the guests who were staying with him.[13]

Beyond the luxuriously hot springs of Iceland, over 4,000 kilometres east as the crow flies, bathing remained a crucial part of Norse culture even as that culture started to shift in different directions and absorb different influences. Evidence for this comes from a peace treaty made between the Byzantines and the Rus in 907. It is preserved in the *Rus Primary Chronicle*, which was first compiled in Kyiv around 1113, and charts the history of Kyivan Rus from its origins in the middle of the ninth century. The Rus seem to have had predominantly Nordic origins, likely from what is now modern-day Sweden. The unlucky crew who ended up buried in their ships on the Estonian island of Saaremaa may well have come from a similar background, but a century earlier. But over time, they assimilated with other cultural groups in this part of the world, although they retained some elements of Nordic identity.

The peace treaty of 907 follows a Rus raid on Constantinople, the glittering and wealthy heart of the Byzantine Empire. The attack was led by Oleg, who ruled from Novgorod (the same place that, several centuries later, would be the home of a tiny birch bark artist called Onfim). If we are to believe the *Chronicle*, Oleg was accompanied on the raid not only by his fellow Rus, but also many others from Slavic and Finnic tribes across the region. Yet named in the peace treaty are Rus with very Norse names, including Oleg (the Old Norse name 'Helgi') as well as Karl, Farulf, Vermund, Hrollaf and Steinvith. And the terms that the Rus and Byzantines came to were also very Norse. For Rus merchants who came to trade peacefully, they were to be given six months of bread, wine, meat, fish and fruit. Even more importantly, 'baths shall be prepared for them in any volume they require'.[14] And although we can never prove it, there's a good chance that the day when the bathhouses were most filled with Rus bodies was Saturday.

Just as not everyone appreciated the fastidious grooming habits of the Scandinavians who settled in England, so not everyone in the east appreciated the frequency of their bathing. But this time, they wanted more of it, not less. The disgruntled individual was Ahmad ibn Fadlān, writing in 922, only fifteen years after the Rus–Byzantine peace treaty was signed. Like the Anglo-Saxon writers who bemoaned the fierce and fabulous hair-care regime of the Vikings, Ahmad ibn Fadlān too was a man of god, a theologian. But his was a different god, since he was a Muslim from the Abbasid Caliphate. He was part of a diplomatic mission sent by the caliph to the Volga Bulgars, around 3,500 kilometres to the north of Baghdad. He wrote an account of his travels and the many peoples he encountered on the way. Among them was a group of Rus traders who set up camp on the banks of the River Itil, close to the north-west shore of the Caspian Sea. Apparently, he didn't think much of their washing habits:

> They are the filthiest of God's creatures. They do not clean themselves after urinating or defecating, nor do they wash after having sex. They do not wash their hands after meals. They are like wandering asses . . . Every day without fail they wash their faces and their heads with the dirtiest and filthiest water there could be. A young serving girl comes every morning with breakfast and with it a great basin of water. She proffers it to her master, who washes his hands and face in it, as well as his hair. He washes and disentangles his hair, using a comb, there in the basin, then he blows his nose and spits and does every filthy thing imaginable in the water. When he has finished, the servant carries the basin to the man next to him. She goes on passing the basin round from one to another until she has taken it to all the men in the house in turn. And each of them blows his nose and spits and washes his face and hair in this basin.[15]

As a practising Muslim who would only have used clean running water for washing, Ahmad ibn Fadlān's horror at these insalubrious bathing habits pours off the page. Let's just be thankful for his sake that he never reached England, because if we are to believe John of Wallingford then the Anglo-Saxons were even more unhygienic than the Scandinavians.

The look of the past

When it came to the Rus he met on the river, Ahmad ibn Fadlān was far more complimentary about what they looked like, regardless of their questionable hygiene: 'I have never seen bodies more perfect than theirs. They were like palm trees. They are fair and ruddy.'[16] He also described how each man covered his body with dark green designs, 'from the tips of his toes to his neck'.[17] It is usually assumed that this is a reference to tattoos, and very occasionally, such images do survive on the fragile skin of the past. Sometimes this is because the bodies were deliberately mummified (as in the case of Ancient Egyptians, where those with tattoos were predominantly female). At other times, this is because the bodies were preserved by ice (such as 'Ötzi the Iceman', discovered 5,300 years after his death in the Alps with his series of sixty-one line and cross tattoos, or the young woman from the fifth century BCE, who lived on the Siberian steppes and whose frozen body was found with tattoos resembling a deer, a sheep and a snow leopard). But nothing comparable has yet come to light from the Viking Age world, and we have to rely on Ahmad ibn Fadlān's words alone.

We might expect the Anglo-Saxons – so concerned with the physical appearances and general sexiness of the Scandinavians who settled parts of England – to have commented on the presence of tattoos if they were popular widely across the Viking world. On the other hand, it's possible that Anglo-Saxons themselves were partial to a bit of body art, which would make it something less to be remarked upon. And indeed, when

William of Malmesbury, born thirty years after the Norman Conquest to an English mother and a Norman father, described the Anglo-Saxons of 1066, he painted a picture of them tattooed and dripping in bling: 'The English of those days wore garments halfway to the knee, which left them unimpeded; hair short, chin shaven, arms loaded with gold bracelets, tattooed with coloured patterns.'[18]

Granted, this isn't meant to be a flattering description of the Anglo-Saxons, so we can't be sure of its accuracy. William also criticised their drinking, their uncouth names and the grating sound of their language. If he is correct, this might explain why Viking tattoos, if they existed, were not remarked upon in Anglo-Saxon sources. Yet such is the power of Viking Age imagery – the interlacing and knots, the gripping beasts, the biting animals, the symbolism, the runes, the mythological tales – that Viking-themed tattoos remain enormously popular today. If potential tattooees are seeking historical authenticity, the best advice might be to make sure the tattoo is coloured a shade of dark green, as Ahmad ibn Fadlān describes (probably from the use of wood ash as pigmentation). Beyond that, until we find a tattooed body from the Viking Age frozen in the ice, we have little else to go on.

Other types of body modification were more unusual in the early medieval world and left more of a trace in the archaeological record. Especially teeth filed with grooves, mostly horizontal, occasionally diagonal, and, in the case of the Viking Age, always in male mouths. In Sweden, more than 130 Viking Age bodies have been found with filed teeth. It seems to have been a phenomenon centred especially on the island of Gotland in the Baltic Sea.[19] This is where many of those with filed teeth had been buried, though interestingly not all of them *came* from Gotland. Thus far, only three more examples of Viking Age filed teeth have been found outside Sweden: two from the island of Funen in Denmark and one in a mass execution site on Ridgeway Hill in Dorset, England.

The bodies from Ridgeway Hill were found in a pit, dug into an old Roman quarry. It contained fifty-four decapitated skeletons, but not quite enough skulls to go round, only fifty-one, all piled together to the side of the bodies. Just like the mass grave in Oxford, Viking Age bodies do not all have easy endings. Also just like the mass grave in Oxford, the bodies in the Ridgeway Hill pit were all male, mostly young and mostly well built. They came from across the Viking world: Norway, Sweden, Iceland, even the Baltic and Kyivan Rus. And they had been executed, somewhere between 970 and 1025, although it's hard to be more specific. One major difference with the Oxford skeletons is that these bodies had no healed injuries from weapons, which makes it harder to identify them as seasoned warriors as opposed to settlers or traders.[20]

The individual with filed teeth was typical of those in the pit, a young male between twenty-five and thirty-five years of age. He had two horizontal lines filed across his two top teeth, one straight across and one curved like a half moon. As yet, no one has looked at his isotope profile to see where he came from (although Sweden is the safest bet). But what is strange is that, despite so many Viking Age filed teeth now in the database, no clear pattern emerges. These bodies must be telling a story through their dental modifications, just as they did in their owners' lifetimes (about identity, about character, about origins). Even so, other than the apparent Gotland connection, we're not yet reading the narrative. For now, these bodies keep their secrets.

Hair and teeth aside, what about the faces of the Viking Age? Those most distinctive and personal arrangements of features, so intimate yet always turned out to the wider world, so obvious and familiar when the person is present, yet so quick to fade in their absence. In an age long before photographs, long before portrait painters began to capture the realistic likenesses, expressions and characters of their subjects, finding out what the

Vikings looked like is no easy task. We have so many personal remnants of the Viking Age, so many colourful historical figures, so many sagas with exquisitely characterised protagonists. And yet, however close we feel to them, we can never conjure up their faces.

We can start with artistic representations. Images of faces and bodies appear in the many art styles that developed over the course of the Viking Age and the centuries that followed. Many are highly stylised: generic faces angled sideways on runestones, playing their part in mythic scenes, or glaring out of the wood they were carved into with blank eyes and exaggerated expressions. But sometimes, lifelike, naturalistic human faces emerge from the soil, head hair twisted into elegant knots, beards and moustaches plaited and twisted. Faces such as these come from the Oseberg ship burial, that famous high-status grave containing two women from 834. There are faces – both human and non-human – peeping out from all sorts of grave goods that were included in the burial, some with bulging eyes, bared teeth and ferocious expressions as if to scare off intruders and protect the

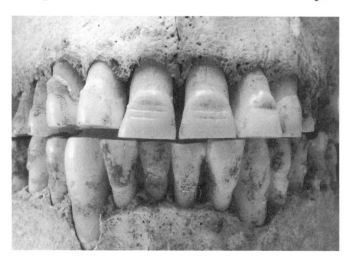

Teeth filed with two horizontal rows, from a skeleton buried at the fortress of Trelleborg in Denmark, 10th century.

women inside. Several little heads – some human, some not – are mounted on the wagon and sled. The human heads have wistful eyes, parted mouths, neat moustaches, meticulously combed hair. Among the faces of toothy dragons, fearsome warriors, even cats, these feel like faces inspired by those of real humans who once felt the sun and rain on their skin.

In some ways, the further away from the Viking Age we get, the closer we can get to the people who lived at the time. Forensic facial reconstruction and DNA analysis can bring us face to face with the past, quite literally. There are two ways of doing it, and both are extraordinarily sophisticated, blending art, science and technology. The old-school method uses a model of the skull, pegs added to determine tissue depth depending on age, sex and genetic origins, and then facial muscles rebuilt around the pegs in clay. Then there are computer-generated models, which create faces so uncannily lifelike and fluid in their expressions – blinking, smiling – that they become equally magnetic and disquieting to behold. Experts in forensic facial reconstruction often work on modern-day police investigations too, where bodies have become too decomposed to identify. The rates of accuracy continue to improve as technology marches on, good enough that the facial reconstructions of these people would likely be recognised by those who knew them. Some of these Viking Age reconstructions are from well-known individuals. St Magnus, once ruler of Orkney in the early twelfth century, stares out at us with his kind eyes, wide nose and full lips. But some features are easier to determine than others: while the forensic artist has given him typically Nordic blue eyes and blond hair, no DNA data was available, so these elements are informed guesswork.[21]

Other reconstructed faces are of unknown individuals whose lives have long since vanished into the darkness of the past, but whose skulls happen to have survived well enough for forensic anthropologists to breathe new life into them. At the Jorvik

Viking Centre in York several of the figures included in the exhibition are modelled on skulls of the actual inhabitants of Viking
Age York.[22] These include the 'Coppergate Woman', who was
probably in her mid-forties when she died and may well have
walked with a crutch since she had hip dysplasia. Kept separate
from other burials, without a shroud or burial goods, it is likely
that she wasn't a high-status individual, but there may well be
another story hiding behind the manner of her burial. What
we do know is that she ended her life very far from where she
began it, having spent her childhood on the coast of south-west
Norway or the very far north of Scotland.[23] Finally, there is the
reconstruction of the older of the two relatives we met earlier
in this chapter, one buried on the Danish island of Funen, one
buried in the mass grave in Oxford. Just as their skeletons were

Carved wooden head
decorating one of the
wagons from the Oseberg
ship burial. Norway, 834.

Reconstruction of the older of the two relatives whose skeletons were brought together at the National Museum of Denmark for the exhibition *Togtet* ('The Raid').

brought together in Copenhagen, so the features of the older man were brought back to life for the same exhibition. Over a thousand years after his death, he was conjured up to stand watch over the bodies of himself and his young kinsman, kitted out not as a warrior but as an everyday farmer with silvering hair and deepening lines on his weathered face. Dressed simply in a brown woollen tunic, holding a little knife and an apple in his soil-tinged hands, this reconstruction reminds us that his body may have known violence, but this was far from the whole story.

Physical needs

Every single body that comes into the world has basic physical needs. The need for getting food and drink into the top end and eliminating it at the bottom end. The need for warmth and shelter. The need for sleep. That ninth-century left-handed mitten that we met briefly in the chapter on travel, lost on the hillside at Lendbreen and frozen in time, is part of that story. So is a fossilised human poo from ninth-century York, or *Jórvík*, as the Vikings called it. At 20 centimetres long and 5 centimetres wide, this monster is the largest piece of fossilised human faeces ever discovered. It is often known as the Lloyds Bank Coprolite because it was found on the site where the bank was planning to build a branch. Usually, historical human faeces are preserved in a big communal mush, such as at the bottom of a latrine. So the survival of a lone turd is actually a marvellous opportunity to find out something about a single individual from the past. Not only a human who fell between the cracks of history, but also the prodigious product of their bowels. And as it turns out, they were not the healthiest of humans. The coprolite consisted mainly of meat, bread and several hundred intestinal worms that would have made life very itchy and sore. Its size suggests that the unfortunate person hadn't pooed in several days, and while the process can't have been much fun, the relief must have been considerable.

The human responsible for bringing this poo into the world probably thought that this was an end to it. Little did they know that its story would still be unfolding over a millennium later. Back in 2003, when the Lloyds Bank Coprolite was being visited by an adoring party of school children, it was dropped by their teacher and broken into three pieces. It has since been glued back together, but the joins are still visible, a reminder that not even a fossilised turd, hardened by 1,100 years in the world, can escape the fate that that the Norns have spun for it.[24]

Since so many bodily functions are universal, it can be hard to link them to specific individuals who lived in the past, especially when we are thinking about people who – runes aside – were not literate and did not write down their experiences of being in the world. But we can move forward to the era of manuscript composition in medieval Iceland, from the thirteenth century onwards, to hear individuals complaining that the basic needs of their bodies are not being met. Disgruntled scribes, scribbling in the margins of their manuscripts, leaving messages that attest to their need for more warmth ('it's bad to write in a northwester'), more light ('darkness has fallen, necklace-bearer'), more food ('you do me wrong, Dori, you never give me enough fish'). Others write of needs that are more of the mind and soul than the body: the need for mental stimulation ('writing bores me'), the need for love ('all hope is lost that she will love me'). Another writes of his bodily limitations, and his desire to be healed of them: 'The poor wretch is ill in his eyes', and 'Jesus, son of Mary, behold the eyes of your slave'. And this brings us to another near-universal truth, for just as every single body that comes into the world has the same basic physical requirements, so we become most aware of our bodies when something isn't working properly.[25]

The world's biggest fossilised human poo, mighty product of 9th-century York.

Sick bodies

Viking Age medicine was rudimentary at best, involving the use of herbs, setting of broken bones, bandaging and cauterising wounds, and bloodletting. Later saga stories include several healers, many of whom were women, attending to those who had been wounded in battle. One of the most informative passages comes from *Óláfs saga helga*, which is part of *Heimskringla*, Snorri Sturluson's compilation of kings' sagas. By this point in the narrative, the king has been killed in battle, and his poet, Thormod, is wounded:

> After this Thormod went off to a kind of storehouse and went in. There were already many men inside there badly wounded. There was a certain woman busy there bandaging men's wounds. There was a fire on the floor, and she was warming water to cleanse the wounds . . . Then said the physician: 'Let me see your wounds and I shall give you some bandages.' After that he sat down and threw off his clothes. And when the physician saw his wounds, then she examined the wound that he had in his side, felt that there was a piece of iron stuck in it, but could not tell for certain which way it had gone in. She had been cooking in a stone kettle there, ground garlic and other herbs and boiled it together and was giving it to wounded men and could find out like that whether they had intestinal wounds, for it smelt of garlic from out of the wound if it was intestinal. She brought this to Thormod, bidding him eat it. He replies: 'Take it away. I am not pining for gruel.' Then she took some tongs and tried to pull the iron out.[26]

We see from this passage that medical intervention might take the form of warm water to clean wounds, bandages, garlic and herbs to investigate – and perhaps try to heal – injuries, and tools for removing whatever had become embedded. We know from surviving skeletons that some injuries could indeed be healed. In the story of Thormod, however, his wounds proved fatal.

When a body had been pierced by a weapon, the cause of the injury was clear. In the case of unseen ailments, other cures had to be sought to battle the unseen forces that had brought about the disease. Supernatural dwarves, elves and demons were thought to be sickness spirits, responsible for many maladies and pains, fevers, epilepsy and malaria (as well as bad weather). These associations existed in many early medieval cultures, not only in the Nordic world but also in Anglo-Saxon England and parts of Germany.

In the last chapter, we met an individual called Bofi, from Kvinneby in eleventh-century Sweden, who suffered from a festering sore. This was thought to be caused by a demon, and the cure was a copper amulet inscribed with runes that called on Thor for protection. Bofi was not the only patient who sought to be cured in this way. Also from eleventh-century Sweden, this time from Sigtuna, comes another copper amulet. This one is a thin rectangle with a hole at one end, designed to be worn around the neck. As in Bofi's case, the interpretation isn't straightforward, but the runes seem to address the 'Thor' or 'ogre' of the wound-fever, which may be a reference to blood poisoning or gangrene. One side of the amulet commands: 'Thor/ogre of gangrene, Lord of demons, flee! You have been found!' The other side is more complex. One possible translation might be: 'Receive three torments, wolf! Receive nine needs, wolf! Three ice(-runes), these ice(-runes) may satisfy you wolf! Benefit from the charm!'[27]

Head pain, blood poisoning, festering sores: human bodies in the grip of affliction while supernatural beings battled for supremacy. And once Christianity gained a firm foothold in medieval Scandinavia, much the same formula continued. We can see this in one more runic inscription, once again from Ribe in Denmark, home to the rune-inscribed skull fragment from the early eighth century. This one, however, is from around 1300. It's a professional-looking piece of work, a five-sided length of pine wood with runes beautifully carved on each of them. Written in the form of an alliterative poem, this lengthy inscription is a cure for 'the trembler', which might be malaria or epilepsy:

> I bid the earth ensure, and the heaven above, sun and Saint Mary, and God the Lord Himself, that he lend me a healer's hands and a lively tongue to bind 'the Trembler' where cures are needed. From back and from breast, from body and from limb, from eyes and from ears, from every (place) where evil can enter. A stone is called 'black', it stands out in the ocean. On it lie nine needs. They must never sleep sweet nor wake warm before you receive a cure for this, where I have found out runes to speak words. Amen and so be it.[28]

Such runic inscriptions seem to be another form of the *bjargrúnar* or 'helping runes' that we met earlier in connection with childbirth. But not all protective runes against malevolent beings are quite as benevolent as they might first appear. That same *bjargrúnar* word appears on one of our old friends, a Bergen rune stick dating to around 1335, with runes carved on all four sides. The context isn't clear, but it begins positively enough: 'I carve *bótrúnar* (runes of remedy), I carve *bjargrúnar* (runes of protection), once against elves, twice against trolls, thrice against giants'. But just when we might start to think that this is another attempt to heal ailments caused by supernatural beings, the tone changes swiftly. The inscription ends with dark menace and magic that seems to curse an unknown female until she submits to the carver: 'you shall never sit, you shall never sleep – love me as you love yourself'.[29] Sometimes, the beings who seek to cause the most pain are neither supernatural dwarves nor elves, neither trolls nor giants, but other humans.

Vulnerable bodies

Such runic prescriptions with their blends of religions, beliefs and superstitions were designed to heal the suffering body. But not all infirmities could be healed. To understand a society's priorities and values, we can look at how it cares for the most vulnerable bodies and minds in its midst. This isn't always an easy task, and what we discover might not be easy knowledge to take on board. In the case of the Viking Age, for example, newborn babies were sometimes put out to die. Infanticide was nothing particular to this period and was carried out far back into prehistory, and in cultures across the world. Infanticide by exposing babies to the elements is mentioned in texts describing Iceland's official conversion to Christianity in around 1000, the same event that had Icelanders running to the hot springs on the way back from the national assembly rather than risk baptism in the freezing cold waters closer to the assembly site. But what about bodily vulnerabilities that continued later in life, bodies that were disabled in one form or another?

Several of the gods had what we today might class as disabilities. Odin was blind in one eye, having famously given up the other in exchange for wisdom. Tyr had one hand, having lost the other in the jaws of the wolf Fenrir. Hod, a son of Odin, was blind. At times – although not always – the stories of how they got these bodily limitations are great myths, seen as something positive and mystical. Once again, Odin speaks to us through *Hávamál*, reminding us with characteristic black humour that life doesn't necessarily stop because of a disability:

> The lame man rides a horse,
> the handless man drives a herd,
> the deaf man fights and succeeds;
> to be blind is better than to be burnt:
> a corpse is of no use to anyone.[30]

1. The skull from the Salme ship burial with the 'king' gaming piece (seen here as a dark oval) between its teeth. Surrounded by the finest grave goods, this individual seems to have been the leader of the expedition. He was also born with fused vertebrae in his neck. Salme, Estonia, *c.*750.

2. The 'Hostage Stone', depicting a bound figure being led away to a ship by men wearing chain mail. It comes from the island of Inchmarnock off the west coast of mainland Scotland, the location of an early medieval monastery. It dates to the late 8th or early 9th century, the same time as the first Viking raids on the British Isles.

3. A reliquary of yew wood and bronze, made to hold Christian relics but apparently pilfered by Viking raiders. Found in the grave of a woman in Melhus in central Norway, early 9th century.

4. A little figure – likely a child's doll – carved from antler, found in the Viking Age trading town of Hedeby, Denmark.

5. A bronze figure with a pointy hat, a pointy beard and a pointy penis. This seems to be the god Frey, who was associated with fertility. Rällinge, Sweden, c.1000.

6. One of the birch bark drawings by Onfim the little artist. It depicts a smaller figure on the right holding out an arm to a larger figure – broken off – on the left. Both have Onfim's signature garden-rake-style arms. Novgorod, Russia, mid-13th century.

7. A left-handed mitten found frozen in the ancient mountain pass of Lendbreen, patched together from whatever textiles were available. Norway, 9th century.

8. Selection of beads belonging to the 'Mountain Woman' (there were over 500 in total). She was not native to Iceland, but her body was found near the old route between Seyðisfjörður and Egilsstaðir. Eastern Iceland, 10th century.

9. Feline carvings from the Oseberg ship burial, which contained the bodies of two women. Several anxious-looking cats have been carved into the back panel of the wooden cart, while other images of cats appear elsewhere in the burial. This may echo the association between cats and the goddess Freyja. Oseberg, Norway, 834.

10. Entrance to the Surtshellir lava tunnels in the Hallmundarhraun lava field, formed by a volcanic eruption in the Langjökull glacier area around the year 930, Western Iceland. Deep inside these tunnels, it seems that early Icelanders performed rituals to placate unseen and unpredictable forces.

11. A gold medallion (bracteate) from the Migration Age. It most likely depicts the god Tyr, who has one hand in the mouth of a wolf-like creature. Trollhätten, Sweden, 5th or 6th century.

12. The Tjängvide picture stone from the island of Gotland. At the top, a figure on an eight-legged horse (probably Sleipnir) is greeted by a woman holding a drinking horn. At the bottom, armed warriors stand on a longship. Gotland, Sweden, c.700–900.

13. A little silver figurine less than 2 cm high. It may represent the one-eyed god Odin, flanked by his ravens and wolves and wearing strings of beads and a long tunic more commonly associated with female atire. Lejre, Denmark, c.900–950.

14. A silver-gilded figurine, 3.4 cm high, holding a sword and shield, her hair pulled into a twisted knot. Her hairstyle is very similar to that of the woman on the Tjängvide picture stone from Gotland. Both women are probably Valkyries. Hårby, Denmark, c.800.

15. Normans displaying their Norse cultural roots through their hairstyles ('with bare neck and blinded eyes', as Ælfric of Eynsham described it). Bayeux Tapestry, late 11th century.

16. Facial reconstruction of St Magnus, who ruled Orkney in the early 12th century. The reconstruction was made using computer software, based on photographs taken of the skull in the 1920s. Since the skull itself had since been interred in one of the cathedral's pillars, no DNA evidence was available. This means features such as eye and hair colour are guesswork.

17. Glass gaming pieces for the popular Viking Age game *hnefatafl*, with the little 'king' piece at the centre. Found in a double chambered grave on the island of Birka, Sweden, 9th century.

18. Sundial from the church of St Gregory's Minster, explaining how Orm Gamalsson had it rebuilt 'in the days of King Edward and Earl Tostig'. This allows us to date it to the decade before the Norman Conquest of 1066, just as Orm's name strongly points to his Norse heritage.

19. A gown made of tough Greenlandic *vaðmál* ('wadmal'), which clothed a woman buried in the graveyard of Herjolfsnes in the Eastern Settlement. This has been radiocarbon dated to between 1380 and 1530, in other words to the very last decades of the Norse settlement in Greenland.

Indeed, this was a period where, if one was not born with a physical disability, then acquiring one was likely only a matter of time, if not from violence or accident, then in the form of degenerative ageing conditions from the wear and tear of life. Even the skeletons of the young males executed on Ridgeway Hill in Dorset attest to this. Although, unlike the Oxford bodies, these ones had no healed weapon injuries that suggested seasoned warriors, several of them had disabilities that would have been quickly apparent. One had broken his leg, which had healed so that it was shorter than the other: he would have walked with a pronounced limp. Another had a chronic infection in his thigh bone, which was twice the size than it should have been and oozed pus. A third had a fractured collarbone that had never knit back together, so that his arm was permanently dislocated. The question is, did these and other disabilities make them a ragtag bunch with weakened constitutions, or, as the researchers have also suggested, robust survivors who were able to thrive despite their bodily limitations?[31]

The archaeological evidence tells us that prominent individuals could be disabled. We have already met two: the leader of the Salme ship disaster with his fused vertebrae, and the older woman buried in the Oseberg ship. She was around seventy to eighty years old at the time of her death, and among other conditions suffered from arthritis and two neck vertebrae that had fused together. While she had developed some disabilities later in life, there were others that she may have lived with since childhood. Special shoes had been made for her: soft leather shaped to the contours of her feet.

What about congenital disabilities among the ordinary humans of the early Nordic world? This chapter ends with one of the most remarkable examples from Viking Age history. It centres on two individuals from the tiny hamlet of Skämsta in Sweden, just over 100 kilometres north of Stockholm. Eight burials were found close together, most likely connected to

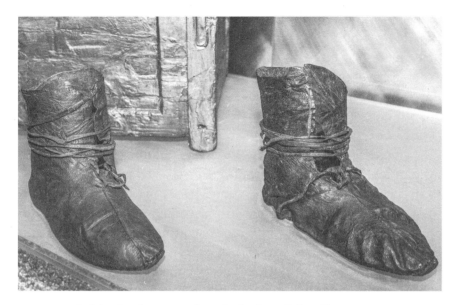

Soft leather boots, made to fit the feet of the older woman
buried in the ship from Oseberg, Norway, 834.

a nearby farm at Tierp. Two of these burials were the bodies
of a male and female who had reached an adult height of no
more than 130 centimetres (4 feet 3 inches). They both had a
condition called spondyloepiphyseal dysplasia, a particularly
rare form of dwarfism. This can be caused by a genetic muta-
tion or inherited from a parent with the same condition, but it
is such a rare condition – both then and now – that the chances
of finding two unrelated bodies buried a metre apart from each
other are infinitesimally small. When the archaeologist investi-
gating these bodies first published her findings in the 1990s, there
was no DNA evidence available to tell her more about how the
two individuals were related. But in 2020, when the bodies were
included in a larger project that analysed the DNA of hundreds
of Viking Age individuals, it turned out that they were siblings.[32]
This is even more extraordinary because it suggests that there
was probably another person with the same rare condition – at

least one parent with the same dominant gene – whose body has not (yet) been found. As they aged, life would likely have become increasingly uncomfortable: their skeletons showed bony knots on their hand joints and knee joints, signs of osteoarthritis, and in the case of the brother, fused vertebrae. But the most remarkable thing is that they *did* age, both living to at least forty to fifty years old.

We have already encountered a male and female dwarf in this book, in the Ribe skull inscription in 'Beginnings'. In this case, they are presented as mythical, malevolent creatures capable of inflicting sickness. There is nothing to suggest an association between these supernatural beings and the siblings with dwarfism who lived at Skämsta. In an age when infant exposure was a practice, runes were a form of medicine and life was undeniably

A double-sided comb made of elk antler, buried with one of the
two siblings with dwarfism. Skämsta, Sweden, 11th century.

tough, these siblings with dwarfism seem to have been ordinary members of the community, who lived and died in apparently unremarkable ways. And when they were buried, it was with precisely that artefact with which this chapter began: the sister was buried with a single-sided comb, and the brother was buried with a double-sided comb made of elk antler, together with a knife. The teeth on one side of this antler comb are larger for general detangling and the teeth on the other side smaller for finer detail, perhaps for removing lice and/or styling facial hair. The style of the double-sided comb made of elk antler means that it probably dates to the eleventh century, which most likely provides a date for the burials themselves. These combs remind us that, at some point in the eleventh century, there lived two humans whose bodies needed upkeep and maintenance, as all bodies do, regardless of whatever is unfolding around them. But in this case, the bodies of the siblings who owned the combs also survive, to tell a story so extraordinary precisely because these people were ordinary.

Chapter 7

HOME

Seeking a home

A ship packed with humans of all ages, restless livestock, preserved food supplies and whatever else could be packed into chests or squeezed on board: furniture, cooking equipment, tools, textiles. Its woollen sail creaking at the seams, wooden planks caked in animal dung and saltwater, it ploughed through the choppy waters of the fjord, a Viking Age Noah's Ark. For the occupants of a floating home seeking land, the terrain was not encouraging. On either side, towering mountains rose sharply out of the deep waters, bare grey rock giving way to snow-dusted flanks and thick white tips. But thanks to the hardy souls who had already visited these fjords and scouted out its resources, they knew that there was land to be settled at the head of the fjord, close to the vast ice cap that extended beyond any reckoning. They also knew that others were settling in this area, which meant two things. Firstly, they would have a community around them. Secondly, they had better get a move on. So, the ship and its occupants kept going, dwarfed by the mountains, storm-tossed, having sailed for many days up the coast from the fjords that had already been settled. They were on their way to their new home.

Eventually, many hundreds of years later, the home they founded would be engulfed when milky glacial waters changed their course. The river buried it under layers of sand and gravel so thick that archaeologists nicknamed it *Gården under Sandet*, which is Danish for 'the Farm under the Sand'. But right now, everything was only just beginning, and there were generations of lives to be lived in this place, a new home to make on the margins of the world.

For the Vikings, making new lives in Greenland was not unlike colonising the moon: the sheer scale of the distance across the ocean, the scarcity of certain resources needed to maintain a farming way of life, and the lack of any existing society to piggy-back off. This was not like other regions the Vikings had settled, such as the British Isles. This difference makes Greenland special, and worth focusing on here. In England, for example, genera-tions of Anglo-Saxons, Romans, Britons and the various peoples who came before them had already worked the land and built up farms over countless generations. We might remember that pivotal entry in the *Anglo-Saxon Chronicle* for the year 876, where the invaders divide up the land of the Northumbrians and start to plough it. These Norse settlers enmeshed themselves in a web of ancient farming systems, of droving and trading patterns, and drew on generations of knowledge about where to find fruits, herbs and nuts out in the woodlands and fields, what resources were in the rivers and fens, by the seashores, out in the bays.[1]

In Greenland, though, the new arrivals had to start from scratch. Their first task was to burn away the scrub birch and willow, making the first deep human marks on the landscape. While this was hard work for the settlers, it makes life easier for modern researchers. The problem with fertile farmland is that, if it's worth ploughing, people will keep doing it. They may also build on it. In the process they churn up, disrupt and destroy a lot of what came before them. This can be challenging for archaeologists trying to find traces of the Viking Age in places where people have continued to live. The islands of the North Atlantic were not as densely populated as southern Scandinavia or the British Isles, and this has led to some chance survivals. For instance, Iceland is home to the remains of one of the first houses ever built by Norse immigrants, uncovered in downtown Reykjavik and now housed in an interactive museum about the island's early settlers. Further east at Stöng, meanwhile, a farmhouse was preserved under lava when Hekla erupted in 1104.

But what survives of the Norse Greenlanders' world is of a different magnitude. This is partly because the inhabitants who came after the Norse settlers – the ancestors of today's Inuit Greenlanders – were hunters rather than farmers, and so did not plough or generally build on the land. It is also because the permafrost and general coldness of the climate has allowed so much organic material to survive: hair, bone, textile, wood, leather and fur. This is what makes Greenland such an extraordinary historical treasure trove for the ephemera of everyday life, such a rich source for our understanding of Norse homes and lives in a way that isn't replicated anywhere else. Even better, it's not just one farmstead, one home, that survives. It's a whole homescape: an interconnected mesh of lives and communities, whose experiences in the world would ordinarily leave little trace. It includes the sorts of people who very quickly get erased from history, especially women. Their hidden labour within the home powered the Viking Age, and their work often involved precisely the sort of organic materials that normally disappear first. So, if we want to grasp the material reality of 'home' in the Viking world, Greenland is the place to start.

Home from home

In Old Norse, the word *heimr* meant both 'home' and 'world', a fitting double meaning for a Viking Age characterised by an era of outward expansion: waterborne raiding and trading, exploration, conquest and settlement. Between around 800 and 1000, many left their Scandinavian homelands and sailed west to explore the islands of the North Atlantic, making new homes in new lands across the water. A shifting climate eased their way: from roughly the late tenth century to the early thirteenth century, the North Atlantic region became a few degrees warmer on average, an event known as the Medieval Warm Period. It is no coincidence that this was also the time of Norse expansion across the islands of that ocean, bringing with them a northern European culture based on livestock and agricultural farming. Among other places, this expansion took them to the islands of Orkney and Shetland, north of mainland Scotland. It took them to the Faroe Islands and on to Iceland. Still further west lay Greenland. Each of these lands would come to be called *heimr* by those who settled them.

One particular name looms large in the history of Norse Greenland: Erik the Red, the first-known European to land on a Greenlandic shore. As is so often the case with such intrepid pioneers, this was not entirely by choice; when he first arrived in 982, it was as an outlaw booted out of Iceland for murder. Rather than try his luck in some familiar country, he had decided to find the land that a certain Gunnbjorn, son of Ulf the Crow, had sighted when driven westwards over the ocean. *Eiríks saga rauða* ('The Saga of Erik the Red') was recorded in thirteenth-century Iceland and is one of two main texts based on oral tales about the Norse settlement in Greenland. The other is *Grœnlendinga saga* – 'The Saga of the Greenlanders' – and together they are known as the Vinland sagas. Many of the narrative details in the sagas are hard to verify, and there is plenty of material there that should not be taken at face value, including an episode where plague strikes and the dead come back to life. However, Erik's voyage west across the ocean fits with the pattern of Norse expansion across the North Atlantic: most new lands were discovered by accident before they were discovered on purpose, and many of the first settlers had fractious relationships with the homelands they left behind.

For Erik, the three years of his outlawry was enough time to scout the farming potential of the fjords that indented the coastline of west Greenland and discover some of the wild resources that the country had to offer. East Greenland, by contrast, he must have swiftly ruled out for settlement: the seas by the coastline are frozen for three quarters of the year, and icy katabatic winds known as *piteraq* – Greenlandic for 'that which attacks you' – sweep down from the ice cap with ferocity. Having said that, the east coast wasn't entirely ignored by later Norse sailors, who might end up there accidentally if their ships were blown off course, or travel there on purpose for hunting. One short Icelandic narrative called *Hemings þáttr* ('The Tale of Heming') includes a guest appearance by a character called Líka-Loðinn – 'Corpse Loðinn' – so called 'because he had carried the corpses of Finnr *feginn* (the Glad) and his crew from Finnsbúðir east of the glaciers in Greenland'.[2] Likewise, the Icelandic annals for the year 1189 report the arrival of Asmund *kastanrazi* (a nickname that has been translated as 'wiggle arse') who had sailed all the way to Iceland from the same location on Greenland's icy east coast.[3]

When Erik finally returned to Iceland three years later, it was to persuade his friends and family to relocate with him. Won over by his vision, they gathered up their belongings, piled what they could into ships and headed west.

Konungs skuggsjá, the Norwegian text written in around 1250, has extensive passages about Greenland's topography, resources and inhabitants. In one section it describes Greenland as 'ice clad beyond all other lands', while elsewhere it alludes to the vast ice cap that covers most of the country.[4] Yet its description of Greenland's climate also shows precisely why tough Norse settlers such as Erik and his wife Thjodhild chose to build their lives and homes out on the edge of the known world:

You asked whether the sun shines in Greenland and whether there ever happens to be fair weather there as in other countries; and you shall know of a truth that the land has beautiful sunshine and is said to have a rather pleasant climate. The sun's course varies greatly, however; when winter is on, the night is almost continuous; but when it is summer, there is almost constant day. When the sun rises highest, it has abundant power to shine and give light, but very little to give warmth and heat; still, it has sufficient strength, where the ground is free from ice, to warm the soil so that the earth yields good and fragrant grass. Consequently, people may easily till the land where the frost leaves, but that is a very small part.[5]

Of this 'very small part' of the country, first to be populated were the fjords close to the southern tip of Greenland, which came to be known as the 'Eastern Settlement'. Erik the Red, Thjodhild and their children made their home in a green, sheltered spot at the head of a fjord and called their farm Brattahlid ('steep slope'). Protected from sea fogs and ocean storms, with fine pastures for growing and grazing, Erik had bagged swathes of prime farmland. Around him, his companions took control of other fjords and started to build their farms.

Erik was also familiar with the coastline further north-west of his new home fields. Located close to the modern-day capital Nuuk, these deep, glacier-fed fjords would become known as the 'Western Settlement'. According to *Eiríks saga rauða*, he had spent his first winter of outlawry there before relocating to the comparatively balmy fjords of the south. It was more than 500 kilometres from the Eastern to the Western Settlement, several days' worth of good sailing. The pockets of farmable land there were harder to work, and the longer, colder, darker winters reduced growing and grazing time considerably. Today, summer temperatures in the region of the Western Settlement might comfortably reach the mid-twenties Celsius, and the climate was similar during the Norse settlement era. But for a medieval European farming community, the real kick in the teeth would have come during the long winters, where temperatures could fall as low as minus fifty Celsius.

Despite this, people started to settle on farms in the Western Settlement not long after the Eastern Settlement, in the first decades of the new millennium. Most probably the limited farmable land in southern Greenland had already been claimed, leaving new homesteaders little choice but to head into less favourable climes. The same thing had happened during the settlement of Iceland a century earlier, which was likewise virgin territory: once the best farming land around the coast had been taken, those who arrived late to the party had to settle for less profitable land further inland. Yet, hard as it was, farming in the Western Settlement was still possible. After all, this was a relatively warm period of history, and the inner fjords offered protection from the worst of the coastal weather. Determined settlers could – and did – make a home here.

And there were additional incentives. According to *Grœnlendinga saga*, Erik the Red claimed that he had named this country 'Greenland' to attract more settlers, looking for land of their own and a place to build farms. Certainly, farmable land was at a premium in the islands of the North Atlantic, where every Norse settler was looking for a place to call home. But whether Erik knew it or not, Greenland's greatest riches lay still further north, and they were not green but white.

Up the coastline, in what the Norse called *Norðrseta*, the 'Northern Hunting Grounds', lay precious Arctic resources. These hunting grounds lay close to what is now Disko Bay, where glaciers calve swiftly from Ilulissat Icefjord and the summer waters are packed with jagged shards of ice. For the Norse settlers, the non-human inhabitants of this region were considerable compensation for life on the edge: a blubbery treasure trove of walrus colonies, lolloping in the shallow coastal waters.

Over time, this supply of precious ivory would come to be the lifeblood of the Norse Greenlanders, together with other Arctic treasures such as hides, furs and eiderdown. Traders would come all the way from Norway for these riches. In return they offered essentials that Norse Greenlanders found virtually impossible to get from their environment: metal, timber and grain. As *Konungs skuggsjá* notes:

> In Greenland it is this way, as you probably know, that whatever comes from other lands is high in price, for this land lies so distant from other countries that men seldom visit it. And everything that is needed to improve the land must be purchased abroad, both iron and all the timber used in building houses. In return for their wares the merchants bring back the following products: buckskin, or hides, sealskins, and rope of the kind that we talked about earlier which is called 'leather rope' and is cut from the fish called walrus, and also the teeth of the walrus.[6]

For much of the lifetime of the colony, walrus ivory would prove the strongest strand in the rope that kept the Norse Greenlanders tethered to the rest of their diaspora further east.

The icy Northern Hunting Grounds would never have been a suitable environment for Norse settlers to make their forever homes. It was still a considerable distance away from the Western Settlement: one calculation suggests that, in a boat with six oars, the journey from the Western Settlement to these Northern Hunting Grounds might take fifteen days. The same journey from the Eastern Settlement might take almost twice as long, at twenty-seven days.[7] But the Western Settlement was not a hunting camp. It was a community of permanent homes, albeit small and scattered. They included the Farm under the Sand, which was one of the first homesteads to be built and one of the last to be abandoned. In total, around 75 settlement buildings have been found in what was the Western Settlement, while around 560 have been found in what was the Eastern Settlement.[8] These numbers must be treated carefully; they were not all occupied throughout the whole period of settlement, and not every building represents a farm. The total population of Norse Greenland seems to have peaked at a few thousand at best – it was never a large enterprise.

Still, it was an enterprise that succeeded for almost half a millennium, a European-style farming and hunting community that survived and thrived in the most marginal of environments. For a time, it kept its place on the international stage, bound by strong trade routes to the rest of the Norse world – especially Norway – and boasting its own bishopric, albeit the most remote in the Christian sphere. Norse Greenland's demise was not inevitable from its inception, and many generations called this land home. Transplanting a version of Norse 'home' here depended on the connections of each and every farmstead to the rest of the Norse world, whether physical, economic or psychological. In terms of that double sense of the word, it would take the *heimr* to make a *heimr*. How the early settlers did this, the choices they made, and how they were forced to adapt, can tell us a great deal about what *heimr* meant to the Norse.

Making a home

When the first settlers reached the Western Settlement, and the site that is now known as the Farm under the Sand, the green pocket of land held great promise. As they neared the head of the fjord, they would have seen tangles of shrubby birch and willow trees clinging to the hillsides, indicating fertile soil underneath (however shallow) and the potential for local wood resources (however meagre). They would have discovered crystal-clear streams snaking down from the mountains, providing ample fresh water for humans and livestock. They could trace the imagined outline of a farmstead on the flat part of the plain, surrounded with infields for growing crops (mostly fodder for the animals). They knew there were rich hunting opportunities up in the mountains, near the ice cap (especially reindeer) and down by the water (especially seal). There was soft soapstone in the mountains, easy to carve and heat, good for cooking equipment and lamps. And of course, they were now much closer to the Northern Hunting Grounds.

As they pulled their ship onto the clay-grey shoreline, they would have been aware of the lack of one crucial resource needed to make and maintain a Norse-style homestead. The local downy birch, grey leaf willow, green alder and mountain ash could be used to fashion tools, utensils and toys, and perhaps use as a limited fuel source. But dwarf birch and willow trees are of little use for building houses and stables, furniture and boats. For this, the settlers would have to rely on driftwood – mainly larch and spruce, which came with the currents all the way from Siberia, wormhole-peppered – and, if possible, timber imported from Norway. This wasn't just a Greenlandic problem; the same was true of all Norse colonies in the North Atlantic. But the further out the colony was, the harder it would be to import wood, and the ancient supplies of driftwood that had accumulated along the shorelines over the millennia wouldn't last forever. The ships themselves that brought the first generations of settlers to the Western Settlement were probably well-travelled vessels, even before they reached Greenland. It's likely that such ocean-going vessels had actually begun their lives in Norway or Britain, where tall trees grew easily and good timber was plentiful. Yet such vessels don't last forever either, even when they are carefully maintained and repaired.

The nearest forests were further west, in modern-day Labrador. The significance of this resource is clear from the name that the new Norse Greenlanders gave the region: *Markland*, which means 'Forest Land'. The trees were discovered barely a decade after the first settlers arrived in Greenland, in around 1000, when the children of Erik the Red led exploratory voyages to the edge of the North American continent. But the irony is that ocean-going vessels were needed to reach such a source of fine timber, which lay at least 1,000 kilometres across the Labrador Sea – as the crow flies, that is, which would not be the preferred route since it meant dangerous open waters full of icebergs, fog, unpredictable currents and violent gales. Centuries later, an entry in the Icelandic annals for the year 1347 illustrates this situation vividly, with the tale of a tiny vessel from Greenland, blown dramatically off course as it attempted to reach this land of forests: 'Then a ship came from Greenland, smaller in size than little Icelandic boats . . . It was anchorless. There were seventeen men on board, and they had sailed to Markland but were later shipwrecked here.'[9]

Small surprise, then, that the settlers in the Western Settlement had to make do with what they had to hand. When the founders of the Farm under the Sand started to build their home, they began with fire: burning away the scrubby trees on the hillsides. The first building they raised on the blackened earth was a typical Norse longhouse, around 12 metres long and 5 metres wide, with a fireplace hearth in the centre, posts supporting the roof, and benches flanking the sides.[10] To make a more even floor they scattered twigs, hay and moss on the ground. The foundations and base of the house were made of stone, and the walls from turf, up to 2 metres thick in some places, to keep out the deep-winter freeze. Then there were the animals to consider: any livestock they had brought with them could graze on the water meadow during that first brief summer, but would need solid shelter and substantial food supplies over the long, harsh winter to come. While they were establishing this rhythm, the new settlers would have to depend on the wild resources that could be hunted, especially seal.

Home is where the hearth is

Who were the inhabitants of the farm who sat around the fire at night? The extended family unit that occupied a Norse home was a fluid, shifting entity, and one that encompassed a variety of blood and non-blood relationships. A married couple would likely form the lynchpin of the household, perhaps together with some of their siblings and older relations and a scattering of children, some related to one or both parents biologically, others fostered. Then there were the farm labourers, some of whom might spend their whole lives at one farm. Others might move between employment on an annual basis: in Iceland 'Moving Days' fell at the end of May, when people could relocate to other farms, although it's not known whether the same custom was followed in Greenland. Multiple households might also live on one farmstead. Each of these units was also part of a wider community together with the other farmsteads scattered across habitable pockets of land around the fjords. In the Western Settlement, the grandest and most powerful residence was Sandnes – meaning 'Sandy Headland' – with its large cattle byres, feasting hall and, most importantly of all, its Christian church. Other households would have gone there for mass, to bury their dead, for communal celebrations and perhaps legal procedures.

In the extreme conditions of the North Atlantic, heat and light were central to any home-building. The hearth was the centre of any longhouse, a focal point for cooking, warmth and company. Not all rooms would be heated, but one particularly ingenious device found in certain Norse dwellings across the North Atlantic is a little box made of stone slabs, with space inside where turf, dung and twigs could be used as a fuel to light a fire. This was particularly useful in rooms where sparks and embers could prove catastrophic, such as where textiles were being produced. In fact, the first buildings erected on this site of the Farm under the Sand did burn down at some point early on, although it's not possible to tell whether this was accidental or intentional. Throughout the Norse settlements of the North Atlantic, fuel depended on what was available locally, turf being the most popular choice once wood became scarcer, and knotted wrack, a knobbly green-brown seaweed widely available on sheltered seashores. Then there were lamps, hollowed out from whatever local material was available – soapstone in Greenland, lava in Iceland – and filled with seal oil.

Near the fireplace at the centre of that first longhouse at the Farm under the Sand, archaeologists found fragments of a quernstone for grinding flour, made from local material, and part of what looked like a stone plate for baking flatbread, which would have been heated by tucking it into the hot ashes of the fire.[11] This discovery is more extraordinary than it might seem, because, together with wood, another everyday product to which the Greenlanders had little or no access was bread. The Norwegian *Konungs skuggsjá* remarks that some of the wealthiest Greenlanders had tried to sow grain as an experiment, but that 'the great majority in that country do not know what bread is, having never seen it'.[12] These optimistic experimenters probably lived in the Eastern Settlement, where pollen records and even a fragment of a plant indicate that early attempts were made to grow barley.[13] Two millstones have been found at farms in the Eastern Settlement, and a minuscule number of charred barley kernels, which suggests some sort of grain was ground at some point. It seems that some of it even reached as far north as the Farm under the Sand. Likewise, grain may have been occasionally imported from further east when the merchants visited. But grain was clearly scarce, certainly compared to agriculturally productive parts of the Norse world such as southern Scandinavia, Britain and Ireland. There is far more evidence for other foodstuffs that could be preserved and stored over the long and hard winters, such as large barrels that could hold fermented dairy products and meat salted with charred seaweed.[14]

The warp and the weft

A circlet of long, honey-blond hair, woven into a loop of approximately 58 centimetres. Two delicately twisted strands crisscrossing to make a chain, once fastened by a button or a bead. The most intimate of artefacts, tucked into a little nook in the wall, then frozen by the permafrost and hidden by a thick crust of sand and silt for over half a millennium.[15] The circlet comes from the latter part of the Farm under the Sand's occupation; the river that would eventually make the site worthy of that name might still have been clear and sparkling when someone wove the hair into this intricate shape. Or perhaps it was already milky with sediment, a sign that the terrain would soon be on the move. It was found in the weaving room, that most female of Norse spaces, and possibly sometimes equated with a word that appears in the Old Norse sagas – *dyngja* – referring to separate women's quarters.

Having said that, in Greenland there are several cases of male names written in runes on textile equipment. One is a square tablet for weaving thick bands to secure warp threads to a loom with the name 'Magni' on it.[16] Another is a soapstone mould for a spindle whorl – a weight to keep the spindle spinning – with 'Didricus owns me' written in Latin, and a couple of cute cartoon faces scratched onto the other side.[17] It is possible that these were written by a woman, inscribing the name of a loved one on her equipment. Or, as is often the case in frontier territories where gender roles blur more easily, perhaps these are owners' marks, and there were men involved in the textile-making process in Norse Greenland. Either way, while we will never know the name of the owner of the blond hair that was twisted into a loop and hidden away in the weaving room, we do know other names of Greenlandic women who spent much of their lives in such spaces, carding animal wool into fluffy softness, tying these cloud-light bundles to wooden distaffs and spinning them into thread on wooden spindles. Most often, it is when they carved their names in runes onto the weighted whorls that kept the spindle twisting and spinning: 'Sigrid made', 'Sigvor owns', 'Thorhild owns me.'[18]

Spinning the thread was only the beginning of the textile-making process. Other items found in the weaving room at the Farm under the Sand testify to the complexity of making cloth: weights, tufts of unprocessed wool, soapstone lamps, combs and needles made from reindeer antler. There were also some of those flat stones fashioned into an open, moveable box, containing wood and dung to burn as fuel, a safer source of heat in this tinderbox of a room. The thread then had to be turned into cloth, usually on a free-standing wooden loom that leaned against the side of the room. The loom that was found at the Farm under the Sand is the largest to be found anywhere in the North Atlantic, almost 2 metres across, capable of producing

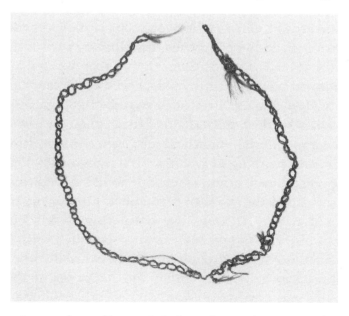

A woven loop of human hair, from the weaving room at the
Farm under the Sand in Greenland's Western Settlement.

sizeable pieces of cloth. Found together with the loom were around eighty soapstone loom weights, designed to hang down and keep the vertical warp threads taut as the yarn was woven in and out, backwards and forwards. Some of the loom weights found on Norse Greenlandic farms do have runic inscriptions, but every inscription that can be read is devotional rather than a personal name, spelling out 'Mary', 'Jesus Christ' and 'Hail'.[19] This is not surprising; Iceland officially converted to Christianity in around 1000, just fifteen years after the settlement of Greenland began, and Norse Greenland had a strong Christian presence from its early years.

Producing cloth was an intensely time-consuming, physical business. It was also one that involved the entire community, from rearing the sheep and goats needed for the wool to hoisting a finished ship's sail or swaddling a newborn baby. The weaving rooms would have been noisy, busy, smelly places, sharp with the scent of lanolin from the wool and urine for treating the cloth. The heavy loom weights would be clanking together constantly as the threads were moved, the weaving swords thudding against the threads to pack them tightly together for a denser, more uniform weave. There would have been infants and children there too, the smallest ones swaddled and feeding while their mothers worked, the toddlers getting under everyone's feet and providing entertainment and annoyance in equal measure, the older ones working in whatever way they could. One long, tapering object made from whalebone found at a farm in Austmannadal, also in the Western Settlement, hints at the presence of children at play. It looks like a weaving sword, but wonderfully, it also has two human figures scratched onto it, both holding little shields and brandishing little swords. These images have more than a hint of Onfim the Artist about them. So perhaps this was a weaving sword that eventually found its way into the hands of a weaving room's youngest members, repurposed as a toy.[20] If so, this is not the only evidence of children in the weaving room. Further afield, in the remains of a Viking Age weaving room at Bjørkum in western Norway, the imprints of little children's teeth were found on birch tar, which seems to be the equivalent of chewing gum.[21]

Across the Viking world, weaving rooms were places where news and gossip could be exchanged, skills passed on to the next generation, and songs and stories shared. They were also places where saga stories might be set in their own right, such as a dramatic turning point in *Gísla saga* where a man overhears his wife and sister-in-law making clothes and talking about past love affairs that should have remained hidden. On another occasion in *Laxdæla saga* ('The Saga of the People of Laxardal'), the character of Bolli returns home having murdered his foster brother, only to be told by his wife Gudrun, 'A poor match they make, our morning work – I have spun twelve ells of yarn while you have slain Kjartan.'[22] (It should be said that Kjartan was Gudrun's former lover, and, as the chief protagonist in the saga, she has played no small part in the events leading up to his death.)

Meanwhile, in the world of Old Norse myths and legends, spinning and weaving weren't only the work of humans. One of the most vividly dramatic scenes in any saga comes from *Njáls saga* ('The Saga of Njal') and is set on the eve of the Battle of Clontarf (fought near Dublin in 1014). In Caithness, at the north-east tip of mainland Scotland, a man sees twelve figures riding towards a *dyngja* (that aforementioned word for women's quarters). He peeps inside and sees that they have set up a

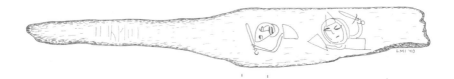

A weaving sword, a children's toy, or both? Sketch of an item made from whalebone, found at a farm in the Western Settlement of Norse Greenland.

grotesque weaving loom, where severed heads are used as the warp weights, human entrails are the warp and weft threads, and swords and arrows are used to move the wool backwards and forwards. The weavers are Valkyries, choosers of the slain, and they are deciding who will live and die in the coming battle. As they weave, they sing a poem that begins:

> A wide warp
> warns of slaughter;
> blood rains
> from the beam's cloud.
> A spear-grey fabric
> is being spun,
> which the friends* of Randver's slayer
> will fill out
> with a red weft.[23]

The existence of these stories is important. They are about women as complex, rounded humans: as friends sharing confidences, as spurned and vengeful lovers, as figures with the ultimate power of life and death. They play these dramatic roles in the narratives even as they spin yarn, weave cloth and cut clothes. And these stories, poems and songs would have filled the weaving rooms and other women's spaces in the home, just as much as they were told around the central hearth on winter nights, or on a ship at sea when the wind dropped.

Sometimes it is hard to get excited about spheres historically associated with hidden women's labour. Mundane, repetitive domestic work has not been given much attention in most traditional history books, and certainly not as much as it deserves, given the fact that very little else would exist without it. Without the textile production that went on within every home, there

---

* An allusion to Valkyries.

would have been no Viking Age at all, no expansion across the islands of the North Atlantic. As we've seen, *heimr* means both 'home' and 'world'. The fact that the Norse were able to transplant one to the other depended on what women did in the weaving rooms, among many other things. You can't sail across an ocean without a sail. Or without tough waterproof clothing. Or, in fact, without any clothing at all. Take away the textiles and the women, and you have some naked men in a rowing boat.* The poet Ottarr the Black knew this: in one poem dedicated to King Olaf Haraldsson of Norway he describes the king in his ship, cutting through the high waves, while 'the sail, which women had spun, played against the mast top'.[24] The king, Ottarr acknowledges with a nod, would be nothing without the women.

Thanks to modern research, we know just how hard those women must have worked. According to one measure, it would take one person at least two years to produce a sail 25 metres squared, which would be enough for a small vessel. It would take that same person nine years to produce a sail 112 metres squared, which would be the size needed for a Viking Age warship.[25] Another estimate focuses on everyday life: a family of five needed 25 to 30 sheep to provide enough wool just to keep them clothed for a year.[26] And according to another calculation, to produce two outfits, one male and one female, a spinner needed to spin around 42,600 metres of yarn.[27] Thanks to the preservation of Norse textiles in the Greenlandic permafrost, evidence of that investment of time and labour survives, with clothes recycled and repaired – stitched, patched, re-patched, reused – until they could only function as rags.

In medieval Iceland, such was the investment in textile production that one type of cloth – *vaðmál* or wadmal, meaning 'cloth measure' – became one of the country's key exports,

---

* Take away the food they cooked, preserved and stored for the voyage, and you have some naked hungry men in a rowing boat. Take away the children that the women gave birth to and cared for, and before long you will have just a boat.

together with dried fish. Wadmal was a coarsely woven woollen fabric in a diagonal twill weave, dense and strong enough to be used as working clothes. From the eleventh century up to the early modern period, wadmal was even used as the main form of currency in Iceland, measured in ells. When Gudrun, the main protagonist of *Laxdœla saga*, taunts her husband 'I have spun 12 ells of wool, and you have killed Kjartan', the ell she refers to is this internationally recognised unit, measuring roughly from fingertip to elbow. In other words, feud and murder might be more stereotypical Viking activities, but they were hardly going to put bread on the table.

Pets and pests

Where humans make their homes, so do certain other animals, some more welcome than others. Human lice and animal ticks were frequent cohabitants on the farms, as might be imagined, and some particularly impressive specimens have been found on farms in the Western Settlement. Other parasites point to generally unsavoury conditions in Norse homes not only in Greenland, but also in a range of other locations including Iceland, York and Dublin: stinking floors covered in decomposing vegetation and meat, the stench of faeces and dirt only partly masked by the smoke from the fire.[28] Also living in the weaving room of the Farm under the Sand, tucked between the hearthstones, were the nests of long-haired house mice.[29] The little skeletons in these nests were the last members of an extensive family tree that stretched back to whenever their ancestors had first arrived in Greenland, tucked up snugly in the cargo of a Norse ship. The presence of mice on the farms might also explain the skeleton of a cat found on another farm, this time in the Eastern Settlement, the first to be identified from a Norse Greenlandic site.[30] The cats of the Viking world were magnificently hirsute creatures with large bodies and thick pelts, like today's Norwegian Forest Cat. Before the Viking Age they were a rare sight in Scandinavia, and it seems that their usefulness on ships and farms accounts for their growing popularity in an age of travel and settlement.[31] Dogs were an even more common feature on Norse farmsteads, used for hunting, herding and security. Most were of a spitz variety, with thick fur and pointed ears and muzzles, such as the elkhound.

Beyond the homestead

Let's step out of the longhouse, leaving behind the rich-smelling cosiness of the hearth and weaving room, and duck through the doorway into the open air. What we see depends to some extent on where we are in the Norse world. The farmsteads built in Greenland's Eastern Settlement took the form of building clusters – living quarters, animal shelters, storehouses, workshops, stables – that were common pretty much wherever the Norse went. The farm itself was the nucleus, surrounded by infields and beyond them outfields. In the infields, crops and animal fodder were grown. In the outfields, animals grazed. In the medieval Icelandic collection of law codes known as *Grágás* (meaning 'Grey Goose'), farmsteads were legally obliged to maintain boundary walls between the infields and the outfields.[32] This reflects the fact that natural resources and territorial units were precious commodities on this newly colonised island, while the movement of livestock had to be carefully controlled. The boundary walls had to be substantial structures, built of stone and turf and measuring the equivalent of 1.5 metres in height and 1.5 metres at the base.[33] Home was more than a state of mind; it was a legally enforced physical presence, inscribed on the landscape itself.

Beyond the farmstead with its infields and outfields, away up in the hills and mountains, lay the summer pastures. These were accompanied by shielings, smaller buildings that could be used for all sorts of purposes – shelter, storage, a place to round up animals, a place for milking – and were occupied mostly during the summer. Variations on this set-up existed across the Scandinavian homelands and the North Atlantic settlements. For instance, shielings of this sort have been found in the mountains of Lendbreen, on the route of the frozen Norwegian mountain pass we met in 'Travel'. But in Greenland's Western Settlement, on the very margins of medieval agriculture, much of this blueprint simply did not work. The pockets of farmable land were smaller, and farmsteads were twice as far apart as in the Eastern Settlement because the soil was poorer and the summers shorter and colder. Rather than the mountains leading to summer pastures, they led only to the vast ice cap that covers most of Greenland. Moreover, no boundary walls have been found surrounding Norse Greenlandic farms. This is probably because the population was so much smaller and scattered; land was cheaper and plentiful, leading to fewer conflicts about who owned what, and less need for regulation of space. Boundary markers, then, so important to the definition of 'home' in other parts of the Norse world, were dispensable here.

Livestock

At every step across the North Atlantic there were different terrains and climates to adapt to, different resources to discover, different limitations to work around. The Norse settlers would arrive, optimistically, with their typical farm of cows and pigs (the two most popular animals), sheep and goats, and horses. Over time, it would become clear which livestock could survive in that particular environment, and which would fade away.[34] Goats and sheep turned out to be the hardiest and most successful livestock for Greenlandic farms, capable of providing both milk and wool. Goats were the unglamorous superstars because they were particularly good at eating twigs and leaves. And indeed, the body of one of these caprine superstars was found at the Farm under the Sand, its skin and wool marvellously preserved by the freezing conditions.[35]

With all due respect to sheep and goats, however, the preferred choice of farm animal for Norse settlers was the cow. In the case of the Western Settlement, where temperatures wouldn't rise above freezing until at least May, cows were a limited but still important option.[36] At the Farm under the Sand, in a small building down in the field close to the river, an accumulation of dung and a large drinking trough made of soapstone indicates that cows were the likely occupants. In the same building was a spade made from whalebone, attached with whale baleen to a wooden handle, and a whale vertebra that was probably used as a milking stool.[37] The harsh Greenlandic winters would have seen the bovine occupants of this shed huddled inside for eight months at a stretch, dung slowly piling up around their hooves, muscles atrophying. Apart from the soapstone lamps that would be lit when people came to check on them, they would be in constant darkness. There would have to be enough fodder to see them through this time, no small undertaking in such a marginal landscape.

But cows mattered because they were the portable wealth of the Viking Age, valuable animals that provided milk, meat, bone, horn and hide. The Old Norse word *fé* means both 'cattle' and 'wealth' (this conflation existed in languages throughout the Germanic world and is preserved today in the English word 'fee', while in Iceland the same word is used for sheep). So it follows that the biggest cow herds in Norse Greenland were kept on the farmsteads with the most resources and highest status. Gardar, in the Eastern Settlement, was the site of the bishopric. In case there was any doubt about this, in the 1920s archaeologists found the skeletons of one of the bishops, complete with his gold ring and a beautifully carved crozier made from walrus ivory. This was probably Olaf, who became bishop in 1246 and died in 1280 or 1281.[38] At its height, there were enough byres to hold up to 100 cows at Gardar.[39] This also meant that there was enough fodder available to keep them going through the winter, speaking to the wealth of the bishopric. Today, the site of the former bishopric is called Igaliku; throughout the summer lush grass still fills the sloping fields and traces of the medieval Norse irrigation channels can be seen coming down from the hillsides.

If goats and sheep were the standout survivors on the Greenlandic farms, and cattle were the higher-status, high-producing livestock of choice, then the animal that didn't stand much of a chance was the pig. They needed large tracts of woodland or

Stones from the Norse Greenlandic cathedral of Gardar in the Eastern Settlement, stacked to form the arch of a doorway. Igaliku, Greenland.

marsh for pannage, or they needed plenty of food and warmth if they were to be kept in a sty. Neither being abundantly available in Greenland, a pig was not a common sight, although occasionally it seems that piglets were brought to farms, perhaps by visiting merchants from the east or from the major farms – such as the bishopric at Gardar – that had the resources to support them.[40] The situation was similar in Iceland, where settlers arrived with pigs but quickly realised that they were on a hiding to nothing.[41] They were much more suited to the few urban centres that existed in the Norse world, such as York, where they were good for general rubbish disposal as well as meat. Most would have been kept in the backyards of the narrow, densely populated houses, with their strict plot boundaries and their buildings of wattle walls and thatched roofs. Among higgledy-piggledy workshops and tangles of kitchen gardens, pigs pottered about, rootling in the squelchy soil, mingling with the chickens and bees. The other surprising pig-farming hotspot of the Viking Age seems to have been the Faroes, where the animals gorged themselves on buttercups in the farm outfields, and left traces of themselves in around 140 piggy place names across the islands, such as *Purkhús* ('pig house'), *Svínstiggjur* ('swine path') and *Galtabólið* ('boar pen').[42]

Wild animals

Whereas livestock brought by the Norse settlers had to adapt to their new surroundings or perish, wild animals were already at home in the extreme Greenlandic conditions. The reindeer migrated long distances overland, while the seals did the same at sea. Large, hooded seals would appear in April and May, with inflatable red bladders on their heads. Harp seals would bob up a month or two later with their silver-grey coats and adorably fluffy-white pups. There were plenty of fish available – Arctic char in the glacial rivers, cod where the waters were deep enough, capelin in the spring when they came into the fjords to breed – although the jury is still out on how much the Norse made use of this plentiful resource. Then there were the wild birds, including auk, and gulls by the seashores and ptarmigan in the mountains. In the cold, dark months, huge populations of guillemot and eider birds would fly from the Arctic north to overwinter in the open waters west of southern Greenland. Up in the mountains lived the Arctic fox – sleek and beige in the summer, a cute white fluffball in the winter – and the Arctic hare with its white fur and black-tipped ears. At the other end of the scale were the biggest wild mammals, not least occasional polar bears, which were most useful for their skins, and whales, which were seized upon eagerly when they were beached on the seashore.[43]

Norse homesteads in other parts of the North Atlantic had different options and preferences. On the Faroes, for example, wild birds – razorbills, guillemots, puffins – were a much bigger part of the Norse diet, as were the fish (especially Atlantic cod, but also ray, salmon, trout and flatfish). Also on the Faroes, the most important communal hunt was for pilot whales (called the *grindadráp*, when whales were driven into shallow bays where they were beached and killed, a practice that continues today).[44] In Greenland, however, the main communal hunt was for walrus, especially for tusks and hide, although walrus meat was also eaten, especially in the Western Settlement.[45]

Archaeologists have found plenty of wild animal bones that tell us what was eaten on the Norse Greenlandic farms and how the location and status of these farms might affect what appeared on the menu. Seal was always the most important food source in Greenland, and for the most part became increasingly important as the climate started to get colder in the mid-thirteenth century. In the Western Settlement, reindeer was more plentiful, most of all at high-status farms such as Sandnes.[46] Meanwhile, although there was far less reindeer available in the Eastern Settlement, those living at the bishopric in Gardar got more of it on their dinner plates than anyone else in the area.[47] According to a four-teenth-century description of Greenland the cathedral owned a 'large island which lies off the fjord and is called Renøe ['Reindeer Island'], so-called because in autumn countless reindeer run there'.[48]

These animals were vital to the survival of the Norse Greenlanders, but they were more than inert resources for the dinner table. Their beauty and vitality are reflected in the occasional fragments of artwork and decoration that survive from the farmsteads. One of these is a well-used wooden chopping board from the Eastern Settlement with a series of vaguely comical walrus heads on one side, as though bobbing suspiciously out of the water.[49] From the same farm but this time found in the midden, a little polar bear carved from walrus ivory, its paws and snout delicately marked, its slightly too-big head thrust out in

A polar bear carved from walrus ivory, found in the boggy midden of a Norse farm in the Eastern Settlement, Greenland.

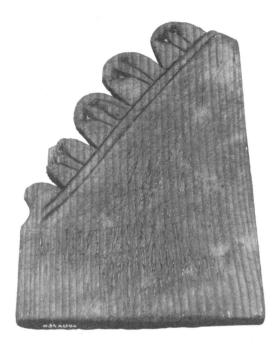

Walrus heads pop up to decorate the side of a wooden chopping board from a Norse farm in the Eastern Settlement, Greenland.

front.[50] As it doesn't seem to have any obvious practical function, most likely it was purely decorative, an ornament holding up a mirror to the natural world in which the Norse Greenlanders were embedded. Other equally intricate ivory carvings have been found in farms from the Western Settlement: a gyrfalcon with its head nestled into its body, a walrus with folded flippers and tusks tucked in, and a polar bear with a graceful domed back, seeming to sniff the ground in front of it. All three were carved in such a way that they could be threaded and worn as pendants, perhaps for good luck in hunting, perhaps in honour of the non-human inhabitants of their homeland.[51] Through their creativity, the Norse Greenlanders were bringing these wild animals into their domestic sphere, recognising their central place in the world they called home. But they were not the only cultural group who saw Greenland as their home.

Adaptations and endings

There were plenty of good reasons for the Norse to sail west – mostly from Iceland – and make new homes in Greenland. Land. Resources. Adventure. A new start. Others had done so before and would do so again, but theirs were different sort of lives and different sort of homes. Prior to the Norse arrival, Palaeo-Eskimo groups had lived and thrived in the north-west corner of Greenland at various points over the preceding millennia, having crossed from Arctic Canada. Traces of the earlier Saqqaq (*c.*2400–800/700 BCE) and Dorset cultures (*c.*800/700 BCE–0 BCE) have been found. In summer, such peoples were nomadic, living in tents weighed down with circles of stones, and a hearth for fire at the centre. In winter they relocated to turf-walled houses, with floors dug down into the earth to conserve heat. They had adapted their way of life to a very cold climate, hunting harp and ringed seals through holes in the ice. Remnants of their existence survive not least in their exquisite artwork, which reflects their world view and the Arctic environment, including intricate ivory carvings of polar bears and seals.[52]

It seems that Greenland was unoccupied by humans from around 0 CE to 700 CE, at which point small groups of Late Dorset culture arrived in north-west Greenland. They start to fade from the archaeological record around 1200, by which point the Norse Greenlanders had been in situ for around two centuries. But at the same time, a separate group was arriving in north-west Greenland and making their way down the coast, towards the Norse settlements. These were the Thule people, ancestors of the modern-day Inuit. With their dog sleds, kayaks and umiaks (both types of boats with skins stretched over frames made from driftwood or whalebone), they were able to cover large distances by land and sea as they hunted, and they prized the bowhead whale above all. At some point, probably after the Norse had been in Greenland for around a century, Norse and Thule hunters met for the first time, probably in the region of the Northern Hunting Grounds. With the European Norse coming from the south and the Inuit Thule from the north, both were nearing the margins of what they could call home, with environmental conditions that could support their way of life. But another tipping point was not far around the corner, and only one of these cultures would survive it.

As the Norse colonised the islands of the North Atlantic, there were always adjustments and adaptations to be made. In Greenland, some of these were fairly straightforward, such as the fact that there wasn't a lot of metal available, so items that might be made of metal elsewhere in the Norse world – such as buckles – were made from whalebone or walrus ivory. Likewise, where there wasn't home-grown wood, then other solutions had to be found. At the Farm under the Sand someone made a door from three planks of worm-eaten Siberian driftwood. It was lashed with whale baleen* and attached to the doorframe with a hinge made of reindeer antler – a perfectly serviceable solution to the problem of needing a door.

There is always a tension between what stays constant and what has to change while still remaining recognisably 'home'. But if a marginal world becomes more marginal, then how far is it possible to adapt until the whole project becomes untenable? The Norse Greenlanders were not the first to find themselves facing this problem, and they certainly would not be the last. By the early 1300s, Greenland was getting a lot colder. The Greenlanders started to weave cloth with different patterns and densities, to protect better against the cold. They also started to include different sorts of fur in their textiles: at the Farm under the Sand, striped cloth was found woven from black goat hair mixed with white Arctic hare fur, to increase the warmth of the

---

* Baleen is the bristly filter system in whales' mouths, made from keratin and used to sieve things like krill and plankton.

final product.[53] And over time, as it became harder to maintain livestock, wild animals made up an ever-larger proportion of the Norse Greenlanders' diet.[54]

And still, gradually, it got colder. Ice cores tell us that the middle of the fourteenth century was the coldest period in Greenland for a millennium.[55] There was less rainfall but more storms and more sea ice, which meant that the crossing from Norway – the dominant power in the Norse diaspora, and Greenland's main trading contact – got harder and more dangerous. In any case, Norway had problems of its own, not least when the Black Death struck in 1349, wiping out close to half of its population. Iceland managed to escape the Black Death until 1402, but when it finally struck, the consequences were brutal. So those further east in the chain of the Norse diaspora were less able and less willing to make the long voyage to Greenland. Meanwhile, the walrus colonies were getting smaller, most likely because they were such an important part of the Norse Greenlandic economy.[56] Hunters were having to go further north and rely increasingly on smaller walruses, often female, to supply ivory for the international market as far as Kyiv and Novgorod. Meanwhile, from the 1200s onwards, elephant ivory was becoming increasingly fashionable in Europe. These combined pressures would have been felt first in the more marginal Western Settlement, with its greater reliance on the walrus hunt, its smaller community and colder climate. The impact would have been felt in each of the little farmsteads where people had lived their whole lives.

In the mountains above the Farm under the Sand, the glaciers began to creep forward. Inland ice increased. The once-clear rivers were now milky and full of sediment. Slowly, sand drifted onto the pastures. But this was one of the last farms to hold out, still occupied until around 1400, when many of the surrounding fjords may have been abandoned for decades. We don't know who the last occupants of the Farm under the Sand were, but we do have names from among the final generations to call this place home. An intricately decorated wooden board with the name of its owner carved on top, a woman called Bjork.[57] A flat piece of wood with regularly carved notches – apparently a prayer stick – with runes that state its owner was a man called Thord.[58] A small whalebone spade found in one of the living rooms, with runes on the handle declaring it to be the property of a man called Bard.[59] They were probably not the very last inhabitants, but they may have lived to see the beginning of the end, experienced the desperately cold winters where the fodder ran out for the livestock, heard the news from unlucky farms where supplies ran out for the humans.

When the last inhabitants of the Farm under the Sand decided to leave, they packed up and took their home with them: beds, furniture, valuables. What was left behind was what they didn't need or couldn't take, including sheep and goats that ran wild on the hillsides for a time. But this was no apocalyptic ending. They closed the door carefully behind them – that baleen-lashed door with reindeer antler hinges, made from three panels of Siberian driftwood – sailed along the fjord one last time, and headed down the coast.

Although the retreat from the Western Settlement seems to have been orderly for the most part, not all farms in the region had such good endings. So marginal was the environment that one bad winter could easily wipe out a community. Just an hour's walk from the Farm under the Sand, the story of another farm had ended in extreme cold and starvation. The larder contained the bones of Arctic hares, ptarmigans, a lamb and a newborn calf, all of which would have provided meagre pickings. Most chillingly, the larder also contained the head of a hunting dog. Close to the larder by the cooking pit was a shaft of animal bone, presumably used as a cooking utensil, with runes that read 'Ljot owns me.'[60] We do not know what happened to Ljot, and we may not want to know. But outside in the hallway was the partial skeleton of one of the hunting dogs – perhaps the same one whose head ended up in the larder – with butchery marks on its bones reflecting a desperate situation.[61] In the same fjord community, even the most magnificent of dwellings, Sandnes, with its feasting hall and church, eventually came to a troubled end. Beneath the collapsed roof timbers of the dwelling house, the partial remains were found of nine hunting dogs. The presence of the nine dogs is unsettling enough, but equally chilling is that no one had come back for the precious wood from the roof timbers.[62] There would be no more Norse homes in the Western Settlement. And by 1500, there would be no more Norse homes in Greenland.

One autumn day in 1990, two Inuit reindeer hunters were crossing a vast barren sand plain where cloudy glacial waters wound their way in ribbons down from the high mountains. Close to the steep outer bank of the river, they found a piece of wood sticking out of the thickly silted ground. In a Norse twist on *Planet of the Apes*, when archaeologists arrived to investigate, they realised that the wood came from the beam of a loom. This landscape, which would have seemed so alien to a Norse settler looking for a place to call their own, had in fact been home to generations of Norse Greenlanders. For buried under the grit and gravel, up to 1.5 metres below the surface, was the Farm under the Sand.

Chapter 8

PLAY

The sound of silence

A pear-shaped, roughly hollowed out piece of alder wood, almost half a metre long. At one end, a rounded bottom to rest against a thigh or nestle in the crook of an arm. At the other end, a little neck and a stumpy head with five straight sides. This is the skeleton of a stringed instrument that was known by many names in many lands, most often a rebec or fiddle. But even when it was made, a skeleton was all it ever was. For it to be played, this musical instrument would have needed a lot of additions: a flat piece of wood covering the concave body to form a soundboard; several – usually three – strings made from animal gut or horsehair, stretched from lower belly to head; a long, low-pitched string in the middle to hold the drone note while the two strings on either side wove the tune around it; a little wooden bridge sitting on its belly, to lift the strings and keep them taut and angled; tuning pegs at the top to keep these strings at the right pitch; a length of springy wood attached to strands of taut horsehair to act as the bow. But there were no holes drilled in the head for the tuning pegs to be slid into position, no sign that a soundboard had ever been attached, and no smoothing out of the wooden belly itself, which was still rough and jagged. The only song that this instrument ever played was the sound of silence.

Even so, the fact that someone seems to have abandoned the job halfway through is exciting. Because it means that it was probably manufactured where it was found. And this would make it not only the oldest known bowed instrument from the Nordic world, but perhaps the oldest ever found in Europe.

Quite possibly, instruments of this type had their origins outside medieval Europe, in Islamic and Byzantine parts of the world. If this is the case, then the place where this half-finished fiddle was found is also important. It came from tenth- or early eleventh-century Hedeby, a major Viking Age town close to what is now the Danish–German border. The town was an international trading centre, a crowded, bustling hive of activity that lay at the heart of the major trading routes between Scandinavia, the Baltic, the Frankish Empire and the North Sea. By around 900, Hedeby's population numbered around 1,500 people. Some were local and others came from much farther afield, including other parts of Scandinavia, the British Isles, the Frankish Empire, southern parts of Europe and Slavic lands. Among this tangle of languages, customs, incomers and outgoers were traders, travellers and skilled craftspeople who manufactured items such as glass and amber beads, metalwork and textiles. For those who called Hedeby home, life was crowded, dirty and very often short. But that doesn't mean that there was no time for play.

The Old Norse verb *at leika* – 'to play' – encompassed many activities, just like its modern English equivalent, including playing a musical instrument, a game, or a sport. It was something done for its own sake, often imaginative, sometimes competitive, and hopefully enjoyable. A verse said to be composed by Earl Rognvald, ruler of Orkney until his death in 1158, captures some of the dimensions of 'play' in the Norse world, not only in Rognvald's time but also stretching back to the dawn of the Viking Age and even earlier. It appears that Rognvald had a healthy sense of his own accomplishments, judging from how he boasted of his many talents: 'I am quick at playing chess, I have nine skills, I hardly forget runes, I am often at either a book or craftsmanship. I am able to glide on skis, I shoot and row so it makes a difference, I understand both the playing of the harp and poetry.'[1]

Rognvald's verse speaks to a general historical truth, that those at the top of the pile tend to have more leisure time and resources than most to cultivate their hobbies and skills. Yet play was universal, and in whatever forms they occurred, the elements that his poem touches on existed in many different walks of life: board games, runes, crafts, sports and of course music.

In the last line of his verse, Rognvald claims to be particularly skilled at playing the harp. In addition to the stringed instrument that never got to fulfil its destiny, another fragment from Viking Age Hedeby seems to be the remnants of a harp. What survives is a tailpiece made of beech wood, although the rest of the instrument has long since vanished into the darkness. On this tailpiece, five holes had been drilled into the thicker, rounder end to hold the strings in place. Most likely, it was once attached to the body of what Rognvald called a 'harp' – the Old Norse word is *harpa* – which we might now think of as a lyre. We tend to use this latter word instead, with its Ancient Greek origin, because such instruments were already ancient by the Viking Age.

According to Ancient Greek myths, lyres were played by gods such as Hermes and heroes such as Orpheus. In Old Norse legends, perhaps the most famous harp player is Gunnar, tied up and thrown into a pit of snakes by his murderous brother-in-law Atli, where he plays the harp to placate them. One version of the story comes from the poem *Atlamál* ('The Lay of Atli'), which possibly originates from Norse Greenland. Here, Gunnar plays the harp with his toes. Unfortunately for Gunnar, one of the snakes doesn't appear to be a music lover – or perhaps it was too much of a music lover, since the sources don't tell us if Gunnar is any good at playing the harp in such an unorthodox fashion – and strikes him in the heart. The image of Gunnar surrounded by snakes and playing the harp was a popular one in the Norse world. Among other places it appears on a twelfth-century baptismal font from Norum in Sweden, where Gunnar stands surrounded by snakes, with a harp below his feet and runes above his head that read, 'Svein made me.'[2] He was also once in the portal of Hylestad stave church in Norway, among a series of carvings from the legend of Sigurd the Dragon Slayer made around 1200. The church no longer survives, but the panel does, and includes the figure of Gunnar, arms bound, a snake at his heart, playing a beautifully intricate harp with his beautifully intricate toes.

In contrast to the fragmentary state of the two stringed instruments from Hedeby, the other instrument found there was practically complete. It was a bone flute with four finger holes for changing the pitch, and another hole nearer the top to channel the passage of the air. In the global history of human music-making, flutes are the oldest instruments found, made from the bones of animals including the cave bear, griffon vulture, even woolly mammoth. The oldest known bone flute is over

Detail of a carving from the 12th-century Hylestad stave church in Norway, showing Gunnar in a snake pit playing the harp with his toes.

50,000 years old and seems to have been made by Neanderthals, a reminder that the desire to play and hear music is a deep and universal human trait, one shared with our early ancestors and across cultures.

Unfortunately, in the case of the residents of Hedeby, not everyone was impressed by their musical skills. Ibrāhīm ibn Ya'qūb was a traveller from Tortosa in Al-Andalus, the Muslim-ruled part of the Iberian peninsula. He came to Hedeby in the 960s, as part of his journey through northern Europe. In his writings he described it as 'a very large city, on the coast of the ocean', where women had the right to divorce their hus-bands and both men and women wore eye make-up to enhance their beauty. Ibrāhīm ibn Ya'qūb is measured and neutral in his description of this culture at the end of the world – until, that is, he gets to their musical talents, or lack thereof: 'There is no uglier song than the groans that come out of their throats. It is like the baying of hounds, only worse.'[3]

Ibrāhīm ibn Ya'qūb came from a different cultural back-ground with different musical traditions. We don't know exactly what he heard to provoke such a strong and uncomplimentary reaction. One possibility is that the people of Hedeby practised a form of throat singing, more commonly associated today with cultures from areas such as Mongolia and Canada. Alternatively, their singing style may have been closer to a Sámi joik, a tra-ditional singing-chanting practised by the people whose cultural region stretches across northern parts of Fenno-Scandinavia. Each joik evokes a specific entity in the world – a person, an animal, an element of the landscape – and given the connections between the Viking and Sámi cultures, this form of singing is something that many in Hedeby might have been familiar with. Or possibly Ibrāhīm ibn Ya'qūb really did hear some truly awful singing by someone very much lacking in musical talent.

Other fragments of musical instruments survive from all over the Norse world, a little orchestra that stretches across many lands and many centuries. In the string section, the top part of a wooden harp, its tuning pegs still intact. Dating from the first half of the eighth century, it was found buried deep down in the earliest layers of the Viking Age town of Ribe in Denmark. Next, heading west across the ocean to a Norse Greenlandic farm in the Eastern Settlement, the wooden bridge of a stringed instrument was discovered. Perhaps once part of a fiddle, it was just under 13 centimetres long, made from juniper wood, and decorated with a double row of zigzag patterns. The bridge was discovered on the same Norse Greenlandic farm as the cat bones from the previous chapter. Although we can't actually date either the remains of the cat or the remains of the musical instrument with enough precision to link the two in time, it's nice to think of the cat lazing by the fire along with the farm's human inhabitants, listening to the fiddle music on long winter evenings. A passage from *Eiríks saga rauða* describes similarly convivial winter pastimes at the farmstead in Greenland owned by Erik himself: 'That winter there was much merry-making in Brattahlid; many board games were played, there was storytelling and plenty of other entertainment to brighten the life of the household.'[4]

Our last member of the string section comes from Sigtuna in Sweden, founded in around 975. Dating to the 1100s, it's an antler tuning peg for a stringed instrument, measuring 129 millimetres long. The peg is inscribed with runes that tells us the name of its maker, its owner, and the instrument it belonged to: 'Listen to the one who made this! Erri made this harp with wholesome hands.'[5] Rognvald, it seems, was not the only proud harp player of the twelfth century.

The woodwind section of this little ensemble includes a cow horn with four finger holes from Västerby in Sweden, dated to the ninth century. Then, from Denmark and Norway, several long wooden instruments called lurs, this time with no finger holes. Made from lengths of hazel and alder wood that were split, hollowed out and lashed back together, these instruments could reach over a metre long. At the more diminutive end of the scale, several other bone flutes have been found in addition to the one from Hedeby. These varied in size and pitch depending on their size, which was determined by the animal they were made from. Some only had two finger holes, more often they had three, and occasionally there might be as many as seven.

Some of these surviving instruments are close enough to their modern descendants that it is easy to see how they would have been played and what they would have sounded like. Indeed, in some cases enough of them remains that they still *can* be played, such as an almost-complete set of boxwood panpipes from tenth-century York, with smoothly worn sides from years of use. Five and a half holes still survive, all drilled at different depths into the wood to produce different pitches. Part of the little case has been broken off and there were probably seven holes originally, but the ones that survive intact still produce the same notes as they did a millennium ago.

Other music-making fragments are more of a mystery, such as what seems to be part of a wind instrument found on the island of Falster in Denmark. Dating from around the eleventh century, it is a length of wood with five finger holes cut low into the wood and raised decorative ridges between each of them. The instrument is clearly missing something to make it playable, but what this might be isn't obvious. Perhaps there were once a mouthpiece at the top and a bell at the bottom, both made of horn, so that the instrument could be played like a shawm (an ancestor of the oboe). Possibly the length of wood was accompanied by a leather bag so that it could be played like bagpipes.

Together, fragments such as these from across the Viking world come together to make an orchestra of different pitches, rhythms and timbres, some familiar to modern ears and others less so. Most of these instruments can be reconstructed: bone flutes produce a high, reedy piping, while cow horns have

Boxwood panpipes from
10th-century York, England.

deeper, rounded tones. Panpipes have a breathy roughness about them, while lurs have a brighter, louder richness. Then there are the plucked strings of the harp with their light, flat timbre, and the low middle-string drone of the fiddle with the wispier tune played around it. Certainly, many of these instruments would have been used for purposes other than pure recreation: to call livestock in from pastures, in warfare, for religious rituals. But at least we have a fairly good understanding of what they would have sounded like when they were plucked or blown. What is far harder to reconstruct is the sound of the oldest and most common musical instrument in existence and the first to be experienced by most humans when they start to tune into the world from the depths of the womb. The human voice leaves no trace in the archaeological record, and yet it is the most intimate and personal musical instrument that anyone can possess, regardless of their place in the world.

When we turn to written sources for help, descriptions of singing and musical performances can only take us so far, as we have already seen from Ibrāhīm ibn Ya'qūb's less-than-complimentary remarks about the residents of Hedeby and their musical talents. Another intriguing little window into what singing might have sounded like, at least in one corner of the Viking world, comes from Gerald of Wales, a clergyman and historian of Welsh and Norman heritage. Writing right at the end of the twelfth century, his *Descriptio Cambriae* ('Description of Wales') includes information about the style of singing practised by those living in northern England, and how it compared to the Welsh: 'In the northern parts of Great Britain, across the Humber and in Yorkshire, the English who live there produce the same symphonic harmony when they sing. They do this in two parts only, with two modulations of the voice, one group humming the bass and the others singing the treble most sweetly.'

What Gerald seems to be describing is a form of two-part harmony, the lower part a drone and the higher part a tune. According to Gerald, this sort of singing had been around a long time, and was so far from an elite custom that even local babies quickly got the hang of it: 'The two peoples must have developed this habit not by any special training but by age-old custom, by long usage which has made it second nature . . . What is even more remarkable, small children sing in parts, and tiny babies do so, too, from the moment they stop screaming and first begin to sing.'

Gerald's conclusion was that this was a particularly Norse style of singing, derived from the Danelaw settlers who had arrived in that part of the country from the ninth century onwards: 'As the English in general do not adopt this way of singing, but only those who live in the north, I think that these latter must have taken their part-singing, as they did their speech, from the Danes and Norwegians, who so often invaded those parts of the island and held them long under their dominion.'[6]

This is a tantalising glimpse into a lost musical world. Even so, it's pretty hard to describe music without a secure and mutually understood frame of reference. For such a frame of

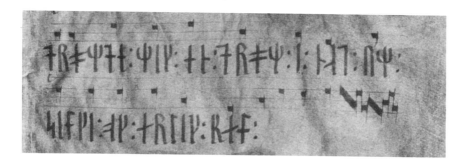

Musical notation and runes from the last page of *Codex Runicus,* preserving the oldest secular verse from the Nordic world. Denmark, *c.*1300.

reference, we need to come forward even further in time, to around 1300, where we find the oldest secular song that survives from the Nordic world. It is recorded in *Codex Runicus,* a manuscript that includes the oldest-preserved Nordic provincial law codes written – very unusually – in runes. On the last leaf of the manuscript are two lines of a verse (also in runes) accompanied by two lines of musical notation.* The words read *Drømde mik en drøm i nat um silki ok ærlik pæl,* which can be translated as 'I dreamed a dream in the night of silk and fine fabrics'. This is a romantically optimistic dream about someone hoping for the finer things in life. Since we are thinking here about the ordinary people of the Viking Age, it is fitting that this verse is not about someone who already has the silk and fine fur, but someone for whom they are – so far – just a dream.

Where eagles soar

Norse culture delighted in wordplay, poetry, storytelling and riddles, and wordsmiths were held in high esteem. Odin was the god of poets: according to one of the myths retold by Snorri

* From the 1930s the tune was used as the interval signal on Danish national radio.

Sturluson in his *Edda*, the wily god stole the mead of poetry from the giants by transforming himself into an eagle. He then flew back home to Asgard with the mead in his belly, pursued by an extremely angry giant. The other gods were waiting with buckets, and when he got safely over the wall Odin spat out the mead into these vessels. Unfortunately, he also squirted some out of his bottom as he escaped his furious pursuer (proving that even gods suffer from squeaky bums when the going gets tough). It was said that anyone who drank the mead that had come out the top end could compose beautiful verses. Anyone who drank the mead that had come out of the bottom end could only compose mediocre doggerel.

We have already seen how the title of this book – 'Embers of the Hands' – is a kenning from the Viking Age itself, born from the inventive mind of Thorarin Skeggjason, eleventh-century court poet to King Harald Hardrada. Skalds such as Thorarin were the elite of the profession, and composers of skaldic verse. This fiendishly complex type of poetry is a form of riddling wordplay where surreal imagery and twisty ambiguities must be unpicked before the meanings reveal themselves. Like cryptic crosswords where the rules need to be known before the clues can be deciphered, skaldic verse delights in alliteration that chimes across the lines, tangling up the word order so that it has to be unpicked like a knot. Within each verse are kennings, hidden in the tangle of words like Easter eggs, word riddles full of unexpected imagery and mythological references. A kenning for 'battle' might be 'the furious rain of sword-points',[7] while a kenning for 'alcohol' might be 'the soothing balm of all torments'.[8] Others are more complicated double-kennings, such as the 'white roof of the reindeer-sea', which refers to the sky (for which you first must work out that the 'reindeer-sea' refers to the land).[9] Likewise, 'the dark betrayer of the wood-bear of old walls' feels like it might refer to some grim and ancient mythological being, but it turns out that the creature is only a cat (the 'wood-bear of old walls' is a mouse, betrayed by the feline that wishes to kill it).[10]

Many names of elite skalds survive today, along with their verses, immortalised as the chief protagonists and supporting cast members in the Old Norse-Icelandic sagas. Often in these stories they are portrayed as socially disruptive, emotionally febrile characters always on the lookout for a scrap, ready to exchange poetic insults and physical blows at the slightest provocation. Practising skalds were often socially elevated characters in their own right, but it's also the case that historical figures of considerable standing were renowned for their poetic skills, not least Earl Rognvald of Orkney (not that you'd find him boasting about it) and even Harald Hardrada himself.

Yet storytelling, wordplay and poetry weren't only the preserve of the upper echelons of society, any more than most other forms of play. The Viking world was full of people who shaped stories to tell around the winter fires on their farmsteads, or during repetitive domestic tasks, or during the less exciting parts of long journeys over sea or land. It was full of those who took delight at playing with words, making vowels and consonants chime together across the lines of poetry, conjuring images out of other images. And it was full of individuals who enjoyed a satisfying brain-teaser or pun. On the one hand, it's hardly a surprise that very little direct evidence of this sort of everyday play survives, not least because so much of it would have been spoken rather than written. On the other hand, it's an utter delight to find any scraps of information at all that remind us that this was going on in people's everyday lives.

The cat and the fiddle

On the same medium-sized farm in Norse Greenland's Eastern Settlement where the remains of the cat and the fiddle were found, an unprepossessing wooden stick was discovered in a little bog by the farmhouse. Around 8 centimetres long and 3 centimetres wide, it most likely dates from the twelfth century. On each side are two neat lines of runes. Although they were carefully set out, it is hard to translate them, but they seem to be two lines of poetry. The runes have been transcribed tentatively as 'hér hafa hælibörvar hart . . .' on one side of the stick, and '. . . ák láðgota lyðum . . . Ræfils' on the other. This isn't an awful lot to go on, but it has been translated as 'Here the praising trees have . . .' and '. . . I have the people of the land-horses . . . Ræfils.'[11] Luckily, the bits that reveal that this is poetry are the bits that are easiest to read and translate. The words that can be made out alliterate (a repeated 'h' in the first line, and a repeated 'l' in the second line), and there are two little kennings hidden among the staves. The first is 'the praising trees', which seems to be a kenning for men or warriors. The second is 'the people of the land-horses', which also seems to be a kenning for men or warriors. True, it's not the finest scrap of skaldic verse in the repertoire; perhaps this particular poet drank from the wrong bucket. But the thrilling thing is that it exists at all. And perhaps the same cat that curled up by the winter fire to listen to fiddle music also enjoyed a bit of poetry when it wasn't earning its keep darkly betraying the wood-bears in the old walls.

Staying with the Eastern Settlement but going back a little further in time, possibly to the earliest decades of the Norse settlement of Greenland (c.985–1025), we find more runes scratched into wood that tell us about other forms of wordplay enjoyed by the Norse Greenlanders. This time, the runes are on a four-sided stick of pinewood around 43 centimetres long, with a natural knot at one end that resembles a birdlike creature. It was discovered in the 1950s by a local from the nearby town of Narsaq who was after some good-quality mud and soil for gardening. Inadvertently, they found themselves digging in the middle of the living room of one of the earliest Norse farms. The runes are on four sides. On the first, transliterated into the Roman alphabet, the runes read: 'o : sa : sa : sa : is : o sa : sat'.[12] Several interpretations of these runes have been suggested, along the lines of 'On a tub saw the person, who sat on a tub', or perhaps 'On the sea that seemed to be, which you did not see on the sea', or 'On the sea, the sea, the sea, is the ambush of the Æsir' (the Æsir being one group of the Norse gods, including Odin and Thor). Whatever the correct interpretation (and perhaps there was never meant to be just one) this is an example of wordplay using homonyms, words that are spelled the same but have different meanings.* The next part of the inscription doesn't seem to play on words but does slip a cheeky little kenning into the mix, and can be translated as 'Bifrau is the name of the maid who is sitting on the blue one'. 'The blue one' may refer to the sea, the sky or even heaven, in which case perhaps Bifrau is a mythological being perched upon it. Ultimately her identity remains a mystery. If these first two sides are tricky, then the third side is even more so: forty-nine runes, meticulously carved but utterly indecipherable. It seems likely that they had meaning, but if it is a code then we don't have the means to crack it.

Whatever the purpose of this stick – suggestions have ranged from the religious to the educational – it is nevertheless the case that someone is getting creative with runes and playing around with words and sounds. And Greenland wasn't the only part of the Norse world where this sort of wordplay was enjoyed. A runic inscription from Bergen in Norway, again on a wooden stick, also has fun with the many meanings of 'sá', and a very similar theme. It can be transliterated as 'huat sa sa er i sa sa sik sa sa (e)r i sa sa : sis(i) . . .', which has been translated as 'what did they see who looked into the tub? They saw themself, they who

---

* Modern Nordic languages have some great examples of this, such as the Icelandic sentence 'Afi á Á á á á á', ('grandpa from Á (a place) has a sheep by a river'), or Scandinavian variations on 'Far? Får får får? Nei får får ikke får får får lamm' ('Father? Do sheep have sheep? No, sheep don't have sheep, sheep have lambs').

looked into the tub'. Likewise, an inscription on a length of bone from Sigtuna in Sweden continues the theme with 'si sa sikh sa i sa sik sa is', which might mean 'See! They who saw themself in the tub, saw themself in the ice.'[13] Most of the surviving evidence comes from the twelfth and thirteenth centuries, perhaps indicating that this sort of wordplay was most popular in the centuries shortly after the Viking Age, or else that this was when it was most likely to be recorded. After all, poems and riddles can circulate for hundreds of years in a culture before there is any written evidence for their existence.

The same might be true of the more extended, traditional riddle form that has existed across cultures and across time for thousands of years: brain-teaser puzzles to be interpreted and solved. From the Sphinx of Ancient Greece to Shakespeare, from the Bible to *The Hobbit*, everyone seems to love a good riddle. And in the case of the last of these, its author, J. R. R. Tolkien, was inspired by a riddle contest from Old Norse legend, held between Gestumblindi (the god Odin in disguise) and King Heidrek. Several dozen riddles pass between them, preserved across three manuscripts of *Hervarar saga* ('The Saga of Hervor'), an Icelandic saga probably first assembled in the thirteenth century, but bringing together older historical and legendary material. Some of the solutions to the riddles are straightforward: fog, ale, hammer, bellows, sun, spider. One asks:

Four are hanging,
four are walking,
two point the way out,
two ward the dogs off,
one ever dirty
dangles behind it.[14]

It's a cow, of course. Other riddles in this contest are more intricate. A slow-moving creature with ten tongues, twenty eyes and forty feet turns out to be a sow pregnant with nine piglets. The solution to another one is a dead snake on a dead horse on an ice floe floating down the river. The riddles in this thirteenth-century Icelandic saga are the largest collection from the Norse world by far. And although the two riddlers here are high-status individuals drawn from the realms of myth and legend and the competition is preserved in a literary form, these riddles and the other examples of wordplay, verbal dexterity and riddle challenges that we have already encountered point to their importance in Norse culture.

Board games

Several riddles preserved in *Hervarar saga* themselves concern another playtime activity, and one for which we have far more evidence: board games, beloved by cultures across the world, for hundreds if not thousands of years before the Viking Age. The Norse called them *tafl*, which simply means 'table' or 'board'. Their favourite was *hnefatafl*, literally 'fist table'. In this respect, the riddle competition in *Hervarar saga* is actually very useful, because it includes riddles that hint at the rules of these games in ways that physical surviving evidence cannot. Each riddle appears in slightly different forms in the three manuscripts that contain versions of *Hervarar saga*, but their solutions are essentially the same. One can be translated as:

> What women are they
> warring together
> before their defenceless king;
> day after day
> the dark guard him
> but the fair go forth to attack?[15]

Later in the competition, the following riddle is posed:

> What is that creature
> that kills men's flocks –
> with iron all about it is bound;
> eight its horns are
> but head it has none:
> there are many that move at its side?[16]

In response to the first of these riddles, the opponent gives the solution of *hnefatafl*, the most popular of all board games played in the Viking Age. They explain their reasoning, in that the darker gaming pieces defend the *hnefi* and the brighter ones attack it. *Hnefi* literally means 'fist' or 'handful', and here refers to the 'king' piece who starts out at the centre of the board, surrounded by his (apparently female) protectors. The solution to the second riddle is given as 'the *húnn* in *hnefatafl*'. A *húnn* is the name for a bear cub, but also here, it seems, a six-sided die, its eight horns being its eight corners. This suggests that at least one version of the game was played with dice, presumably rolled to determine how many moves a player could make.

The family of 'hunt-and-chase' games include not only *hnefatafl*, but others that were widespread in other parts of Europe and beyond. These included Nine Men's Morris, an enormously popular board game in the Nordic world where the goal was to get three of your pieces lined up in a row and kick your opponent's pieces off the board. Such games started to make their way north many centuries before the Viking Age, under the influence of the Roman Empire. The Roman version was *Ludus Latrunculorum*, or 'Game of Little Bandits', a two-player board game based on military strategy. We know that versions of this game had reached parts of Scandinavia by around the year 300 because of an Early Iron Age grave cairn in western Norway that contained a cremated body and grave goods. Located at Ytre

Fosse, 20 kilometres north of Bergen, the site is perched high above the dramatic waters of an ancient shipping route that ran up the length of Norway's coastline. The area is scattered with high-status grave mounds that indicate its strategic, political and economic importance. If anyone were going to be sent to their eternal rest with state-of-the-art gaming pieces either imported from or inspired by sophisticated southern cultures, it would be someone who held power here. Among the cremation goods were eighteen gaming pieces and an oblong die – a 'stick die' – all made of bone.[17]

Around a century later, two similar stick dice were deposited into the famous sacrificial bog at Vimose in Denmark, which we first met in the Prologue with its Roman-era war gear and the little wooden comb with runes. These dice were accompanied by several more in the traditional 'cube' shape and many dozen gaming pieces made from amber, bone and glass. There were also four wooden gaming boards, etched with the grids and lines

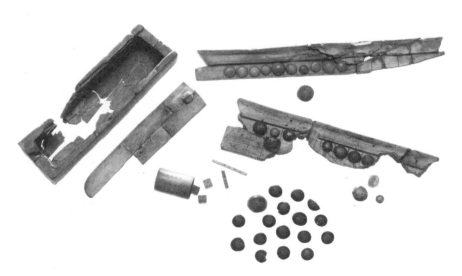

Gaming board, gaming pieces and dice cast into the boggy waters of Vimose, Denmark. In total, four gaming boards have been found amongst the offerings.

needed to play various board games. Life as a warrior could be chillingly exhilarating – as the existence of the Vimose sacrifices testify in the first place – but it came with its fair share of waiting around and empty time that needed to be filled. And board games slipped easily into that space, just as they had for so many cultures before them.

As we move through the centuries towards the Viking Age, we can see the growing popularity of these board games in the north. We can also see how their reach spread, gradually filtering through different elements of society. The Golden Horns of Gallehus are – or rather 'were', since they were stolen and melted down by an unscrupulous goldsmith in 1802 – a pair of elaborately decorated golden horns from early fifth-century Denmark, which places them very firmly in elite territory. Very early runes inscribed round the top of one of the horns tell us that 'I, Hlewagastir, son of Holtir, made the horn.'[18] Among the images that cover the pure gold surface, two naked figures stand on either side of a square gaming board. Lining the edges of the board are little circular shapes, which are either decoration or the gaming pieces about to sally forth and commence battle. Below the board, a creature – most likely a faithful hound – sits upright, observing the action.

Another image of two figures playing a board game takes us into the Viking Age itself. Rather like the golden horns of Gallehus, the Ockelbo runestone from Sweden – around 200 kilometres up the E4 motorway from Stockholm – also didn't have much luck. Having been moved inside a church for safety in the nineteenth century, it was then caught up in a fire in 1904, which destroyed both the church and the runestone. Like the golden horns, all that remains of the runestone are early sketches. Among the images carved into the stone are two figures seated on either side of a gaming board. One of them is in the process of taking a cheeky swig from a drinking horn: we have clearly caught them in a moment of leisure.

Illustration of the Golden Horn of Gallehus. The horn itself is lost to the world, but thanks to antiquarian illustrations made prior to its demise, we know that amongst the images on the horn were two naked little figures playing a board game.

So board games began in the Norse world as an elite pastime. Even the gods played them. The mythological poem *Völuspá* ('The Prophecy of the Seeress') starts by recounting the creation of the world and finishes just after the destruction of the gods at Ragnarok. The seeress who narrates the poem tells how, as soon as the gods have built their altars and forged precious things, they happily play board games in the meadow. At the end of the poem, after the final fatal battle, those who survive return to the meadows and find the gods' golden gaming pieces in the grass. Climbing down the rungs from gods to mere mortals, but still the rich and powerful ones, it is no coincidence that scattered among the dead buried in the Salme ships in Estonia, from the dawn of the Viking Age, were several hundred gaming pieces made from cow bone, whalebone and walrus ivory. No ship's crew needed that many gaming pieces: these were as much status symbols – and perhaps diplomatic gifts – as they were a leisure activity. The fact that a king piece – a *hnefi* – with its iron nail driven through the top was placed in the leader's mouth strengthens the possibility that these were items of social significance.

We also might remember from 'Beginnings' that the Salme dead mostly came from the Lake Mälaren area of Sweden, close to what is now Stockholm. The lake itself is dotted with islands, including Birka (meaning 'Birch Island'), which was founded as an international trading centre around the same time as the Salme disaster. From its origins in around 750, Birka was the spider at the centre of a vast web of connections and links that extended all the way from Arctic Greenland to South Asia, and perhaps even farther. This made it a hub for the powerful, the wealthy and the well connected. Several high-status graves from Viking Age Birka contain exquisite and delicate gaming pieces made from coloured glass, amber, horn and bone. One particularly fine set contains eight little globes of opaque, blue-black glass, and seventeen more of the same size, but lighter and more marble-like, swirling with shades of blue and white. Most likely, they are to play *hnefatafl*. To return to the riddle from *Hervarar saga*, these are the women who fight without weapons, the 'dark ones' and the 'bright ones' that either protect their lord or attack him. The 'lord' himself is there too, twice the height of the other pieces, transparent green glass body decorated with swirls of blue, and a head with two blobby blue eyes, an equally blobby blue nose, topped with a circlet crown. Once, they were played as a game for the last time. And then they lay hidden under the black earth of Birka for over a thousand years, friends and foes together.

Gaming pieces are scattered across the Norse world, made not only from glass but also from antler, amber, walrus ivory and bone. They have been found everywhere from Greenland to Kyiv. At Baldursheimur, a farm in northern Iceland, a very different but equally well-crafted gaming set was found in a tenth-century grave. The ensemble was accompanied by a die, just as with the earlier sets found in Norway and Denmark, this time rectangular in shape, and made from bone. The twenty-four smaller pieces were made from walrus ivory. With their bulbous bottoms, rounded sides and pointy tips, they have a dumpling-like quality, lined up together like a collection of tiny cream-coloured breasts. The central figure is of a different character altogether: craggier, greyer and more weather-beaten, in part because he was made from whalebone that has split and pitted over the centuries. Not quite 4 centimetres tall, he sits hunched over, clutching his long, forked beard and staring with hollow eyes.

Not every game played during the Viking Age had to be such an ornate affair. Everyday items such as shells, pebbles or bones might serve as perfectly good gaming pieces, and these are unlikely to survive in contexts that make it possible to identify them us such. One possible exception is a collection of five sheep ankle bones – astragali – in the remains of a little building at

Gaming set from northern Iceland, a gnarled king piece made from whalebone, and 24 smoother counters made from walrus ivory. Baldursheimur, Iceland, 10th century.

Pálstóftir in the highlands of Iceland. The building was part of a small tenth-century shieling, where livestock would be brought during the summer months from the main farm down in the valley. There would have been sheep to milk and care for, craft-work to carry out, wool to spin. Even so, the summer days were very long, and there would have been empty time to be filled. The fact that the little cubic ankle bones were found grouped together suggests that they were once kept in a pouch made of leather or fabric, long since rotted away. We can't know exactly what they were used for, but astragali have been used for both divination and gaming purposes by cultures throughout the world, where they are known by names such as knucklebones and scatter jacks.

Especially when everyday items were used as gaming pieces, the only thing that would be required was the appropriate board, scratched into whatever wood or stone was available. From Tof-tanes in the Faroe Islands, an oak dish or serving plate, split in two down the middle, seems to have been reused as a game board. On one side are the remains of a rather wobbly grid for *hnefatafl*, with a cross in the middle marking where the king starts the game. The other side is set up for an (equally wobbly) game of Nine Men's Morris.*

A short voyage south-east from the Faroe Islands brings us to Orkney, off the north coast of mainland Scotland. We have already met Earl Rognvald earlier in this chapter, one-time ruler of Orkney, whose first boast was his skill and speed at playing board games. But several gaming boards found on Orkney are of a suitably rough-and-ready nature to show that Orcadians from many walks of life enjoyed such games. At the north-west tip

---

* There's even a Nine Men's Morris grid carved onto one of the stone slabs of Charlemagne's throne in Aachen, not because the Carolingians were magically able to play on a vertical surface, but because the grid was already there when the stone was brought from its original location. A popular suggestion is that this original location was the Church of the Holy Sepulchre in Jerusalem.

of Orkney's largest island – Mainland – is a promontory called Buckquoy, jutting out into the sea to create the Bay of Birsay. This sheltered, fertile spot was prime farming territory, first for the Pictish settlers and later for the incoming Norse. The question of what happened to the Picts in Orkney when the Norse arrived is yet to be satisfactorily answered, although a substantial DNA study looking at population genomics across the Viking world points to at least some degree of assimilation between the Picts and the Norse.[19] But whoever was living here was doing more with their free time than sharing genes. Because at Buckquoy, not one, not two, but *three* rough sandstone slabs were discovered in the Norse settlement phase, all with *hnefatafl* grids roughly scratched into them. In fact, the markings were so rough that, in the case of two of the boards, the archaeologists didn't realise their significance and chucked them onto the waste stone pile. It was only when heavy rains arrived that the muck was washed away and the grids came to light.

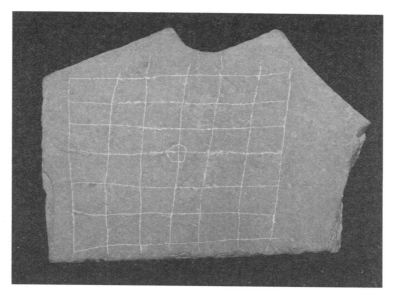

One of three rough-and-ready hnefatafl gaming boards
scratched into stone, found at Buckquoy, Orkney.

At the diagonally opposite end of Mainland is the Brough of Deerness, a dramatic sea stack that towers around 30 metres above the water. Only accessible via a narrow path that winds up the cliff, this was once an attractively defensible stronghold, and a seat of considerable power. The Brough was occupied from the sixth to the twelfth centuries. Pictish settlers were the first to call the sea stack home, followed by Viking incomers, until it had grown into a settlement with about thirty buildings. It was here that archaeologists discovered yet another chunky slab of sandstone with a *hnefatafl* grid scratched into the soft surface and a circular depression in the middle where the king piece would start the game. The board game was found in a building that seems to have had a living-room function, with a central hearth for a cosy fire and a bench on one side, the perfect location for a game of *hnefatafl* when the day's work was over.

Child's play

Back in Hedeby, among the noise of musical instruments and singing/howling of its inhabitants, another sort of play was happening, most likely closer to ground level. Because the dark soil of Hedeby has given us not only musical instruments, but also what seem to be children's toys. These include several small human figures. One, carved from antler, has an open, smiling face, arms pressed into their side and fingers splayed on their tummy – the perfect size to be grasped by a loving little fist. Another possible toy is a miniature boat, rather like the one from Dublin, each careful scrape still clearly visible where the alder wood was hollowed out to make the vessel. From across the Norse world, other little bits and pieces have come to light: spinning tops, horses, swords, other boats, other dolls. They're a reminder that, regardless of how long a child is deemed to be a child or what other social expectations are placed on them, playing is a cornerstone of the human experience, a way to imagine and create, make sense of the world, test boundaries, learn skills and internalise the values of the society you have been born into. At the same time, the sorts of possessions often most beloved by children are those even less likely to survive the centuries: the little bits of cloth that were their comforters, the repurposed household items that were their favourite toys, the interestingly shaped sticks, stones and leaves that they picked up as they made their way through the day.

As these small humans got older and reached adolescence, they would have discovered different sorts of games to be enjoyed. One such pastime might have been ice skating. Hundreds of ice skates made of animal bones survive from all over the Viking world, or at least those bits where ponds, bogs and water meadows were likely to freeze over reliably. To be skateable, the ice had to be free of snow and reliably thick enough to support the weight of a human, which was unlikely to be the case on a large frozen lake or meandering stream. This meant

Little wooden horses from Norse Greenland, one with a rider perched on top.

that, while skis were the best way of covering long distances effectively during the winter months, skates may have been intended often for fun. And this fun may have been enjoyed predominantly by older children and adolescents. Researchers analysed 290 bone skates from Birka (home to that beautiful gaming set with its blobby-eyed king) and 389 bone skates from Sigtuna (home to the tuning peg carved with runes). They found that the majority of Birka's skates were made of cow bones, and the majority of Sigtuna's skates were made of horse bones. This meant that, on average, an ice skate from Birka was 20 centimetres long, while an ice skate from Sigtuna was 22 centimetres long. Even allowing for toes poking over the front of the skate and heels jutting off the back, this is really quite small. If we remember the youthful foot outlined on the Gokstad ship plank from 'Travel', it was only 22 centimetres long. The researchers combined what they had found with written accounts of skating down to the twentieth century, many of which also describe skating as a youthful pastime. So it is possible that out of the hundreds of ice skates found across the Viking world – and indeed beyond, because humans have skated on ice for thousands of years – many may be the remnants of generations of Viking Age children and teenagers, wrapped up against the cold, mucking about on the ice, competing against each other, and generally having a lovely time.[20]

Sometimes skates were strapped to the bottom of shoes with leather cords. Sometimes the skater would balance carefully on the bone without any need for binding. In terms of how the skates were used, we have to rely on later images and descriptions from the early modern period, which suggest that skaters propelled themselves along with a long wooden pole between their legs, tipped with a metal spike so that it could bite into the ice. In his *Historia de Gentibus Septentrionalibus* ('A Description of the Northern Peoples'), published in 1555, the Swedish cleric Olaus Magnus illustrates his writing with wonderfully lively woodcuts, many featuring ice and snow in their various incarnations. In one of these, figures push themselves over the frozen water, bone skates on their feet and poles in their hands. Just in case there's any doubt as to how much skill is involved, the figure on the far left has just taken a tumble and landed sprawling on the ice.

Olaus Magnus's written description of skating also makes it clear that this is a competitive sport:

> The prizes are silver spoons, copper pots, swords, new clothes, and young horses, but more often the last. The rest are outrun by those competitors in the race who attach to the soles of their feet the shin-bones of deer thoroughly smoothed and greased with pork fat, since, when the cold drops of water rise as it were through the pores of the ice during fierce cold, the bones smeared in this way cannot be hampered or kept in check, as iron can however much it is polished or greased.[21]

Woodcut illustration from Olaus Magnus's 'Description of the Northern Peoples' (1555), featuring three figures upright on their ice skates with poles in their hands, and another who has taken a tumble.

Sports

In the Viking Age too, a variety of competitive sports were popular, some more familiar to us today than others. Here we have rather less to go on than in the case of skating, simply because little material evidence survives. Our main sources are the Old Norse-Icelandic sagas, which started to be recorded in thirteenth-century Iceland but often had longer oral tales stretching back through the centuries to the early years of the settlement. It's hard to know where we stand in terms of historical accuracy when we have no other information to go on. But if we're guided by the sagas, sports were clearly an important part of life, including horse fighting, ball games, tug of war, wrestling and swimming. Other sports are less familiar today, such as animal-skin throwing (which seems to be a version of piggy in the middle) and pot scrapers (apparently involving doing something mysterious and nasty with pot scrapers made from horn, since the description of the game being played in *Harðar saga* ('The Saga of Hord') ends up with six players dead). In these narratives, the participants are always male, which may well reflect the social reality of who played such sports.

These sporting games might be played as the equivalent of an evening kickabout on the farmstead (the Old Norse word is *leikar*, simply meaning 'games'). At other times, the games were longer, more organised events, where competitors and spectators would come from all around (*leikmót*, meaning 'game meetings'). These might take place over several weeks and coincide with important points in the year, such as midwinter, midsummer, autumn nights, legal and religious gatherings. Because these sports appear in the context of dramatic saga narratives, they're usually a means by which a feud is started or escalated, and things rarely go smoothly. Sometimes simmering tensions spill over, and what starts as a friendly game quickly becomes deadly. Horse fights are particularly bad for this, since the men stand behind the horses with sticks, such as in this description from *Grettis saga* ('The Saga of Grettir'):

> Then the stallions were brought out; the horses were kept tied together at the edge of the riverbank, just above a deep pool. The horses fought well and it was a good show. Odd goaded his horse on vigorously, while Grettir kept his horse back, holding its tail with one hand and the stick he used to goad it on with the other.[22]

However, it's not long before the two competitors are using their sticks on each other, until one is sent crashing backwards into the pool with three broken ribs. Ball games rarely end better in the sagas, especially in *Gísla saga* where a feud between in-laws gets out of hand. On two occasions in this story, organised ball game competitions turn very sour very fast:

> One day, a great crowd of people came to see the game because they wanted to find out who was the strongest and the best player. And it was the same here as anywhere else – the more people arrived to watch, the greater the eagerness to compete. It is reported that Bork made no headway against Thorstein all day, and finally he became so angry that he broke Thorstein's bat in two. In response to this, Thorstein tackled him and laid him flat out on the ice.[23]

We can assume that not all sports were quite so ill-tempered and deadly as they appear in the sagas. But from these saga descriptions, it's clear why we don't have any other evidence for such games, because they rarely leave identifiable traces in the archaeological record. In the case of feats of strength, we do have one final piece of evidence to add to the pile, albeit one that amounts to little more than a tangle of topography and tradition. It's a very Icelandic piece of evidence too, which centres on the Icelanders' reputation as a nation of fiendishly strong physical specimens, and Iceland's geological fame as a land of ice and fire. The sagas include tales of characters such as Finnbogi the Strong, star of *Finnboga saga ramma* ('The Saga of Finnbogi the Strong'), who is asked to demonstrate his strength in front of his friends and relatives:

> Finnbogi went over to where a large rock stood firm in the ground. He pulled it up, though most people thought it unlikely it could be lifted on account of its size. He took two stones and placed them on top of the big stone, lifted them all up to his chest and walked a considerable distance. He then hurled them down so that the big stone sank no less than two ells into the ground. We have heard it said that little sign of the big stone is now to be seen, but one can see the two which he placed on top of it. Thorgeir offered him his thanks. 'It's very likely that this demonstration of strength, which you say is not great, will be remembered for as long as Iceland is inhabited, and that your name will be known to everyone.'[24]

Finnbogi may well have been content knowing that a saga bearing his name was still doing the rounds a millennium after he lived, but unfortunately in terms of his strength and name being remembered as long as Iceland is inhabited, he was up against stiff competition from another saga hero. Dotted over Iceland are giant boulders that seem to have come from nowhere, rocks called glacial erratics that have been carried long distances by glacial ice and set down in the landscape. Today, these are named for another saga strongman, not Finnbogi but Grettir, whom we met a few paragraphs earlier breaking the ribs of his opponent during a horse fight. Grettir's story is one of super-strength and intense vulnerability, as he roams the wastes of Iceland for twenty years as a hunted outlaw, fighting monsters while being frightened of the dark. On three occasions in the saga, enormous rocks are said to be named after him because only he could lift them. The first time comes shortly after he has been sentenced to outlawry:

> When they rode back from the Assembly, the chieftains rested their horses at Sledaas before going their separate ways. Grettir lifted up a boulder lying in the grass there, which is now called Grettishaf (Grettir's Lift). Many people went up to look at it and were astonished that such a young man could lift such a huge rock.[25]

Across Iceland, many huge stones throughout Iceland are still named for Grettir: Grettishaf ('Grettir's Lift') or Grettistak ('Grettir's Take').[26] These names don't necessarily date back to the periods in which the sagas were set and written down, but they reflect how stories and characters have become embedded in the landscape. And there are other stones – not named for Grettir – that reflect the Icelanders' love of demonstrating their physical strength. So-called 'lifting stones' can be found in various places around the island, all with tales and traditions attached to them.

Today Iceland continues to breed muscle-bound giants. They dominate international strongman and strongwoman competitions out of all proportion to the size of their small island population, in a way that connects them all the way back to the first settlers. Often, their feats of strength still involve the lifting of large stones. But now we turn back to another stone from another time and another place, far smaller and lighter than those lifted by powerful Icelanders, but no less significant on account of its diminutive size. A stone that takes us east across the North Atlantic and back to a tiny island off the western coast of Scotland, to find the people of the Viking Age who are more invisible to us than perhaps any others.

Chapter 9

UNFREEDOM

Between the lines

The little figure and their captor are heading towards the ship. His arms are stretched out in front, possibly bound together. There seems to be a rope around his neck, and perhaps a hood covering his eyes. He trails behind the wild-haired warrior, half the size. A diminutive figure who seems to be very much alone, bringing up the rear on the end of the pole.

We are back with the Inchmarnock hostage stone that we met in 'Beginnings', with its gossamer-thin lines of precise sketching. But this time, fade out the tall, punk-haired, bearded figure wearing what looks like chainmail. Fade out his scabbard, his long, narrow body, his spidery legs wrapped in crisscrossed bindings. Fade out the legs of his two companions. Focus on the small figure who has just become portable property, just like the reliquary that dangles from his wrists. Who knows where his journey will lead him. Will he be ransomed, or enslaved? To see what happens next, we would have to follow him onto the longship, and across the water. Which, of course, we can't. He may have never existed. But even if he didn't, countless others like him did.

We don't know if the Inchmarnock stone depicts a specific event or is meant to be a generalised image of Viking raiding.

Either way, it's a story that was repeated many times in coastal communities dotted around the waters of western Europe and far beyond. For instance, the chronicler Jābir ibn Hayyān wrote an account of a bloody attack by the *Nordomanni* ('Norsemen') on Seville in 844: 'Meanwhile the Norsemen – may God curse them – had arrived, ship after ship, and occupied the city of Seville. They spent seven days there, killing the men and enslaving the women and children.'[1]

Captives and enslaved people were there from the beginning of the Viking Age. They have been there from the beginning of this book, too, often hidden between the lines, depicted on the Inchmarnock hostage stone, embedded in the Irish annals and their records of captives seized. The women taken from Étar in 821. Tuathal and the reliquary of St Adomnán, carried off from their monastery in 832. The Abbot of Armagh and his companions, taken by the Vikings to their ships. Some were sold back to their communities if the ransom was high enough. Others were sold on to slavers.

Slavery has been a constant, almost invisible presence in the various facets of everyday human life that have been explored in this book. When we're thinking about those who fell between the cracks of history, this is most consistently and inescapably true of the enslaved. Their lives were not exceptions to the rule: one estimate suggests that between 20 per cent and 30 per cent of the Scandinavian population were enslaved around the year 1000.[2] Yet if we're trying to find traces of their lives from the ephemera that survive the centuries, then there is precious little to go on. Nevertheless, we have to try find them, hidden between the lines.

There was a saying that echoed around the early Nordic world: *með lögum skal land byggja* ('the land shall be built by law'). Variations on this phrase appear in several of the Scandinavian law codes, and in the Icelandic classic *Njáls saga*, where the hero of the story states, 'our land shall rise with law, but perish with lawlessness'.³ Law and legal rights were of primary importance for the free people of the Viking world. But their lands were also built on the labour of those who had no rights according to the law, and the sale of those humans who were traded on to other places. Where enslaved people appear in the law codes, it is as property to be protected for someone else's benefit, like cattle. In the Viking Age and the centuries that followed, *þræll* ('thrall') was the term used most often to describe them, and generally referred to males. The most common female equivalent was *ambátt*, which could also gesture more specifically towards a sexual relationship with whoever owned them. Over time the meanings of such words expanded, until the word 'thrall' in particular became a term of abuse (such as in *Njáls saga*, where one of the characters tells another, 'it's bad to have a thrall as a best friend').⁴

It isn't possible to describe a 'typical' thrall or *ambátt* in the Viking period, since slavery itself could take many forms, as it can today. One excellent working definition of enslavement identifies four characteristics: removal and relocation by force, an inability to leave the workplace, compulsion to work under threat, and little or no pay.⁵ Much of this also holds true for the Viking Age, but the circumstances of enslavement were variable. They depended on what roles the enslaved people were assigned, who controlled them and the social context in which they found themselves. Once again we are talking about a vast geographical and chronological scope. Imagine the experience of a woman taken with her children from their home in the city of Seville, to be traded as chattel in the frighteningly foreign slave markets of the Irish Sea; or of someone born into slavery within a Norse household and trained up in a valuable skill such as carpentry; or of an Icelandic farmer who had fallen on hard times and temporarily surrendered their freedom in order to pay off a debt. This last example reminds us that there was a blurred line between free and unfree. Most people, even if legally free, were enmeshed in a tight web of social obligations: to their family, to their neighbours, to their social superiors. This web must often have stifled any real chance of 'freedom' in the sense that we would understand it. Many of them may have had lives that were harder than the lives of some unfree people.

Bindings

If we want to find material evidence of enslaved people and their lives, where should we look? For people taken during raids or battles, we might expect the most obvious marker of their captivity to be shackles, either for wrists, necks or ankles. Written sources point us in this direction. In an eleventh-century verse written by a Norwegian court poet called Valgard, King Harald Hardrada – that later failed claimant to the English throne in 1066 – is praised for his bloody harrying of Denmark. The verse includes the lines: 'fair women were captured, a lock secured the girl's body, many a maiden went before you to the warships, bright fetters bit greedily into the flesh'.[6]

However, it turns out that locks and fetters are rarely found in the archaeological record. Going back to the Inchmarnock hostage stone, the little figure appears to be bound, but with a thin line of rope rather than a metal chain. In contrast, the precious reliquary appears to be attached securely to his waist with a metal chain, which the artist has depicted like a wobbly length of intestine. This makes sense: metal chains were heavy and expensive, captives were plentiful, and there was plenty of rope available on ships for the purposes of everything from rigging to mooring. So, when shackles are discovered, they are the exceptions rather than the rule. To find those exceptions, we have to return to some of the places we have already visited in previous chapters.

Last time we were on the island of Birka in Sweden, it was in 'Play', for an exquisitely blobby glass gaming piece and teenagers' ice skates. Last time we were in Dublin, in 'Travel', it was for images of boats found close to the River Liffey. And last time we were in Hedeby on the Danish–German border, in 'Play' again, it was for musical instruments, children's toys and ice skates. In each of these places, iron shackles have also been discovered, most from around the tenth century. This makes perfect sense: the harbours of Birka, Dublin and Hedeby were international trading hubs where slavers would come to buy, sell and transport their human cargo to the next location.

Written records back up the existence of enslaved peoples in chains passing through these sorts of locations. *Vita Rimberti* ('Life of Rimbert') is the hagiography (saint's life) of a ninth-century missionary and bishop of Hamburg-Bremen. Rimbert made several attempts to convert the Scandinavians to Christianity, initially travelling north with his mentor Anskar. Two of their most important mission centres were Birka and Hedeby, and the *Vita Rimberti* includes the following scene in the latter place:

> When he came on a certain occasion to the Danish region where he had built a Christian church, in a place called *Sliaswich* [Schleswig, i.e. Hedeby], he saw a multitude of Christians being led captive in chains. Among them were holy nuns, and one of them, as she saw him from a distance, seemed to venerate him by kneeling and bowing her head often, praying that she might be redeemed through his mercy. And so that he might understand that she was a Christian, she raised her voice and began to sing psalms. The bishop, moved to tears with compassion, prayed that God would help her, upon which the chain with which she was bound broke from her neck at once.[7]

Vita Rimberti was written within a few decades of Rimbert's death in 888 by an anonymous author, with the aim of presenting Rimbert as a powerful saint worthy of veneration. Its primary audience would have been monks and nuns, who would have immediately identified with the unfortunate captive nuns in the story. To this audience, the astonishing thing would have been the miraculous bursting of the neck chain, which we have to take with a large pinch of salt. The backdrop, however – a busy Viking trading port where a miserable gang of bound captives was a common sight – is all too plausible.

This is the great challenge of searching for enslaved people through material evidence: iron chains aside, legal status does not leave an obvious archaeological trace. But if we cast our eyes back over what we have already seen through the preceding chapters, perhaps we can use written sources as a kind of light, shining it into the dark cracks, peering inside to see that enslaved people have been part of the story all along, hidden from view.

Neck chain found at Birka in Sweden, 10th century.

Human cargo

Let's head east from Hedeby, across Sweden and across the Baltic Sea, to the lands of the Rus. We have encountered them in various guises already, as the people who ruled Novgorod and Kyiv from the ninth century onwards. To start with, they were of Nordic stock – mostly Swedes – but over time they became an increasingly mixed group of east Slavic, Baltic, Finnish and Scandinavian cultures. The Rus operated on the tangle of waterways that flowed south across the Continent. In the west they navigated the vast Dnieper river, which starts in the peat bogs and hills of north-west Russia, flows through Kyiv, and eventually drains into the Black Sea. On the other side of the Black Sea lay Constantinople, the beating heart of the Byzantine Empire, and a major destination for Rus raiders and traders coming from the north.

We met the Rus in 'Bodies', on the pages of a Rus–Byzantine peace treaty from 907. Here, the Rus had distinctly Nordic-sounding names and the terms of the treaty included unlimited baths. The agreement was designed to encourage the Rus to come to Constantinople in order to trade, not raid. But in another Byzantine source, we discover that among the goods that the Rus were transporting and trading in Byzantium were chained humans. *De Administrando Imperio* ('On the Governance of the Empire') is a 'How to be an Emperor' manual written in the middle of the tenth century. The author was none other than the Byzantine emperor himself, Constantine VII, who was more qualified than anyone to write such a text. In it, he describes the series of treacherous rapids and narrow, rocky barrages on the Dnieper that had to be navigated by travellers heading south. When the river becomes impassable, Constantine notes, the Rus drag their boats onto the land, take up the goods that they have on board, and 'conduct the slaves in their chains past by land, six miles, until they are through the barrage'.[8]

Further east, the other major watercourse was the River Volga, coursing with its many tributaries down to the Caspian Sea. At the end of the tenth century, the Arab geographer Al-Muqaddasi listed the goods that were taken up and down the Volga. Here, enslaved people are just another trading item, squeezed in among the livestock and furs: 'Sable, grey squirrel, ermine, mink, fox, marten, beaver, spotted hare, goatskins, wax, arrows, birch wood, tall fur caps, fish glue, fish teeth, castoreum oil, amber, tanned horse hides, honey, hazelnuts, falcons, swords, armour, maple wood, Saqalib slaves, sheep, cattle.'[9]

We have already met the Rus on the Volga too, also in 'Bodies', where Ahmad ibn Fadlān's account of his travels includes less-than-complimentary notes regarding their hygiene practices. But he also leaves his readers in no doubt that the Rus that he encountered during his travels in 921 were also enslavers, who would pray to their gods to send them rich merchants to buy their human wares and sable skins. According to his account, they had sex with their slave girls in company, while dead slaves were left to be eaten by dogs and birds of prey. And, most infamously, they would sacrifice slaves so that they might follow their masters into the next world. We'll come back to that last point later.

Settlers and pioneers

Individuals enslaved by those of Nordic extraction – whatever name they went by, Viking, Rus, or something else – might end up in the flesh markets of the Mediterranean and Middle East, especially if they had been captured during raids and warfare. It's an impossible task to follow them there, to find names of individuals, discover something about the lives they lived. We meet with marginally more success if we look closer to home, in the Scandinavian homelands and the North Atlantic colonies. Here too, in so many of the stories told in previous chapters, enslaved people were hiding in plain sight.

Back in 'Belief', we met Ingolf, striking out across the North Atlantic from Norway in the year 874. According to *Landnámabók* ('The Book of Settlement'), he was one of the first permanent settlers of Iceland. But Ingolf did not arrive alone. For one thing, he sailed alongside his blood-brother Hjorleif, who was also planning to settle in Iceland. And they were both accompanied by enslaved people. Earlier in the narrative, *Landnámabók* explains where Hjorleif acquired them: 'He plundered all over Ireland and took a great deal of loot, including ten slaves called Dufthak, Geirraud, Skjaldbjorn, Halldor, Drafdrit – the rest of them aren't mentioned by name.'[10] Of the five named individuals, the first has a Gaelic name, the next three have Norse names, and the last sounds like they have been given a disparaging nickname (*draf* might be translated as pigswill or hogwash, while *drit* is dirt or shit).

Back to Iceland. While Ingolf made landfall, Hjorleif got separated, and his ship drifted along the coastline until they ran short of drinking water. At this point, we hear about the slaves for the first time: 'What the Irish slaves did was to knead together flour and butter, saying it was good for thirst. They called the mixture *minthak*.'[11]

'Minthak', it seems, is a corrupted form of the Irish word *menadach*, a porridge-like mixture of fat and flour.[12] Eventually they find land where they can spend the winter, at which point Dufthak – the first slave mentioned – hatches a plot to kill Hjorleif and his companions. Having murdered them all in a woodland, the slaves seize the wives, boats and possessions of the dead men and escape to some nearby islands. Ingolf arrives with his own slaves – Vifil and Karli – and, having seen what has happened, sets off to take vengeance. *Landnámabók* notes: 'Ingolf killed every one of them. The place where Dufthak met his death is called Dufthaksskor. Many of the slaves jumped over a cliff that's been called after them ever since, as have the islands where the slaves were killed, which were named *Westmanna Islands* since the men came from the west.'[13] Of course, from the point of view of Iceland, Britain and Ireland lie to the east, not the west. But this is a fossilised term for the Gaelic-speaking populations of these islands, originating with the Norse inhabitants of Scandinavia and Britain.

These 'Westmanna Islands' (*Vestmannaeyjar* in modern Icelandic) lie off the south coast of Iceland. They now include Surtsey, the island born of an underwater volcano in 1963 and named for the fire giant Surt whom we also encountered in 'Belief'. The name given to these islands is a reminder that hand in hand with the story of Iceland's first official settlers is a darker tale of slave revolt and death.

Looking west from Iceland, we have already met those who set out across the North Atlantic to settle Greenland, led by the socially disruptive figure of Erik the Red. His story is also inextricably linked to the story of his slaves. According to *Eiríks saga rauða*, when Erik arrives from Norway and settles in Iceland, his slaves cause a landslide to fall on a nearby farm. One of the relatives of the farm owner kills the slaves, and for this, Erik kills the relative. This is the first of the killings that lead to Erik's three-year outlawry, during which he explores the fjords of Western Greenland and dreams of making a new home in this new land.

The children of Erik the Red continued to push back the boundaries of the world, sailing further west across the North Atlantic from Greenland. With them came enslaved people. Their names are given as Haki and Hekja, two Scots given to Leif Eriksson by the Norwegian king, Olaf Tryggvason. In *Eiríks saga rauða*, they are said to dress in a garment called a *kjafal*, with a hood on top but no arms. It has been suggested that this too – like the *minthak* made on the approach to Iceland – is a corrupted Irish word, possibly *cochall*, a type of hooded cloak.[14] The pair are said to run faster than deer and are sent ashore to explore the new land. Three days later, they return with wild wheat and grapes in their hands, and it is this discovery that leads to the Norse christening the new land *Vínland* (*vín* means 'wine', and *vínber* are grapes). In the other saga about the voyages to Greenland, called *Grœnlendinga saga*, the story changes. Once again it seems that a slave was responsible for discovering the grapes that gave the land its name. This time his name is Tyrkir, a German-speaker from the lands to the south of Scandinavia. Leif Eriksson addresses him as *fóstri minn*, 'my fosterer', a term sometimes used of slaves who lived at the farmstead in close proximity to the other members of the household. The saga notes that 'Tyrkir had spent many years with him and his father and had treated Leif very affectionately as a child.'[15] If he were enslaved, then it appears to be a different sort of enslavement to that presented in the story of Haki and Hekja, or indeed the experiences of the enslaved as recounted in the settlement stories of Iceland.

The voyages to Vinland took place around the year 1000. Archaeological evidence found at the site of L'Anse aux Meadows in Newfoundland has long confirmed that the Norse did reach the edge of North America, lending credence to many of the facts presented in the Vinland sagas. Yet both sagas were only written down in the thirteenth century, based on information that had been passed down the generations by word of mouth. Plenty of the episodes that take place in these two texts are not what we would count as historically verifiable, including a winter haunting where plague victims return from the dead. Similarly, we can't say whether or not Haki, Hekja and Tyrkir were historical figures or fictional characters. Even so, just as in the story of the settlement of Iceland, enslaved people play crucial roles in the story of the Norse discovery of North America.

Workers

The roles that enslaved people played in this era of history were as varied as the lives they lived. But if we focus on those who were embedded within the Nordic world itself – because they had been born into slavery, fell into slavery through debt, or were captured and brought there rather than sold on – then it is true that most people lived on farmsteads. This is the world that their lives would have revolved around, and it provides a framework for the sort of work they performed day-to-day.

Last time we visited the Norwegian stave church at Bø in Telemark, it was in 'Love', in the context of hidden lusts, and a runic riddle that spelled out the name GUDRUN. One of the clues in this riddle was 'the thrall's misfortune', and the answer was *nauð*, the name for the N-rune, meaning 'need, distress, bondage'. A similar sentiment is expressed in the Icelandic rune poem which is preserved in a late medieval manuscript from around 1500, but probably dates from at least the thirteenth century. (The rune poem tradition is older than this: others survive from the Nordic and Anglo-Saxon worlds in manuscripts dating back to the ninth and tenth centuries). Each runic letter is accompanied by a short poem explaining its meaning, and the poem for the N-rune reads: *Nauð er þýjar þrá ok þungr kostr ok vássamlig verk* ('*Nauð* is the suffering of the slave and heaviness of being and toil of work').[16] Such runic clues reflect a basic reality: for the most part, everyone had to work in whatever way they could, but the dirtiest and nastiest tasks would have fallen to the unfree members of a household.

Back in 'Home', we explored the daily tasks that went on inside and outside the farm. For the most part, it is likely that enslaved people would have been there too. Indeed, a passage from the Frostathing Law recorded in medieval Norway described a typical farm in Trøndelag as being one that comprised twelve cows, two horses and three thralls.[17] Surely, the lives and experiences of thralls are embedded in some of the artefacts discovered in the ground during archaeological investigations, especially when they lack embellishment or runic inscriptions that might mark them out as the possessions of more socially elevated, educated members of the community. Yet the thralls themselves remain invisible. When the soil is brushed away from a Viking Age wooden distaff, it is unlikely that we will discover the social status of whoever held it, spinning threads from clouds of wool. Likewise, how can we know whether the person who sat down on a whale-vertebra milking stool in the darkness of a Greenlandic winter and milked the cows was free or unfree? Written sources – be they legal or literary – sometimes hint at the sorts of tasks reserved for thralls: heavy, boring, dirty, uncomfortable and monotonous roles such as spreading muck in the fields, cutting and carrying firewood, grinding corn, cooking food. The bigger the farmstead and the land, the more labour that was needed, and the more thralls that might belong to the household. Beyond that fact, much becomes guesswork. For instance, we might also remember from 'Home' that the bishopric at Gardar in Greenland had space for around 100 cows. Does this mean that more enslaved people lived here too?

Companions

Unfree members of a household could also undertake more intimate roles within the home, not only as co-workers but also as companions and caregivers. Going back through the chapters, we find evidence of this in the saga stories particularly. One unfree saga character meets her death in a way that illustrates her close emotional connections to another member of the household. We have already been introduced to the stroppy but brilliant saga hero Egil. In 'Travel', we read how the young Egil composed a verse that begins 'My mother said'. Yet we know from the next episode recounted in the saga that his mother was not the only woman involved in his upbringing. The incident takes place at the regional games, and this time Egil is in his twelfth winter. Together with his friend, Egil is pitted against his own father, Skallagrim, a sore loser who becomes preternaturally strong and furious at sunset.* Skallagrim kills Egil's friend and is about to do the same to his own child, when an enslaved woman called Thorgerd steps in. She is described as strong as a man and very good at magic, and the saga notes that she had 'fostered Egil when he was a child'.[18] When she intervenes to save Egil from his out-of-control father, Skallagrim kills her. Like Leif and his foster-father Tyrkir who travel together to the edge of North America, here is a saga story where there appears to be true emotional intimacy between both parties.

Thorgerd is introduced as Skallagrim's *ambátt*, that 'female slave' word that can also shade into a sexual meaning. The concept of consent is so far removed from the power dynamic that exists between an unfree individual and the person who controls them, that it is essentially meaningless. There is nothing in Ahmad ibn Fadlān's eyewitness account of the Rus slavers to suggest that the enslaved women are treated as anything other than property: 'If a merchant enters at this moment to buy a young slave girl from one of the men and finds him having sex with her, the man does not get up off her until he has satisfied himself.'[19]

In 'Love', we thought about the implications and experience of pregnancy for women. Of course, this was also true of women who were enslaved. There are several clauses in provincial law codes that discuss the penalties for impregnating someone's slave. But the reason these clauses exist is not to protect the enslaved individual. They exist to protect the

---

* This is something of a family trait: Skallagrim's own father was Kveldulf ('Night Wolf'), described as a great shape-shifter who would grow nastier as evening approached, hence his nickname.

person who normally benefitted from her labour. According to a passage in the Westrogothic Law from Sweden, the person who had impregnated someone else's female slave was responsible for her until she was able to grind grain and milk animals again. The Gulathing Law from Norway has a similar provision, but the test this time is that the postpartum woman is able to carry two buckets of water from the well.[20] Nothing in these law codes, first compiled in the late twelfth and early thirteenth centuries, suggests that welfare for the pregnant woman was remotely in the minds of the lawmakers. And nothing suggests that their situation would have been any better in the centuries before the law codes were written down.

Sacrifice

There were several ways that an individual's enslavement might come to an end. They might die of natural causes or accidents, as most probably did, but they would be unlikely to receive the sorts of burials that would leave clear archaeological traces. Much less commonly but more dramatically, they might be sacrificed to join their master or mistress in the next world, and there is enough evidence to suggest this happened in certain circumstances. Alternatively, if they were especially lucky, they might earn their freedom by paying off the debts that led to their enslavement in the first place, or be granted their freedom by their legal owner. We start with the darkest of these outcomes.

At the end of 'Travel', we briefly came across the Valkyrie Brynhild, lover of Sigurd. In the poem *Helreið Brynhildar* ('Brynhild's Ride to Hel'), she is burned on a funeral pyre and travels to Hel on a wagon draped with tapestries. But here too, enslaved people were present, hovering at the edges of this legendary tale. The preceding poem in the *Codex Regius* manuscript is *Sigurðarkviða in skamma* ('A Short Poem about

Sigurd')*. The poem ends with the dying Brynhild's instructions on how her funeral is to be arranged, so she can accompany Sigurd (whom she calls the 'southern man') to the next world:

> Let the pyre be hung with shields and tapestries,
> skilfully patterned foreign weaving, and many foreign slaves;
> burn the southern man beside me.
>
> On the southern man's side
> burn my maids adorned with jewellery,
> two by his head and two hawks,
> then everything will be orderly.

As she starts to fade, she instructs those listening:

> So five serving-girls accompany him,
> eight servants of good family,
> the slaves who grew up with me, my patrimony,
> which Budli gave to his child.[21]

Next to the ornate grave goods of shields, tapestries and hawks, it is murdered humans who are to accompany the lovers to the afterlife: foreign slaves, maids adorned with jewellery, five serving girls, eight servants of good family and the slaves who were given to Brynhild as a child.

This poem only survives in a thirteenth-century Icelandic manuscript, set down almost three centuries after the country converted to Christianity. We cannot take the words as fact. Yet here we are on the edge of finding actual individuals who experienced lives of enslavement, and died to accompany those who owned them to the afterlife. This brings us back to Ahmad ibn Fadlān and the Rus slavers that he met on the river in 921.

---

* Although at seventy-one verses there is nothing particularly 'short' about it.

Because what his account is most famous for is a description of an enslaved young woman who 'volunteers' to join her master in death ('When a great man dies, the members of his family say to his slave girls and young slave boys: "Which of you will die with him?" One of them replies: "I will.""')[22] We simply don't have enough information to know how voluntary such a decision was, or the accuracy of Ahmad ibn Fadlān's interpretation. Perhaps even if we had been there as eyewitnesses ourselves, we still wouldn't know. In any case, the account takes us through her final days, and up to her final moments:

> I saw that the girl did not know what she was doing. She wanted to enter the pavilion, but she put [her head] between it and the boat. Then the old woman seized her head, made her enter the pavilion and went in with her. The men began to bang on their shields with staves, to drown her cries, so that the other slave girls [would not be frightened] and try to avoid dying with their masters. Next, six men entered the pavilion and [lay with] the girl, one after another, after which they laid her beside her master. Two seized her feet and two others her hands. The old woman called the Angel of Death came and put a cord round her neck in such a way that the two ends went in opposite directions. She gave the ends to two of the men, so they could pull on them. Then she herself approached the girl holding in her hand a dagger with a broad blade and [plunged it again and again between the girl's ribs], while the two men strangled her with the cord until she was dead.[23]

It is possible that we have already met such a victim of this practice, back in Norway, in the sumptuous Oseberg ship burial from 834, which appeared in 'Travel' and 'Bodies'. There were two women in the ship. The traditional interpretation is that the younger of the two – who was in her fifties – may have been chosen to accompany the older, echoing Brynhild's instructions:

'burn my maids adorned with jewellery'. It's not a straightforward case. If one were indeed subservient to the other, this is not reflected in what she ate, because both women enjoyed high-status diets, including lots of meat. Skeletal evidence suggests that the older woman died of natural causes. In the case of the younger woman, very few bones survive, certainly not enough to help us determine whether she was enslaved. But there are some mysterious facts to consider. Several weeks before her death she had broken her collarbone, although the fracture had started to heal in the meantime. There's also the possibility that the younger woman may have had ancestors from the Black Sea region, somewhere near modern-day Iran or Iraq (the first time her genetic material was tested, this seemed to be the result, but subsequent tests haven't replicated the result and there is not a lot of her body left to test).[24] Perhaps this too echoes the legendary Brynhild's words, when she commands that the funeral pyre be furnished with 'many foreign slaves'.

There are instances where the circumstances surrounding a double – or even triple – burial may lead us to suspect that something untoward has occurred. An example with certain parallels to Ahmad ibn Fadlān's account comes from Ballateare on the Isle of Man, and a tenth-century burial. The huge mound – around 12 metres across – contained the body of a male, probably in his twenties, who was buried with weapons to accompany him to the next world. His coffin had been sealed, a shield and two spears placed on top before the mound started to be built up with sand and turf. But before it was completed, it seems that there were other rituals to be carried out. Near the top of the mound was the body of a woman, also probably in her twenties, the back of her skull sliced off with a sharp weapon as though she had been killed from behind while she knelt. She was placed face down in the uppermost layer of the mound together with cremated animal bones, before the mound was finally covered over. Why her body was found much further up the mound than the male in his coffin isn't immediately obvious, but there are various possibilities, not least that she was sacrificed together with the animals as part of a final ritual to close the mound.

From the tenth-century Isle of Man let us sweep eastwards and back in time to a different grave, this one on the Swedish island of Birka around the year 800. The focus of whatever took place here seems to be a man aged forty to fifty, buried with grave goods including a selection of weapons and beads. An elk antler had been placed close to his left shoulder, and because of this unusual feature he's often known as the 'Elk Man'. But he wasn't alone in the grave. Flung across his lower legs was the body of a younger man, between twenty to thirty years old, tall and powerfully built. He had been decapitated, and his head placed by his chest. He had no grave goods himself, but that's hardly surprising, because it appears that he *was* one of the grave goods for the older man.

Ten kilometres as the crow flies to the north-east of Birka, in what are now the suburbs of Stockholm, another Viking Age grave was found at Grimsta. This time, the focus seems to have been a male of uncertain age, who had been cremated. Found with him were the skeletons of two young males, one in his late teens, the other in his twenties. Both had been decapitated. One skull had an open wound that hadn't healed, and so may have been what killed him. It is hard to come up with a reasonable explanation for the three additional bodies in the graves at Birka and Grimsta that does not involve human sacrifice.

There is an intriguing footnote to the two Swedish burial sites that takes us back to 'Bodies', and the deliberately filed teeth – mostly horizontal grooves, mostly Swedish, always male – that have been discovered in the mouths of over 130 skeletons. Both the decapitated skeleton buried with the 'Elk Man' at Birka, and one of the two decapitated skeletons buried with the cremated body at Grimsta had such modifications on their teeth.

They fit the general pattern, in that they were both male, and both found in Sweden. But beyond that, we still can't read whatever narrative these filed teeth are telling us. If we assume that these individuals were killed because they were the 'property' of the dead men, then it is likely that their teeth could tell us something about their identities, their characters and their origins. We don't have the answers yet, but perhaps one day we will.[25]

Freedom

There were occasions where a favourite slave might accompany a dead person into the next world, willingly or not, where presumably their relationship could continue as it had in life. But there were other occasions when such a death was where they parted ways, not only with their owner but also with their slave status. Runestones commemorating the dead have appeared occasionally in previous chapters, such as in 'Play', with the Ockelbo runestone in Sweden, depicting two figures playing a board game. Casting our eyes west to Hørning in Denmark, we find a runestone raised by someone called Toki, to commemorate the person who freed him from slavery: 'Toki the Smith raised this stone in memory of Thorgisl, the son of Gudmund, who gave him gold and freed him.'[26]

The runestone probably dates to somewhere around 1000. It is as much a statement of Toki's success as it is a testament to Thorgisl's good character and generosity. Toki is defined by his profession: a smith, a skilled craftsperson. The very fact that he had the resources to commission a runestone suggests that he had become a wealthy individual of some standing. In fact, he seems to have commissioned more than one runestone, because 30 kilometres away in Grensten, another runestone was raised that reads: 'Toki the Smith raised this stone in memory of Refli, the son of Asgi, the son of Bjorn. May God help their souls.'[27]

Some of the saga narratives we have already encountered in this chapter also include stories of enslaved people being freed by those who owned them. Returning to the story of Ingolf and Hjorleif in *Landnámabók*, after the darkness of the slave revolt and the killings, Ingolf gives freedom to Vifil, the enslaved person who helped him track down his foster-brother's killers. Likewise, in *Eiríks saga rauða*, before Erik himself appears in the narrative, the whole saga begins with the story of Aud the Deep-Minded, one of the great first settlers of Iceland. The saga tells us that when she sets out from Orkney:

> Accompanying her on her journey to Iceland were many men of good family who had been taken prisoner by Vikings raiding around Britain and were called *bondsmen*. One of them was named Vifil. He was a man of very good family who had been taken prisoner in Britain and was called a bondsman until Aud gave him his freedom. When Aud gave her crew farm sites Vifil asked her why she had not given him a farm site like the others. Aud replied that it made no difference, he would be considered just as fine a man wherever he was. Aud gave him Vifilsdal and he settled there. He had a wife and two sons, Thorgeir and Thorbjorn. They were promising men and grew up with their father.[28]

Despite this positive saga portrayal, to be freed wasn't always the same as having always been free, both in terms of social pecking order and legal rights. Going forward a few pages in *Eiríks saga rauða*, we meet Einar, the son of a slave and a person of great talent and potential. He proposes marriage to Gudrid, who will later marry one of the sons of Erik the Red (and, after his death, sail to the edge of North America where she even gives birth). But when Einar sends word to Gudrid's father that he would like to marry her, he reacts furiously: 'I never expected to hear such words from you, telling me to marry my daughter to the son of a slave . . . She'll not go back with you, since you think her worthy of such a lowly match.'[29] Certainly, enslaved people, freed people and the children of enslaved people can be prominent characters in the sagas, but often the taint of slavery follows them into their supposed freedom.

This was more than ingrained social hierarchy and prejudice against former slaves. A freed person – *leysingi* – didn't automatically receive the rights enjoyed by those who had never been unfree. Norwegian law codes note that such a person was still beholden to their former master, not only for their own lifetime but for several generations afterwards. Any inheritance that they had to pass on, any contracts they wanted to enter into, were

Runestone raised by Toki the Smith to commemorate Thorgisl, 'who gave him gold and freed him'. Hørning, Denmark, c.1000.

also tied to the family who once owned them. Freedom was not a binary state, and it might take a very long time for the descendants of a former slave to truly escape the shackles of their past.[30]

Endings

The story in his hagiography tells us that the Christian missionary Rimbert prayed so hard for the enslaved Christians at Hedeby that the chain holding the ring around the nun's neck broke. The runestone raised by Toki the Smith to the one who freed him is inscribed with a Christian cross. Aud the Deep-Minded is famous for being a baptised Christian as well as one of the first settlers of Iceland, putting up crosses on the hills of her new homeland so she could pray to her one God. Freeing enslaved people may have been seen as an act of Christian charity, but it should be noted that in the tale of Aud the Deep-Minded and in the case of Toki's former owner Thorgisl, they both owned humans and made use of their labour in the first place. Around Aud's time – that is, in the late ninth century – Christian clerics in the Carolingian Empire were making objections to the slave trade – but specifically in cases where Christian slaves were being sold to non-Christians (mainly Muslims) in the Mediterranean. They seem to have had no problem with slavery per se. Hence it is unsurprising that the closest neighbours of the Vikings were just as familiar with slavery and just as dependent on it. In ninth-century Anglo-Saxon England, even at a time when the English and the Danes were at each other's throats, this was the one thing they could agree on. Last time we met Alfred and Guthrum in 'Bodies', they were drawing up a peace treaty that cemented the borders between England's Anglo-Saxon and Danish territories. This same ninth-century agreement included a clause that stated neither side would harbour the other's runaway slaves, and another clause to the effect that everyone purchasing slaves, horses and oxen had to know their guarantor. Elsewhere, there are several references to runaway slaves in various Anglo-Saxon law codes, with punishments for slaves 'stealing themselves' including hanging and stoning to death.[31]

Another figure last encountered in 'Bodies' is Ælfric of Eynsham, who was writing a letter to Brother Edward accusing him of adopting an unpatriotic Scandi-chic hairstyle. He also wrote the *Colloquy*, a teaching tool for young Anglo-Saxons learning Latin, where a series of characters and their crafts are introduced. Among the monks, cooks, merchants and hunters is the character of the enslaved person, out ploughing the fields. He says:

> I work too much. I go out early, driving the oxen towards the field, and yoke them to the plough. There is no winter so severe that I dare stay at home, for fear of my master. With the oxen yoked, and the plough share and plough coulter fastened, I must plough an entire field or even more . . . I have a boy who goads the oxen with a cattle prod, and he is hoarse from cold and from shouting . . . And still, I have more to do. I must fill the cowsheds with hay and water, and muck them out . . . It is a lot of work because I am not free.[32]

While this is the dialogue of an imagined character rather than an actual person, it is a rare case where someone from the very upper echelons of Anglo-Saxon society attempts to give an authentic voice to the lived experience of those at the bottom – even if, at the same time, this only underlines how elusive that experience is to us.

Ælfric of Eynsham's *Colloquy* was written almost exactly a century before *Domesday Book*, which was compiled on the orders of William the Conqueror in 1086. And here, among the lists of property owners, priests and livestock, there were enslaved people, perhaps making up somewhere between a tenth and a third of the English population.[33] Under William, a law was introduced banning the sale of slaves into foreign lands, and especially to non-Christians. Whether this made any difference to those who led enslaved lives and were counted in *Domesday Book*, we cannot tell. Nevertheless, in England, the practice of slavery did start to decline.

Over time, the same happened in Scandinavia. And yet, in later decades and centuries, we still see evidence of prominent Christians freeing – but let's not forget, therefore owning in the first place – enslaved people. Dating to 1201, the will of Archbishop Absalon of Lund contains clauses that grant freedom to several enslaved members of his household, including Eskil his bath attendant, the women and children 'whom Niels the stable-keeper had made unfree and put into thralldom', and Christian the cook 'who was unlawfully taken as thrall'.[34] We may wonder about the lives lived by Eskil, Christian, and the unnamed women and children. How did they come into the possession of Absalon and Niels? Had Eskil ever known a life without enslavement? How and where was Christian captured? And what happened to them all after they were freed? So this chapter ends as it began, with a captured Christian, one scratched onto a piece of slate, one inserted into an archbishop's will. In our beginning is our end. But if beginnings are hard to pinpoint, then so are endings, and this leads us to the inevitable question: when did the Viking Age actually end?

Chapter 10

ENDINGS

Three endings, centuries apart. Three artefacts (and their companions) from three moments in time, each reminding us that there is no one conclusion to any history. The first comes from Yorkshire, England, in the decade leading up to the politically transformative events of 1066. The second looks to the islands to the north and west of the Scottish mainland, from around the 1200s. The third looks west across the North Atlantic to Greenland, perhaps in the early decades of the 1400s. Each represents a step that takes us out of the Viking Age as we know it, and each tells its own story about those caught up in the flow of history. This time, there are a few names, but mostly there are traces of humans through their physical remains, their writing, their possessions, their artwork. And we start with a church sundial, hidden in the shadows like a clock that has wound down for the last time.

Ending 1 : Sunset

Today, it lurks in a crooked little porch, beneath the struts of a timber roof. An unknowing visitor could easily miss it. However, a glance upwards and they would soon spot the wide slab, over 2 metres across and half a metre high, embedded in the grey wall of weathered limestone. Peering closely, they would make out a semicircle carved with lines and angular letters, flanked on each side by panels containing more text. They might even recognise the semicircle as some kind of sundial, albeit one that has not seen the sun for a long time, and is missing its gnomon (the long point that casts a shadow). And if they stepped back outside the porch and studied the rest of the building, they might recognise that this retired sundial is very old, in fact older than the porch in which it hides, older even than most of the unassuming church in which it is embedded.

Strip away the porch, the petite square tower to the left of the building, the pointy-roofed chancel to the right, all from the post-medieval period. Strip away the fifteenth-century buttress and windows. Strip away the roof and every other tweak and addition of forty generations. What remains is a tall stone box of age-worn stones, a muddle of grey, brown and off-white, set in rough courses that were, for the most part, laid out almost a thousand years ago. This is the ancient core of the church. Back then, when the limestone glowed between bands of fresh mortar, a visitor's eye would have been drawn to the sundial before anything else.

The church stands at the foot of a steep-sided, thickly wooded valley that leads up to the wild heathland of the North York Moors. Picture it on a bright afternoon, with the high sun casting its shadow on its whitewashed surfaces. On the sundial itself painted letters shine, as sturdy and sharp-cornered as the church itself: 'This is the day's sun-marker, at each hour,' they say. And below: 'Hawarth made me, and Brand the priest.'[1]

But the most interesting information is offered by the panels to the left and right. Together they tell the story of the church and its creators:

ORM GAMAL SVNA BOHTE SCS GREGORIVS MINSTER
ÐONNE HIT WES ÆL TOBROCAN & TOFALAN & HE
HIT LET MACAN NEWAN FROM GRVNDE XPE & SCS
GREGORIVS IN EADWARD DAGVM C[Y]NG & [I]N TOSTI
DAGVM EORL[2]

That is:

> Orm, son of Gamal, bought St Gregory's Minster when it was
> completely ruined and collapsed, and he recently had it built
> from the ground for Christ and St Gregory in the days of King
> Edward and in the days of Earl Tostig.

Only a handful of sundials survive from the Anglo-Saxon period.
None is so well preserved as this example at Kirkdale, and none
of the others tells us so much about itself. It allows us to recap-
ture a moment in history – and to touch down in the first of our
endings.

The sundial itself was created as part of a new beginning.
Orm, we are told, bought and rebuilt a derelict church in the
reign of Edward the Confessor and Earl Tostig. The latter figure
helps us date the construction project with rare precision, since
we know he became earl of Northumbria in 1055 and was driven
out of his earldom in 1065. Orm's masons did not start from
scratch, but set up a workshop on the site where they recycled
whatever decent building materials lay around. These included
several gravestones that were incorporated into the rebuilt
church, the oldest dating as far back as the eighth century. The
sundial itself, in fact, was carved into the side of a recycled stone
coffin. So we know that there was a cemetery and church here
already by the eighth century, and likely even earlier.

This little church stood through momentous changes in
Northumbria, not least the fall of York to the so-called Great
Heathen Army in 866 and the settlement of much of its

hinterland by Scandinavian invaders and their families. Standing quietly beneath the moors, the church was prominent enough that these settlers named the whole valley after it. Kirkdale, from Old Norse *kirkja* ('church') and *dalr* ('valley'), the name by which it is still known. Even after the expulsion of the last Viking king of York in 954, when Northumbria was absorbed once and for all into the kingdom of England, tumultuous events were yet to come. Scandinavian raids continued, until in 1013 the king of Denmark, Svein 'Forkbeard', crossed the sea to lead a new full-scale invasion. Northumbria bowed to him straight away, perhaps because so many of its leading figures, being of Danish or Norwegian descent themselves, were as happy to be ruled by a Danish king as by a West Saxon one. Having pushed King Æthelred – he of the St Brice's Day massacre – into exile and taken the throne of England, Svein died suddenly in February 1014 and was eventually replaced by his more famous son, Cnut. Kirkdale, along with the rest of England, found itself drawn into a North Sea empire that lasted until 1042. Then, once again, an Anglo-Saxon king took the crown: Edward the Confessor.

There is no evidence that the Norse who settled this part of the Vale of Pickering caused any disruption to the church at Kirkdale. On the contrary, the fabric of the present church includes recycled tenth- or eleventh-century sculpture of distinctive Anglo-Scandinavian design, and the church itself seems to have been rebuilt in the late tenth century.[3] In other words, Scandinavians living nearby, following their conversion to Christianity, seem to have patronised the church, worshipped in it, and chosen to be buried beside it. Disaster struck at some point in the early- or mid-eleventh century when the church was destroyed by a fire that left its sandstone foundations burnt a bright red.[4] It's impossible to say what caused this destruction – an arsonist, or a butter-fingered priest with a candle? – but the result left the building largely ruined. That is, until Orm Gamalson appeared on the scene.

The names of Orm and his father Gamal are Old Norse (meaning 'snake' and 'old' respectively), which strongly suggests Scandinavian heritage. And while the sundial inscription is in Old English, the word for 'sundial' itself, *solmerki*, appears to be an Old Norse loanword.[5] Taking this all together, we can build a picture of Orm, blurry as it is. His name does not prove he spoke Old Norse or regarded himself as 'Scandinavian' in any sense. Nor can we be sure that his forebears came to England with the first wave of Danelaw settlement; they might equally have arrived in the eleventh century during the reigns of Cnut and his son Harthacnut, or at some point in between. We do know, however, that he was a man of substance, a success story of the Anglo-Norse cultural and political fusion that defined much of northern England at this time.[6] We also know that his success would not long outlive the creation of the Kirkdale sundial. From our perspective, he was living at the end of an era: that of Anglo-Saxon England. And this era was about to end suddenly and brutally.

The year 1066 is among the most famous dates in English history, and famous enough that it is sometimes used to mark not just the interface between Anglo-Saxons and Normans, but also the end of the Viking Age itself. There is a pleasing symmetry to this. We began with broken stones in the ruins of a monastery on a tiny Scottish island. We end with the broken stones of another Christian building, but this time being rebuilt. And rebuilt by someone connected by heritage of sorts to the punk-haired figures depicted on the hostage stone. This gives us a sense of completeness and resolution, even redemption. The Viking as poacher turned gamekeeper. A fitting place to end.

And 1066 has much to recommend it as a watershed date in English history. The death of the heirless King Edward the Confessor on 5 January 1066 led to a succession crisis that spanned the English Channel and the North Sea. The decisive Battle of Hastings, on 14 October of that year, was momentous by any measure, and its two antagonists – Harold Godwinson and William of Normandy – are rightly famous (or infamous) even today. If we are looking for an end date for the Viking Age, though, our most important figure in this drama is Harald Hardrada, and the most important battle was at Stamford Bridge on 25 September, when he was killed by the army of Harold Godwinson.

Harald Hardrada deserves to be much more than a footnote in English history. As king of Norway, he saw himself as the successor to the Danish King Cnut and heir of the North Sea empire that had disintegrated only twenty-four years earlier. To understand why Harald gets pinned up as a poster child for the end of an era, recall the typical characteristics of the Viking Age that we have covered in previous chapters: raiding and warfare, runes, travel and exploration, paganism and Christianity, international settlement and trade, skaldic verse, wordplay. Harald has it all. He was not only the ruler of a Scandinavian kingdom, but also had an adventurous youth of exploration, raiding, trading and diplomacy on the international stage. According to his saga, he served in (and possibly even led) the elite Varangian Guard, the personal bodyguards of the Byzantine emperor. He composed poetry. He was Christian, but at a time when what this meant was more fluid and negotiable. Few figures personify our idea of the Viking Age so completely. All of this ended in the blood-soaked mud of Stamford Bridge.

The world around him had also changed since the era of the first Norwegian raids in the British Isles. By 1066, battles were being fought between monarchs and would-be monarchs, rather than by simple raiders and petty rulers in search of booty and fame. If we think about religion, this is the period when Christianity truly dug itself into the Norse world. Our later textual sources tell us that Denmark formally converted to the faith under Harald Bluetooth around 960, Norway under Olaf Tryggvason from 995, and Iceland in 1000. Sweden received its first bishops around the same time, although the conversion period here lasted into the twelfth century. The year 1066, then, seems as good a point as any to bring the Viking Age to a close.

But if we return to that image of history as a great untamed river, then this ending is a neat canal lock. Perhaps too neat. The deaths and religious conversions of kings are significant to the people at the top, but to what extent they impacted the lives of most people is up for debate. Take conversion. On the one hand, we can find evidence for Scandinavians converting to Christianity throughout the Viking Age. Often this was for political or economic reasons, and often the conversion may have been less than heartfelt. (According to a Carolingian writer, one ninth-century Dane sneakily went through the ritual of baptism twenty times – because on each occasion he was gifted a fine white linen tunic from the imperial wardrobe.)[7] Yet we see Christians among the first Norse settlers of Iceland, and not just among the enslaved arrivals. On the other hand, certain pre-Christian beliefs and customs lingered, whether in the shadows or openly, long after conversion had officially occurred. The whole process was messy and drawn-out, making it impossible to define any point at which the Vikings truly 'became' Christian.

We find a bigger problem with 1066 if we expand our view beyond England to the wider world of Norse influence, where the date has rather less significance. Why should the defeat of a Norwegian army on the banks of a small river outside York mark an epochal change in the life of a farmer in Greenland, a shepherd in Iceland or a leatherworker in Sweden? They might raise an interested eyebrow at such news should it reach them, but their primary concerns would likely be the weather, their bodily health, the prosperity of their trade, their relationships with friends and family, and the demands of their own immediate lord. This is not to say that the impact of Harald Hardrada's death did not send ripples of some sort through the Norse world, but rather that life for most people usually ran with a different sort of rhythm, where change was slow and gradual, played out over generations, not overnight.

Ultimately this presents us with a challenge. Is it possible to hold these two perspectives at once, the micro and the macro, to connect the rivulets of everyday human experience with the grand flow of history? This brings us back to Kirkdale, and to the new sundial installed in the decade before 1066. Its inscription records the names of the two people who actually created it: Hawarth (probably the stonemason) and Brand the priest (who perhaps directed Hawarth and wrote the text). They are two figures who would otherwise be lost to history. It also records the name of Orm Gamalson, most probably of Scandinavian heritage and of significant local standing. And then there is Earl Tostig himself, in 'whose days' the church was rebuilt.

We now find ourselves among the major-league players in the fateful political game of 1066. Tostig was brother to Harold Godwinson and to Queen Edith, Edward the Confessor's wife. This made him a member of what was indisputably the most powerful family in England. Yet even these family connections did not save him from being driven out of York in the autumn of 1065 by an alliance of Northumbrian nobles, furious that he had assassinated several of their peers and oppressed the earldom with heavy taxes. Harold Godwinson attempted to mediate between his brother and the Northumbrian leaders, but it was hopeless; they would not have him back, and issued a sentence of outlawry upon him for his crimes. Harold had no choice but to concede. Tostig and his wife fled to the Continent, where he ultimately allied himself to King Harald Hardrada of Norway. He accompanied Harald across the sea to Northumbria in 1066, faced his brother's army at Stamford Bridge, and died with the Norwegian king.

From this tangle of international alliances and family feuds emerges an important point: 1066 was never as simple as

Anglo-Saxons versus Normans versus Vikings. For one thing, the mother of Harold, Edith and Tostig was Danish, which made them all half-Danish. In fact, one of their uncles on the Danish side had been married to a sister of King Cnut. Small surprise, then, that Tostig, faced with rising hostility within Northumbria, had hired himself a bodyguard of Danish mercenaries. The names of the parties themselves illustrate the cultural fusion that had taken place in Northumbria especially: just like Orm and Gamal, Tostig himself bore a Norse name. If we bring in the Normans – or, more properly, 'Northmen' – we find a similar story. They may have taken on the language, religion and naming customs of the Franks, but they were aware of their own Nordic origins. Duke William was the direct descendant of Rollo, the Norse-raider-cum-royal-vassal who had been granted the region of Normandy by the Frankish king back in 911. No matter who had won in 1066, then, someone of Norse descent would have sat on the throne.

There is nothing special about the British Isles in this regard. We find the same sort of shifts and fusions at the other end of the Norse-settled world, among the Rus in what is now Ukraine and Russia. In 'Bodies' we came across Norse names in the Rus–Byzantine peace treaty – which, coincidentally, was made in 911, precisely when Rollo was striking a similar deal with the Franks. Like the Normans, the Kyivan Rus quickly acculturated and adopted the customs of their new environment. By 943 they were ruled by a prince with a Slavic name, Sviatoslav, whose parents had borne the unambiguously Old Norse names Yngvar and Helga (which were themselves transmitted into Slavic tongues as Igor and Olga). We are told that Sviatoslav eventually went as far as adopting the Slavic gods Perun and Volos.

So whether we look to Northumbria, Normandy or the vast steppes and rivers of the east, and whether we look at the mundane rebuilding of a local church or at the great movers and shakers of the eleventh century, we find a common tale: peoples merging, cultures evolving, and languages and names mixing until no clear boundaries – or endings – remain.

Ending 2 : Checkmate

Not all endings are really endings. Some are transformations. And sometimes, the objects that survive from such periods face forwards and backwards in time, Janus-like, the cultural hinges between one era and another. To usher us in, a glum little figure, staring anxiously into the distance, apparently in the throes of existential angst. She is a queen, resting her weary cheek in her weary hand: heavy indeed is the head that wears the crown. And she is not alone in her apparent disquiet. Several of her fellow monarchs look equally glum. A short, portly bishop grips his staff tightly, perhaps preoccupied with spiritual matters, perhaps preoccupied with tummy gas. Warriors bite the rims of their shields, but could just as easily be biting their fingernails. A solemn, anxious ivory army of seventy-nine chess pieces, most carved from walrus tusks, some carved from whale teeth. Discovered on the Isle of Lewis in the Outer Hebrides, they are, in many ways, a Viking Age icon. But they date from the decades around 1200, a century and a half after Harald Hardrada met his end at Stamford Bridge.

Much is mysterious about these chess pieces. One way or another – and this seems to be a case where recollections may vary – they were discovered in 1831, in a sandbank on the west coast of Lewis, in a hoard that also included fourteen other gaming pieces and a belt buckle. The chess pieces that are known about – eight queens, eight kings, fifteen knights, sixteen bishops, thirteen rooks – suggest that originally there might have been at least four complete chess sets. But if this is the case then not all the pieces survive or are yet accounted for, a state of affairs underlined by the fact that a new, rather gnarled chess piece surfaced in 2019, having apparently been tucked away in an antique dealer's desk drawer for decades.

How did they end up hidden in the sand? No one needs that many chess pieces for their own use, and in any case they don't show signs of the sort of wear and tear that might come from being played with regularly. More likely, they were brought here by a merchant who planned to sell them on to high-status individuals for a hefty profit. Perhaps they were hidden by the merchant themselves, to avoid paying tax while the pieces were moved to their next location. Perhaps they had been stolen. Perhaps they were stashed in the sand for safety, at a time of social unrest or political uncertainty. Whatever the reason, no one ever came back to claim them.

Where did the raw materials come from? Greenland was the source of most walrus ivory at this time, and this is the most likely origin. But if most of the pieces did indeed begin life in the icy Northern Hunting Grounds far to the north of Greenland's Western Settlement, then they had a long journey ahead of them. A clue to where they might have been carved lies round the back of the royal pieces, in the exquisite detailing on their thrones, where animals with gaping jaws and wings gnaw on intertwining loops and tendrils. Similarities have been noted between this artistic style and the Romanesque stone carvings from the medieval city of Trondheim in Norway, which was also an important centre for ivory carving. Another theory is that the chess pieces were made in Iceland; those who support this theory point to the existence of Margret the Skillful, a thirteenth-century figure featured in *Páls saga biskups* ('The Saga of Bishop Pal') who was said to be the most accomplished ivory carver in the country.[8] Either way, the important point is that their journey took them from their point of origin as raw materials to a Nordic centre of carving excellence, and from there to their final resting place in the Hebrides.

Despite the uncertainties that surround their origins and

journey through the centuries, what is certain is that these magnificent little figures bear witness to the international links that stretched all the way across the North Atlantic and beyond, links that developed during the Viking Age and were still active by the time the chess pieces set out on their travels.

At the time the Lewis chess pieces were hidden in the sand, the Scottish islands to the north and west of the mainland were still part of the Norse political and cultural sphere. Lewis was part of the chain of islands known to the Norse as the *Suðreyjar* or 'Southern Isles'. This encompassed the Hebrides (including Lewis itself), the Clyde islands (including tiny Inchmarnock where the Hostage Stone was discovered) and the Isle of Man. Their name contrasted with the *Norðreyjar* or 'Northern Isles', which was the Norse name for Orkney and Shetland.

A glum queen from the large collection of Norse chess pieces found on the Isle of Lewis, Scotland, *c*.1200.

Norse influence and settlement in these islands began in the late eighth century, as part of their westward expansion from Scandinavia. Sitting at the intersection between the North Sea, the Irish Sea and the Atlantic Ocean, they were crucial stopping-off points for travellers moving between major trading centres such as Bergen and Dublin, or striking out further west for the Faroes, Iceland or Greenland. The chess pieces fit neatly within these lines of contact: made of (probably) Greenlandic raw materials, carved in (possibly) Norway, and transported to Lewis on their way to a final destination they never reached.

Yet the chess pieces in themselves represent a cultural shift, the result of new influences that had spread from southern and eastern lands and made their way through Europe. As we saw in 'Play', the Viking Age board game of choice was *hnefatafl*, although other brands of board games were certainly available. The hoard from Lewis does indeed include fourteen gaming pieces that could be used for such purposes, but they are greatly outnumbered (and, let's be honest, outclassed) by their far more famous chess piece companions. Still, the pensive little faces of the chess pieces look both forwards and backwards in time. Bishops dressed in liturgical vestments clutch their croziers and bestow blessings: these holy men embody the contemporary Christian establishment. But on the chess board they stand next to berserkers, those fearsome, semi-legendary warriors of the Viking Age past who were said to work themselves up into a battle fury by biting on the rims of their shields, and fought either naked or wearing animal skins. By the time the chess pieces were carved, berserkers had been long-since consigned to outlawry in Nordic law codes, and their main role was as colourful characters in saga stories. In 'Beginnings', we came across Snorri Sturluson's *Ynglinga saga* in the context of the Salme ship burials in Estonia. We return to it now, because several berserkers also feature in this legendary account of the earliest Scandinavian rulers, and they are linked to the god Odin:

Odin could bring it about that in battle his opponents were struck with blindness or deafness or panic, and their weapons would cut no better than sticks, while his men went without mail and were as wild as dogs or wolves, biting their shields, being as strong as bears or bulls. They killed the people, but neither fire nor iron took effect on them. That is called berserk fury.[9]

Odin's chosen warriors and Christ's bishops, the Viking Age and the High Middle Ages lining up together to do battle. Endings, like beginnings, are rarely straightforward.

Tick forward a few decades, to the year 1263, and more changes were afoot in and around Scotland's western seaboard. The Battle of Largs was a series of skirmishes fought on 2 October on the Scottish mainland. Largs is less than 20 kilometres – as the crow flies – across the water from Inchmarnock, although to sail from Inchmarnock to Largs one would have to take a detour south around the Isle of Bute, which sits in the middle. The battle was fought between the armies of King Alexander III of Scotland and King Hakon IV of Norway, both of whom wanted control of the Scottish islands. Much of our information from the Norwegian perspective comes from *Hákonar saga Hákonarsonar* ('The Saga of Hakon Hakonsson'). The saga seems to have been written very soon after Hakon's death, on the orders of his son Magnus, who commissioned the Icelandic historian Sturla Thordarson – nephew of Snorri Sturluson – to write it. Sturla tells us that the autumnal weather leading up to the Battle of Largs was especially stormy: ten Norwegian ships were wrecked during a gale, and many more were driven onto the shore during violent hailstorms. In fact, the weather was so bad that they thought it had been raised by witchcraft, illustrated by this verse included in the saga: 'The sorcery-strengthened hailstorm blew around the battle-eager men on the ships.* The twisted storm** drove the very vigorous crew with war-shields towards [the shores of] Scotland.'[10]

Writing around a century later, the Scottish chronicler John of Fordun provides a brief account of the battle from the other side. Hakon is described as arriving at Ayr Castle, a little down the coast from Largs, with 160 ships and 20,000 fighting men, 'for he said that all the Scottish islands lying between Ireland and Scotland were his by right of inheritance'.[11] Having taken the castles of Bute and Man, he sacks the churches along the seaboard. And at this point, divine intervention bites him on the behind, for, 'at God's command, on the very day that both the kings had appointed for battle, there arose at sea a very violent storm, which dashed the ships together'.[12] Despite the fierce fighting that followed, the result of the Battle of Largs was inconclusive. Hakon withdrew to Orkney, where he planned to wait out the winter weather. But the year ended badly for him and he died there, his army scattered throughout the islands he had hoped to reclaim. The campaign died with him, and within three years the Southern Isles had been signed over to Scotland and become the Western Isles.

If Harald Hardrada's attempt to take England in 1066 is seen as a watershed moment for the Viking Age, then there are certainly parallels to be drawn with Hakon's attempt to cement Norway's power in the Scottish Isles, only three years short of the 200th anniversary of the Battle of Stamford Bridge. In both Norse and Scottish accounts of the events leading up to the battle, there are also parallels to the early Viking raids on the coastal communities around the British Isles. John of Fordun

---

* Except, because it's a skaldic verse and therefore never makes things easy, it doesn't actually say 'the ships'. It says 'the troop-inhabited surf-skis of the sea', which is a kenning for 'ships'.
** Although 'storm' would be far too straightforward for a skaldic verse. What it actually says is 'the harm of the land of the surge', which is a kenning for 'storm'.

Lewis chess pieces, shield-biting berserkers lined up alongside
Christian bishops. Isle of Lewis, Scotland, c.1200.

describes the Norwegian fleet sacking the churches along the
Scottish coastline. Even Sturla Thordarson has them attacking
the islands around Loch Lomond, and slaughtering people and
cattle on the Isle of Mull ('the dwellings of faithless farmers
burned', as one of his verses begins).[13] If we are going to char-
acterise the Viking Age with the sort of seaborne Scandinavian
raiding activities that define the start of this period, then here we
have them, almost 500 years after the islands around the British
Isles were first attacked.

With this landmark battle between the kings of Scotland and
Norway, we have jumped back into a larger historical narrative
of big endings featuring big players on the big stage. But how
would the events of October 1263 have affected most ordinary
people on the ground? Again, for the most part, the answer is
– probably not much, unless they were part of the communities that were sacked. When the kings of Scotland and Norway
clashed with their armies on the beach at Largs in 1263, most
people were probably more concerned with what the recent
stormy weather meant for the fishing vessels out at sea, the
livestock in the fields, and the ground that had to be ploughed
and sowed before winter. For those further up the chain of
command, the repercussions were greater. John of Fordun notes
that, after news of King Hakon's death started to spread, King

Alexander sent troops into the islands to kill those who had supported King Hakon's campaign. The Scottish king himself set out for the Isle of Man to secure homage and military support from Magnus Olafsson, ruler of the island. His submission to the Scottish king marks a turning point: Norwegian political influence in the islands west of Scotland was now a thing of the past.

Just as the islands provided connections and stopping-off points on the way to different parts of the world, so those who lived there continued to face in many different directions, in terms of their loyalties, their identities and their cultural backgrounds. This was true of many prominent leaders, which is why King Alexander quickly dealt with the island chieftains who had supported the Norwegian cause, and travelled to the Isle of Man to demand the loyalty of Magnus Olafsson. Magnus himself was a member of the Crovan dynasty, a Norse-Gaelic family who ruled the Isle of Man and the Hebrides (at least some bits of them) between the eleventh and thirteenth centuries (at least some of the time). The same mix of Gaelic and Norse heritage also existed among ordinary people, no more so than on the Isle of Man, an extraordinarily multifaceted, mixed society that brought together elements of both cultural traditions. This can be illustrated by around thirty-five runestones that survive from the Isle of Man, dated from between the tenth and the twelfth centuries. Many of them are stone crosses, and so clearly rooted in a Christian tradition. But several contain pagan imagery that might ring bells for those versed in Old Norse myth. Back in 'Belief', we already encountered the fragments of one stone cross from the tenth or eleventh century, including runes that read 'Thorvald raised this cross.'[14] Yet at the bottom right corner, a human figure stands with a bird perched on one shoulder and a wolflike creature swallowing their right leg. A likely suspect is the god Odin with one of his ravens, being devoured by the wolf Fenrir at Ragnarok.

The same collection of runestones also includes different alphabets from different cultural traditions: not only Norse runes but also ogam, a series of short horizontal or angled lines carved either side of a longer vertical stem for the consonants, and notches carved on the stem for the vowels. Ogam was used to record early forms of the Irish language that was spoken in Ireland and parts of western Britain and Scotland, including the Isle of Man, between around the fourth and sixth centuries. Ogam inscriptions after this date were based on information about the alphabet that had been transmitted through manuscripts, and so were deliberately archaic. This might tell us something about how those who commissioned and carved the stones wanted to be perceived, as having a foot in both cultural camps.[15] For instance, a stone from the churchyard of Kirk Maughold, on the north-east tip of the island, features two lines of runes followed by a line of ogam. The first line of runes can be translated as 'John the priest carved these runes' and the second is a series of runic letters arranged alphabetically. The third line is the first two groups of ogam signs, again in alphabetical order.[16] This is a conscious representation of two alphabets from two different cultural traditions, coming together in one carving.

Other mixed inscriptions from the Isle of Man tell us more about the individuals who inhabited this culturally mixed community. Directly across from Maughold, on the western side of the island, is the churchyard at Kirk Michael, another resting place for several of these inscriptions. On a stone known as MM 130, lines of ogam and lines of runes coexist on the grey surface, just as, or so it seems, the mixed communities of the island did. The runic inscription might be translated as: 'Mael-Lomchon put up this cross in memory of his foster-mother Mael-Muire, Dubgall's daughter, the woman whom Adisl was married to. It is better to leave a good foster-son than a bad son.'[17]

As well as the coming together of Norse and Gaelic alphabets, this particular stone reveals a coming together of Norse and Gaelic personal names, all within one family group. It seems likely that the foster mother (Mael-Muire), her foster child (Mael-Lomchon) and her father (Dubgall) all have Gaelic names, while the husband (Adisl) has a Norse name. From this, we can't tell whether this was a mixed-heritage family or whether Gaelic and Norse names had both become part of the same naming stock on the Isle of Man. But other inscribed stones testify to other family groups with similarly mixed names, such as Thorleif (a Norse male name) who raises a runestone to his son Fiacc (a male Gaelic name).[18] Other runic inscriptions have only Gaelic names, and yet they too were written in runes.

This suggests that these different naming and alphabet traditions were active within at least some parts of the Manx community between the tenth and twelfth centuries when these stones were carved, a cultural mix that produced stones with Christian and pagan iconography, Gaelic and Norse alphabets, and Gaelic and Norse names within family groups. And so the cultural and ethnic diversity of the Isle of Man, which was a product of the Viking Age, did not end with the death of a particular ruler or a change of regime. For these communities, there was no clear ending, not even necessarily a transformation, more of a continuation as the present ticked into the future and gathered the past into itself.

Other possible endings wait on other islands. The same King Hakon who died in Orkney after the Battle of Largs had also been casting his eyes further west, beyond the *Suðreyjar*, across the Atlantic Ocean to Iceland. And here, his political campaigning was rather more successful. Throughout much of the thirteenth century, Iceland had been embroiled in a bloody civil war, where the country's most influential families tussled for power. The tight and fractious connections between Norway and Iceland were stretched to breaking point, with some prominent Icelanders looking to the Norwegian king to support their cause. King Hakon died before he was able to seal the deal, but

by the end of 1264 all Icelandic chieftains had sworn their alle-
giance to Hakon's son, King Magnus. Iceland had been brought
into a union with Norway, but the country's role was decidedly
that of the smaller sibling. And with that, the Icelandic Free State
– which had existed since the island was first permanently settled
back in the 870s at the dizzy heights of Viking Age expansion –
ceased to be.

Was this an ending that most Icelanders would have recognised? Perhaps it is significant that these were the decades when
Icelanders began to write down their sagas in earnest, after
centuries of oral storytelling that passed these tales down the
generations. Sagas were written about many subjects, settings
and times, but the most popular, numerous, and frequently
re-copied were those that we know today as the *Íslendingasögur*
('Sagas of Icelanders'). And those are the sagas that are firmly
set in the first centuries of the settlement, when Iceland was a
fiercely independent country. It is probably no coincidence that
these sagas have so much to say about how the first Icelandic
settlers left Norway to escape the tyranny of King Harald Fairhair, who wanted to take their lands and become ruler of the
whole country. It is probably no coincidence that the sagas have
so many plucky young heroes who travel abroad to royal courts
and prove themselves the equal of any monarch. So perhaps this
was when the Viking Age was well and truly over for the Icelanders, when they lost their political independence and started
writing down the stories of their ancestors in manuscripts rather
than telling them to each other around the winter fires. Perhaps
this is the point when the present becomes the past, when it is
solidified in the written historical record.

More islands, more possible endings. This next one brings us
back towards the British Isles but takes us forward another 200
years. The Northern Isles of Orkney and Shetland were always
an important Norse cultural base. They too had been settled
by Scandinavians in the ninth century (and possibly earlier than

that) when the Viking Age was in full swing. In both the endings represented by Harald Hardrada in 1066 and Hakon Hakonarson in 1263, Orkney played a key role. Hakon, of course, died there, and upon leaving Norway, Harald had made a beeline for Orkney, where he gathered extra troops before pushing south to fight for the English crown. The Northern Isles remained in Scandinavian hands until 1468, when Christian I, the impoverished king of Norway and Denmark, signed a marriage alliance between his daughter Margaret and the Scottish king, James III. Not having enough cash for her dowry, Christian pledged the islands of Orkney and Shetland. For James, this was a case of no take-backsies: in 1472 the Northern Isles officially passed to Scotland.

Yet Norn, the form of the Old Norse language that was spoken in the Northern Isles, survived for centuries after the islands passed to the Scottish crown, perhaps dying out by around 1800. This linguistic heritage had its roots firmly in the Viking Age settlement. As the Norn-speaking inhabitants of the Northern Isles gradually faded away, collectors came to record their vocabulary, poems, riddles and prayers, like butterflies pinned in the display cases of museums. One of the riddles comes from Unst, the northernmost island in Shetland (and it is no coincidence that the same island was also home to around sixty Viking Age longhouses). It translates as:

Four hang, four walk,
Four point up to the sky,
Two point the way into the farm,
And one hangs down behind.[19]

If this riddle seems strangely familiar, and a cow instantly springs to mind as the solution, this is because the riddle is almost identical to the one from the riddle competition between Odin and Gestumblindi. And the Northern Isles still bear strong marks of their Viking past. The motto on Shetland Council's coat of arms reads 'með lögum skal land byggja', a version of that 'the land shall be built with law' saying that also appears in *Njáls saga* from medieval Iceland and the Frostathing Law from medieval Norway. This isn't a continuous legacy from the Viking Age: the council voted to adopt the motto when it was formed in 1890.[20] Like Shetland's famous winter fire festival, Up Helly Aa, this is a harking back to a Nordic history and heritage that began to gather steam in the Victorian era.

But at least there were descendants of the Viking Age settlers still left to hark back to the past. Not all Viking Age settlements made it down to the present day. Some were snuffed out. And this brings us to our third and final ending.

Ending 3 : The world will end in ice

For centuries the frigid sea had been eating away at the shoreline, gnawing inch by inch into the sandy earth as the seasons froze and thawed the soil. It did not stop when it came to the grave-yard, but continued, relentless, as first the boundary wall tumbled into the foam, and then the first of the burials. For a long time nobody was there to see. Later, people came, and from the muddy bank they pulled such scraps of the dead as had not yet been claimed by the ocean: bones, planks of wood, mud-bound lengths of cloth. From the grassy earth above the shoreline they took fallen building stones and grave markers. Later still, others were drawn by the curiosities said to be buried in the soil, and found a skull bearing strands of fair hair. Another hacked at the bank with a boat hook until he came across more grisly treasures: a coffin, most of a decayed body, and clothing that his helpers tore as they dragged it free from the clinging earth.

More years passed. The sea gnawed away until it took a corner of what was left of the church. There it stopped, its appetite sated for now. Then to the half-eaten graveyard came new visitors, strangers to this little spit of land that lies between surging ocean and cloud-high granite peaks. They dug with purpose, enduring the cold, the wet, the wind, the monstrous crashing of the waves. They pulled more bones from the earth, more crosses and coffins. But more precious by far were the clothes: weirdly preserved by the drift ice that cradled the coastline, bound to the earth itself by the delicate roots of crowberry and dwarf willow. They teased the cloth from the ground, peeled it from the bones, laid each piece on sackcloth, wrapped it and packed it in crates with moss from nearby streams. They loaded it onto a ship and took it three thousand kilometres across the sea.[21]

Some of what was excavated at Herjolfsnes can now be seen on the first floor of the National Museum of Denmark in Copenhagen and in the Greenland National Museum and Archives in Nuuk. Gowns, stockings, hoods and caps, painstakingly conserved and restored, are displayed in brightly lit cases. No other archaeological site has revealed such a treasure trove of medieval European clothing, and this collection is all the more haunting because it is so mundane. These are not the clothes of the rich and powerful, but of ordinary people who lived, worked and died on the tough southern tip of Norse Greenland. One of the best-preserved garments belonged to a woman who found her final resting place in the shadowy north-east corner of the graveyard. She was buried not in a coffin – wood was a precious commodity in that windswept, rocky place – but with a sealskin laid over her. She was clad in a short-sleeved gown that is known by the prosaic catalogue number of D10581. The waist had ripped when they pulled it over her body. Radiocarbon dating suggests this happened sometime between 1380 and 1530, in the very last decades of the Norse settlement in Greenland.[22]

We can learn much from something that is at once so ordinary and so extraordinary. The gown was woven from Greenlandic *vaðmál* ('wadmal'), that coarse, thick wool fabric

made from the coats of the hardy sheep and goats that the original settlers would have brought from Iceland. Now the colour is
a dull reddish brown, but when new it would have been a lighter
brown, with tannin-dyed warp and undyed weft. Its constituent
parts were carefully cut and stitched together, with panels added
to ensure a good fit and an originally white patch sewn on the
front, probably a quick repair job. In the rugged climes of Greenland, where resources were limited, a decent piece of clothing
could not be wasted. We sense this, too, from the lack of decoration and the slightly asymmetrical measurements. It was a
working garment: tough, dependable, well worn and appreciated before it was deposited in a grave. And there it wrapped
itself around the last person to wear it, cradling her as she was
taken back into the earth.

For other endings, the winds that fanned the flames of the
Viking Age may have long since calmed, but the final embers
were not so easily extinguished. Out in the North Atlantic, in
Norse Greenland, they continued to glow. We have already seen
that there are many lenses through which to view the Viking
Age. If we think of it as a time of expansion and settlement,
political and social influence, linguistic and cultural connected-
ness, then we have already seen from the case of the Northern
Isles that we need to look to the fifteenth century.

Herjolfsnes, where the preserved clothes were discovered,
lies very close to the southernmost tip of Greenland. From the
very start of the Norse presence in the country, it was there.
In fact, its settlement appears in the opening paragraph of
Grœnlendinga saga:

> Herjolf decided to accompany Erik the Red to Greenland and
> left his farm. One of the men on Herjolf's ship was from the
> Hebrides, a Christian, who composed the verse of the Sea
> Fences. It has this refrain:

I ask you, unblemished monks' tester,*
to be the ward of my travels;
may the lord of the peaks' pane**
shade my path with his hawk's perch.***

Herjolf farmed at Herjolfsnes. He was the most respected of men.[23]

Later in the saga, Herjolf's son, Bjarni, commands the first ship to sight Vinland when they are blown off course on the voyage from Iceland to Greenland. They sail up close and see small hills and forests, then continue further and see flat, wooded land. Bjarni's crew says that they should land to pick up timber and water, but Bjarni decides that they shouldn't go ashore, a decision for which he is later criticised. Later on, Erik's son Leif (the Lucky) buys Bjarni's ship from him, and uses it to mount an expedition to Vinland. But back to the founding of Herjolfsnes, of which the saga states: 'There on this point Herjolf, Bjarni's father, lived and it was named for him and has since been called Herjolfsnes (Herjolf's Point). Bjarni now joined his father and ceased his merchant voyages. He remained on his father's farm as long as Herjolf lived and took over the farm after his death.'[24]

After Bjarni, the farm was taken over by another generation then another, and the world expanded, and so did Herjolfsnes. This was the first important landing site that the storm-tossed merchants could reach once they had crossed the ocean from Norway and Iceland, and the settlement did very well out of its geographical position. The years rolled on. After around 1200, the ships kept coming from the east, but gradually their numbers dwindled as the sea storms worsened and ice started to block the shipping routes into the settlements. By the middle

---

* More kennings. The 'unblemished monks' tester' is Christ.
** The 'peaks' pane' are the heavens.
*** His 'hawk's perch' is his hand.

of the 1300s, there was trouble brewing further north in the Western Settlement – the location of the Farm under the Sand – where farmsteads were being abandoned. Around the same time, ships carrying plague had arrived in Norwegian ports over the summer of 1349, eventually wiping out around a third of the country's population and severely disrupting the supply lines that the Norse settlers in Greenland relied on. Slowly, the thread that connected them to the rest of the Norse world was starting to fray. But it did not break. And part of the reason we know just how long these connections continued is precisely because of the clothes that were found in the graveyard at Herjolfsnes.

Clothes are often obvious visual markers of a historical age, sometimes down to a precise decade or less. From neck ruffs and codpieces to corsets and stovepipe hats, clothes are shorthand for a range of cultural and chronological associations. More often than not, the further back in time we go, the more reliant we are on textual descriptions and artistic images to know what sorts of clothes people wore, because such organic materials rarely survive. Remarkably, it seems that we also have visual clues to what the Norse Greenlanders were wearing during the later centuries of the settlement, through wooden carvings made by the ancestors of today's indigenous Inuit Greenlanders. One was found in an early Inuit house at the archaeological site of Okivilialuk, close to the southern tip of Baffin Island. Perhaps dating to the thirteenth or fourteenth century, the little wooden figure is about 5.5 centimetres high.[25] Its dress echoes several of the garments found in the graves at Herjolfsnes, with its short sleeves, full skirt folds and possibly even a yoked hood covering the head and extending down over the shoulders. The borders of the dress are outlined, seeming to chime with the decorative edges of many of the Norse garments from the graveyard. Two other carved wooden figures were found – separately – at locations on Greenland's west coast, considerably further north than the Norse settlements but likely within the region that they knew as the Northern Hunting Grounds. The larger is 7.4 centimetres tall and shows a bulked-out figure in a yoked hood, a top and trousers. The smaller is a little shorter at 5.8 centimetres high, and seems to be wearing a long dress and a yoked hood. It has been suggested that they date from the very last decades of the Norse Greenlandic settlement, perhaps the 1400s.[26]

Herjolfsnes was not a complete backwater, even as the ships coming from the east became fewer and less frequent. Other clothes from the graveyard testify to professional textile working that was informed by the latest European fashions. When the last generations of Norse Greenlanders were buried in the graveyard at Herjolfsnes, it seems that they were still in contact with western Europe, and able to replicate at least some of the more recent trends. Hoods with liripipes – those long tails hanging down the back – were a particular feature of western European fashion in the fourteenth and fifteenth centuries, and there are several examples of such items among the burials, once

Two wooden figures, apparently carved by the Inuit inhabitants of Greenland and depicting the dress style of the Norse Greenlanders.

a light-grey colour, now stained brown like all the other clothes. But there was also continuity with past generations of Norse Greenlanders. These clothes were made from thick wadmal, the coarse woollen fabric most suited for working in inhospitable weather. And this was produced with the same textile techniques and farming practices that had been transmitted down the decades and centuries, as the settlement adapted to the conditions of their homeland out on the margins.

Eventually, this homeland faded away. At some point, the last person was laid to rest in the Herjolfsnes graveyard. As for the clothes they were buried in, there came a time when every tool that had been used to produce them was set down and never picked up again. The last person stepped away from the weaving loom and never returned. The knives, shears and needles used to cut and sew the wadmal were left to go blunt. The last generation of sheep and goats were left to wander the lonely hillsides over the short summer months, then face the bitter Greenlandic winter alone.

A wadmal hood with liripipe hanging down behind, which were fashionable in Europe in the fourteenth and fifteenth centuries. Herjolfsnes, Norse Greenland.

We don't know what the end of Norse Greenland looked like. But we know that it ended. The last surviving reports – via Iceland – are a witch burning that took place in 1407, and a wedding that took place in 1408.[27] The latest clothing from Herjolfsnes seems to be a few decades later than that. And then, a shrinking back. Silence. Forgetting. Is this when an age truly can be said to be over, when there is no one left alive to remember it?

Yet we remember. Sometimes we don't remember everything accurately and sometimes the remembering changes in the telling. And over the years, the past has a tendency to get boiled down to important dates when important things happened to important people. But the personal, intimate parts of people's lives matter every bit as much as the famous, dramatic, narrative-defining ones. It's through these little fragments of lives lived, the bits and pieces that fell between the cracks in the floorboards, that we are able to reach out through space and time, to the humans of the past. We listen to the brief flashes of their stories like blurred radio signals that cut out and pick up interference from other stations. Among the white noise, the vanished moments sucked into time, are lives lived, events experienced, emotions felt. And so we bear witness to those who came before us, gather them into our own stories, give them new meanings and new voices.

Author's note

For each chapter I have included Endnotes and Further Reading. Endnotes are for direct quotations (of textual sources, statistics and so on), whereas Further Reading lists the other works I have used for the chapters. Full references are listed in the Bibliography.

In the case of primary sources, rather than using my own translations, I have provided published translations where possible, so it's possible to follow them up in case readers want to explore more of a particular source.

Icelandic authors are listed according to their given names, since rather than surnames they tend to have patronyms or matronyms.

Throughout the book, I have given Old Norse personal and place names in their anglicised form (for instance, 'Gyda' instead of 'Gyða' and 'Erik' instead of 'Eiríkr').

Endnotes

Prologue

1 Personal communication with Michael Lerche Nielsen, Department of Nordic Studies and Linguistics, University of Copenhagen.
2 Inscription recorded as Fyn 19 in the RuneS database.
3 Cole, 'Runes and Rye', p. 7.
4 Schulte, 'Runology', p. 89, Looijenga, *Texts and Contexts*, pp. 84, 160–61.

Chapter 1: Introduction

1 Adapted from Larrington, *Poetic Edda*, p. 22.
2 As Judith Jesch argues in *The Viking Diaspora*, 'In this book, the Viking Age is a little arbitrarily defined as the period from 750 to 1100. At the same time, it is recognised that many aspects of the Viking Age can only be understood through a consideration of evidence emanating from the following centuries' (p. 10).
3 See Jesch, 'What does the word "Viking" really mean?', https://theconversation.com/what-does-the-word-viking-really-mean-75647.
4 I cut my academic teeth in the Department of Anglo-Saxon, Norse and Celtic at Cambridge University, where the 'Norse' of that title does exactly that.
5 Helle, 'Introduction', p. 1.
6 See Jesch, *The Viking Diaspora*, pp. 75–7.
7 Whitelock, *English Historical Documents*, p. 185.
8 Whitelock, *English Historical Documents*, p. 186.
9 Whitelock, *English Historical Documents*, p. 199.
10 For more on the Scandinavian influence on English vocabulary, see the Gersum Project: www.gersum.org.
11 See Jarman, 'The Viking Great Army in England'.
12 For recent developments in radiocarbon dating see Van der Plicht, 'Recent Developments in Calibration for Archaeological and Environmental Samples'.
13 See Kuitems, 'Evidence for European Presence in the Americas'.
14 See Margaryan, 'Population Genomics of the Viking World' and

Rodríguez-Varela, 'The Genetic History of Scandinavia from the Roman Iron Age to the Present'.

15   See Grönvold, 'Ash Layers from Iceland in the Greenland GRIP Ice Core Correlated with Oceanic and Land Sediments' and Magnús Á. Sigurgeirsson, 'Dating of the Viking Age Landnám Tephra Sequence in Lake Mývatn Sediment, North Iceland'.

Chapter 2: Beginnings

1   See Nordström, 'Dvärgen på Ribekraniet'. Inscription recorded as Sjy 39 in the RuneS database.
2   Larsen, 'The Ribe Skull Fragment', p. 45.
3   Whitelock, *English Historical Documents*, p. 899.
4   See Sindbæk, 'Glass Beads and Beadmaking' and Barfod, 'Splinters to Splendours'.
5   Skre, 'Development of Urbanisation', p. 83.
6   Margaryan, 'Population Genomics', p. 939.
7   Finlay, *Snorri Sturluson. Heimskringla. Volume 1*, p. 34.
8   Translation adapted from Finlay, *Snorri Sturluson. Heimskringla. Volume 1*, p. 34.
9   Forsyth, 'Text-inscribed Slates', pp. 130, 138–9.
10   Translations adapted from Downham, 'Vikings in Irish Chronicles, 794–902', currently available at https://www.celt.dias.ie/publications/online/vikings-temporarily-removed/.
11   See Lowe, 'Non-text-inscribed Slates', p. 156.
12   Raffield, 'Male-biased Operational Sex Ratios'.
13   Heen-Pettersen, 'An Insular Reliquary', p. 72.
14   All entries taken from the Irish Annals database: 'CELT. Corpus of Electronic Texts', https://celt.ucc.ie/.

Chapter 3: Love

1   Inscription recorded as N B149 in the RuneS database.
2   Inscription recorded as N B308 in the RuneS database.
3   Barnes, *Runes*, p. 114.
4   Inscription recorded as N B584 in the RuneS database.
5   Inscription recorded as N B11 in the RuneS database.
6   Inscription recorded as N B368 in the RuneS database. For more, see Liestøl, 'Correspondence in Runes', pp. 21–2.
7   Inscription recorded as N A74 in the RuneS database.
8   Inscription recorded as N A104 in the RuneS database.
9   Inscription recorded as N 337 in the RuneS database.
10   Inscription recorded as N A199 in the RuneS database.

11 Meulengracht Sørensen, *The Unmanly Man*, p. 18.
12 Finlay, 'Monstrous Allegations', pp. 23, 26; Meulengracht Sørensen, *The Unmanly Man*, pp. 17–18, 80.
13 Jochens, *Women in Old Norse Society*, p. 65.
14 Meulengracht Sørensen, *The Unmanly Man*, p. 26.
15 Inscription recorded as N A322 in the RuneS database.
16 Inscription recorded as N B111 in the RuneS database.
17 Inscription recorded as N B390 in the RuneS database.
18 Inscription recorded as N A39 in the RuneS database. These runes come from a rune stick where four different people have written inscriptions on four different sides. This section takes the form of an alliterative verse: 'They are both / in a booth together, / Clumsy Kári / and the wife (*kona*) of Vilhjálmr'. See Knirk, 'Love and Eroticism', p. 218.
19 Inscription recorded as N B644 in the RuneS database.
20 Inscription recorded as N B465 in the RuneS database.
21 Simek, *Runes, Magic and Religion*, p. 144.
22 Simek, *Runes, Magic and Religion*, p. 144.
23 Tschan, *History of the Archbishops*, p. 208.
24 Tschan, *History of the Archbishops*, p. 207.
25 Jacobsen, 'Pregnancy and Childbirth', pp. 96–7.
26 Larrington, *Poetic Edda*, p. 164.
27 Larrington, *Poetic Edda*, pp. 199–200.
28 Recorded as Bh 58 in the RuneS database.
29 Imer, 'Lumps of Lead', pp. 31–2.
30 Inscription recorded as N 631 in the RuneS database. The word 'incalue' doesn't appear anywhere other than this inscription. While RuneS and other runic databases translate it as 'hairless one', it could potentially mean 'not bald'. See Simek et al., *Runes, Magic and Religion*, p. 180.
31 Jón Steffensen, '*Margrétar saga*', pp. 277–8; Jochens, *Women in Old Norse Society*, p. 81.
32 Fiddyment, 'Girding the Loins?'
33 See Graham-Campbell, 'The Vikings in Orkney', pp. 130–31. See also the National Museum of Scotland website, 'Westness Brooch-Pin', https://www.nms.ac.uk/explore-our-collections/stories/scottish-history-and-archaeology/westness-brooch-pin/.
34 Melnikova, 'The Cultural Assimilation of the Varangians into Eastern Europe from the Point of View of Language and Literacy'.
35 Recorded as N199 in the Gramoty birch bark database. See Schaeken, 'Learning to Read and Write', p. 111.

36 Recorded as N200 in the Gramoty birch bark database.
37 Recorded as N206 in the Gramoty birch bark database.
38 Onfim drew five birch bark illustrations where he didn't include any writing with them, and these aren't catalogued in the Gramoty database.
39 Recorded as N210 in the Gramoty birch bark database.

Chapter 4: Travel
1   Inscription recorded as N B55 in the RuneS database.
2   See Thomav, 'Four Scandinavian Ship Graffiti from Hagia Sophia'.
3   Christensen, 'Ship Graffiti', p. 20.
4   Jesch, *Ships and Men*, p. 168.
5   Jesch, *Ships and Men*, p. 172.
6   Scudder, *Egil's Saga*, pp. 77–8.
7   Hermann Pálsson, *Book of Settlements*, p. 49.
8   Imer, *Peasants and Prayers*, p. 234.
9   See Star, 'Ancient DNA Reveals the Chronology of Walrus Ivory Trade from Norse Greenland' and Barrett, 'Walruses on the Dnieper'.
10 Barrett, 'Ecological Globalisation'.
11 Imer, *Peasants and Prayers*, pp. 7, 242–3.
12 See Pilø, 'Crossing the Ice'.
13 See Secrets of the Ice: https://secretsoftheice.com.
14 'The Hunt for the Lost Mountain Pass' https://secretsoftheice.com/news/2020/04/16/mountain-pass/.
15 See Vedeler, 'Out of the Norwegian Glaciers'.
16 See Finstad, 'Prehistoric and Medieval Skis from Glaciers and Ice Patches in Norway'.
17 See 'The Best-Preserved Pair of Skis from Prehistory', https://secretsoftheice.com/news/2021/10/05/the-best-preserved-pair-of-skis-from-prehistory/.
18 Larson, *The King's Mirror*, pp. 103–4.
19 See Orange, 'Norwegian youths who "ruined" 5,000-year-old rock carving could face prosecution', https://www.telegraph.co.uk/news/2016/07/31/norwegian-youths-who-ruined-5000-year-old-carving-could-face-pro/.
20 Faulkes, *Snorri Sturluson: Edda*, p. 23.
21 Faulkes, *Snorri Sturluson: Edda*, p. 24.
22 Larrington, *Poetic Edda*, p. 30.
23 Larrington, *Poetic Edda*, p. 28.
24 Larrington, *Poetic Edda*, p. 18.
25 Slightly adapted from Larrington, *Poetic Edda*, p. 14.

26 Slightly adapted from Larrington, *Poetic Edda*, p. 13.
27 Rannveig Þórhallsdóttir, 'Fjallkonan'.
28 Larrington, *Poetic Edda*, p. 50.
29 Personal communication with Ellen Marie Næss, Museum of Cultural History, Oslo.
30 Price, *The Viking Way*, pp. 94–5.
31 Larrington, *Poetic Edda*, p. 187.
32 Regal, *Gisli Sursson's Saga*, p. 15.
33 Faulkes, *Snorri Sturluson: Edda*, p. 53.

Chapter 5: Belief

1 Hermann Pálsson, *Book of Settlements*, p. 21.
2 Wieners, 'Haze, Hunger, Hesitation', p. 2.
3 See Vafþrúðnismál ('Vafthrudnir's Sayings'), stanzas 51–2, in Larrington, *Poetic Edda*, p. 45.
4 Hermann Pálsson, *Book of Settlements*, p. 94.
5 Smith, 'All that Glitters'.
6 See Guðmundur Ólafsson, 'Surtshellir'; Smith, 'Ritual Responses'; Smith, 'All that Glitters'. Also personal communication with principal investigator Kevin Smith, Smithsonian Institution's Arctic Studies Center, National Museum of Natural History.
7 All verses from Taylor, *Tale of the Mountain Dweller*, with slight adaptations.
8 Ármann Jakobsson, 'Bergbúa þáttr', pp. 18–20.
9 Sayers, '"ok er hann einhendr"', p. 245.
10 See Brink, 'Mythologizing Landscape' and Brink, 'Myth and Ritual in Pre-Christian Landscape'.
11 Hultgård, *The End of the World*, pp. 150–52.
12 For more on these various representations see Lindow, 'Old Norse Mythology as Sacred Narrative'.
13 Translation slightly adapted from Faulkes, *Snorri Sturluson: Edda*, p. 47.
14 See Abram, *Myths of the Pagan North*, pp. 31–50, where the dating of these picture stones is discussed.
15 Heide, 'Loki', p. 75.
16 Heide, 'Loki', p. 66.
17 Heide, 'Loki', pp. 88–9.
18 Warner, *Ottonian Germany*, p. 80.
19 See Magnell and Iregren, 'Veitstu Hvé Blóta Skal?'
20 Lucas, 'Bloody Slaughter'.
21 Cole, 'When Gods Become Bureaucrats', p. 190.
22 Kunz, K., *Eirik the Red's Saga*, p. 6.

23 See Price, 'Seiðr', in his *The Viking Way*, pp. 55–190, and especially pp. 115–8 for the Oseberg burial.
24 See Fulk, 'Sigvatr Þórðarson, *Austfaravísur*'.
25 Fulk, 'Sigvatr Þórðarson, *Austfaravísur*'.
26 See Simek, *Runes, Magic and Religion*, pp. 65–6.
27 Larrington, *Prose Edda*, p. 32.
28 Staecker, *Rex regum*, pp. 237–9.
29 Staecker, *Rex regum*, pp. 410–12, 523, 524.
30 Hermann Pálsson, *Book of Settlements*, p. 97.
31 Finlay, *Snorri Sturluson. Heimskringla: Volume 1*, p. 199.
32 Grønlie, *Íslendingabók. Kristni Saga*, p. 48.
33 Grønlie, *Íslendingabók. Kristni Saga*, p. 4.
34 Grønlie, *Íslendingabók. Kristni Saga*, p. 9.
35 Simek, *Runes, Magic and Religion*, p. 128.
36 Inscription recorded as N B241 in the RuneS database. Translated in Macleod, *Runic Amulets*, p. 31. See also Mitchell, *Witchcraft and Magic*, p. 66.

Chapter 6: Bodies
1 Inscription recorded as E 4 in the RuneS database.
2 See Abels, 'Alfred the Great'.
3 Fulk, 'Anonymous Poems, *Eiríksmál*'.
4 Whitelock, *English Historical Documents*, p. 900.
5 Clayton, 'An Edition of Ælfric's Letter', pp. 281–3.
6 Clayton, 'An Edition of Ælfric's Letter', p. 283
7 Vaughan, *Chronicle Attributed to John of Wallingford*, p. 60.
8 Whitelock, *English Historical Documents*, pp. 239–40.
9 Whitelock, *English Historical Documents*, p. 641.
10 See Loe, *Given to the Ground*, chapter 3.
11 See Margaryan, 'Population Genomics'.
12 Vaughan, *Chronicle Attributed to John of Wallingford*, p. 60.
13 Hermann Pálsson, *Book of Settlements*, p. 72.
14 Cross, *Russian Primary Chronicle*, p. 65.
15 Lunde, *Ibn Fadlān*, pp. 46–7.
16 Lunde, *Ibn Fadlān*, p. 45.
17 Lunde, *Ibn Fadlān*, p. 45.
18 Mynors, *William of Malmesbury*, p. 459.
19 See Arcini, 'The Vikings Bare Their Filed Teeth' and Arcini, 'Markers of Identity', in her *The Viking Age*, at pp. 74–83.
20 Loe, *Given to the Ground*, p. 63.

21 McKenzie, 'Face of Orkney's St Magnus', https://www.bbc.co.uk/news/uk-scotland-north-east-orkney-shetland-38892669.
22 See Tuckley, C., 'The Vikings of JORVIK', pp. 90–92.
23 'The People of Jorvik', https://www.jorvikvikingcentre.co.uk/the-vikings/the-people-of-jorvik/.
24 Jeffery, 'Museum's broken treasure not just any old shit', https://www.theguardian.com/uk/2003/jun/06/artsandhumanities.arts1.
25 Soffía Guðný Guðmundsdóttir, 'Book Production', pp. 54–7.
26 Finlay, *Snorri Sturluson, Heimskringla. Volume 2*, p. 261–2 (with Thormod's name anglicised).
27 This is a slightly simplified version of the translation provided (with discussion) by Simek, *Runes, Magic and Religion*, p. 126–7.
28 Simek, *Runes, Magic and Religion*, p. 142.
29 Inscription recorded as N B257 in the RuneS database.
30 Larrington, *Poetic Edda*, p. 22.
31 Loe, *Given to the Ground*, p. 213.
32 See Arcini, 'Two Dwarves'; Arcini, *The Viking Age*, p. 67; Arcini, 'Reconnecting Relationships': https://the-past.com/feature/reconnecting-relationships-uncovering-genealogy-in-archaeology/.

Chapter 7: Home

1   See Griffiths, 'Living in Viking-Age Towns'.
2   Faulkes, *Hemings þáttr*, pp. 30–31.
3   See Grove, 'The Place of Greenland', p. 39.
4   Larson, *The King's Mirror*, p. 124.
5   Larson, *The King's Mirror*, p. 149.
6   Larson, *The King's Mirror*, p. 142.
7   McGovern, 'Arctic Frontier', p. 306.
8   Arneborg, 'Norse Greenland Dietary Economy', p. 2.
9   Barraclough, *Beyond the Northlands*, p. 130.
10 Berglund, 'Farm Beneath the Sand', pp. 297–98.
11 Arneborg, 'Norse Greenland Dietary Economy', p. 7.
12 Larson, *The King's Mirror*, p. 142.
13 On the pollen record see Henriksen, 'Norse Agriculture in Greenland'. For the fragment of barley (found in a midden at the site Ø35), personal communication with Georg Nyegaard, former deputy director at the Greenland National Museum and Archives, and excavator at the Farm Under the Sand.
14 Berglund, 'Farm Beneath the Sand'.
15 Østergård, *Woven into the Earth*, p. 108.
16 Imer, *Peasants and Prayers*, p. 340.

17   Imer, *Peasants and Prayers*, p. 186.
18   Imer, *Peasants and Prayers*, p. 74.
19   Imer, *Peasants and Prayers*, pp. 76–7.
20   Imer, *Peasants and Prayers*, p. 159.
21   Cartwright, 'Making the Cloth', p. 172.
22   Kunz, *The Saga of the People of Laxardal*, p. 79.
23   Cook, *Njal's Saga*, p. 215.
24   Townend, 'Óttarr svarti', p. 747. Quoted in Dommasnes, 'Spun on a Wheel', which is one example of a good analysis of the importance of women's textile production.
25   Jørgensen, 'The Introduction of Sails', p. 178.
26   Nyegaard, 'Dairy Farmers' p. 41.
27   Andersson, 'Tools, Textile Production and Society', p. 82.
28   Griffiths, 'Living in Viking Age Towns', p. 9.
29   Berglund, 'Farm Beneath the Sand', and personal communication with Georg Nyegaard, former deputy director at the Greenland National Museum and Archives, and excavator at the Farm Under the Sand.
30   Berglund, 'Farm Beneath the Sand', and personal communication with Georg Nyegaard, former deputy director at the Greenland National Museum and Archives, and excavator at the Farm Under the Sand.
31   Nyegaard, 'Dairy Farmers' pp. 33–4.
32   See Árni Einarsson, 'Viking Age Fences'.
33   See Toplak, 'The Warrior and the Cat'.
34   McGovern, 'Demise of Norse Greenland', p. 332.
35   Berglund, 'Farm Beneath the Sand', p. 303.
36   Madsen, 'Behind the Ice', p. 19.
37   Personal communication with Georg Nyegaard, former deputy director at the Greenland National Museum and Archives, and excavator at the Farm Under the Sand.
38   Arneborg, 'Greenland and Europe', p. 313; Arneborg, 'Norse Greenland Dietary Economy', p. 15.
39   Arneborg, 'Greenland and Europe', p. 313; Arneborg, 'Norse Greenland Dietary Economy', p. 14.
40   Nyegaard, 'Dairy Farmers', p. 42.
41   During Iceland's initial settlement period in the ninth century, up to a quarter of animal bones belonged to pigs. By the twelfth to the thirteenth centuries, that proportion was down to 3 per cent. See Arge, 'Pigs in the Faroe Islands', pp. 23–4.
42   Arge, 'Pigs in the Faroe Islands'.

43 See Arneborg, 'Norse Greenland Dietary Economy'.
44 Church, 'Puffins, Pigs, Cod and Barley'.
45 Arneborg, 'Norse Greenland Dietary Economy', p. 7.
46 See McGovern, 'Vertebrate Zooarchaeology of Sandnes V51'.
47 Smiarowski, 'Preliminary Report', p. 13.
48 Mathers, 'Fourteenth-Century Description of Greenland', p. 80.
49 Nyegaard, 'Dairy Farmers', pp. 36–7.
50 Nyegaard, 'Dairy Farmers', pp. 37–8.
51 Gulløv, 'Natives and Norse', p. 321.
52 Gulløv, Grønlands Forhistorie (2004).
53 Hayeur Smith, 'Dress, Cloth'.
54 Nyegaard, 'Dairy Farmers', p. 46; Arneborg, 'Human Diet', p. 129.
55 Arneborg, 'Norse Greenland Dietary Economy', p. 4; Barlow,
    'Interdisciplinary Investigations', p. 490.
56 Barrett, 'Ecological Globalisation'.
57 Imer, Peasants and Prayers, p. 206.
58 Imer, Peasants and Prayers, p. 208.
59 Imer, Peasants and Prayers, p. 201.
60 Imer, Peasants and Prayers, p. 265.
61 Barlow, 'Interdisciplinary Investigations', p. 492.
62 McGovern, 'Decline of Norse Greenland', p. 337.

Chapter 8: Play

1   Jesch, 'Nine Skills', p. 5.
2   Aðalheiður Guðmundsdóttir, 'Gunnar and the Snake Pit'.
3   Lunde, Ibn Fadlān, p. 163.
4   Kunz, Eirik the Red's Saga, p. 12
5   Lonnert, 'Harpan', p. 96 of main text and p. 25 of appendix 1.
6   Thorpe, Gerald of Wales, pp. 242–3.
7   Attwood, 'Anonymous Poems, Gyðingsvísur', pp. 521–2.
8   Gade, Sturla Þórðarson, Hákonarkviða', p. 720.
9   Gade, Sturla Þórðarson, Hákonarkviða', pp. 719–20.
10 Clunies Ross, 'Anonymous Poems, Bjarkamál', p. 505.
11 Imer, Peasants and Prayers, pp. 82, 275.
12 Imer, Peasants and Prayers, pp. 250–51.
13 For both runic inscriptions see Imer, Peasants and Prayers, p. 80.
14 Tolkien, Saga of King Heidrek, p. 43.
15 Tolkien, Saga of King Heidrek, pp. 37–8.
16 Tolkien, Saga of King Heidrek, p. 39.
17 See 'Gaming in the Roman Iron Age', available online https://www.
    uib.no/en/culturalhistory/135652/gaming-roman-iron-age.

18 Spurkland, *Norwegian Runes*, p. 22.
19 Margaryan, 'Population Genomics', pp. 392–3.
20 Edberg, 'Bone Skates and Young People'.
21 Foote, *Olaus Magnus*, p. 58.
22 Scudder, *Saga of Grettir*, p. 96.
23 Regal, *Gisli Sursson's Saga*, p. 21.
24 Kennedy, *Saga of Finnbogi*, p. 258.
25 Scudder, *Saga of Grettir*, p. 70.
26 Lethbridge, 'Medieval to Modern', pp. 81–3.

Chapter 9: Unfreedom

1   Lunde, *Ibn Fadlān*, p. 106.
2   Jón Viðar Sigurðsson, 'Viking Age Scandinavia', p. 59.
3   Cook, *Njal's Saga*, p. 82.
4   'Illt er at eiga þræl at eingavin', Einar Ól. Sveinsson, ed., *Brennu-Njáls saga*, p. 128.
5   Reséndez, *The Other Slavery*, p. 10.
6   Gade, 'Valgarðr á Velli', pp. 307–8.
7   My translation. Latin from Waitz, *Vita Rimberti*, chapter 18, p. 95.
8   Somerville, *Viking Age*, p. 281.
9   Lunde, *Ibn Fadlān*, pp. 169–70.
10 Hermann Pálsson, *Book of Settlements*, p. 19.
11 Hermann Pálsson, *Book of Settlements*, p. 20.
12 Hermann Pálsson, *Book of Settlements*, p. 20, fn. 14.
13 Hermann Pálsson, *Book of Settlements*, p. 21.
14 Breeze, 'Irish Etymology'.
15 Kunz, *Saga of the Greenlanders*, p. 23.
16 Old Norse from Page, 'Icelandic Rune Poem', p. 28.
17 Zachrisson, 'Bonded People', p. 103.
18 Scudder, *Egil's Saga*, p. 78.
19 Lunde, *Ibn Fadlān*, p. 47.
20 Myrdal, 'Milking and Grinding', p. 297.
21 Larrington, *Poetic Edda*, p. 186.
22 Lunde, *Ibn Fadlān*, p. 50.
23 Lunde, *Ibn Fadlān*, p. 53.
24 See Holck, 'The Oseberg Ship Burial, Norway'.
25 The archaeological material is covered most thoroughly in Brink, 'Thralls in the Archaeological Material: Can We Excavate Slavery?', in his *Thraldom*, pp. 232–70.
26 Inscription recorded as MJy 84 in the RuneS database. Brink, *Thraldom*, pp. 105–8.

27 Inscription recorded as MJy 11 in the RuneS database. Brink, *Thraldom*, pp. 105–8.

28 Kunz, *Eirik the Red's Saga*, p. 2.

29 Kunz, *Eirik the Red's Saga*, p. 4.

30 See Jón Hnefill Aðalsteinsson, 'Position of Freed Slaves'.

31 See Fontaine, 'Slave Resistance in Early Medieval England'.

32 My translation, Latin from 'Aelfric's Colloquy' in Gem, *An Anglo-Saxon Abbot*.

33 Brink, *Thraldom*, pp. 57–8.

34 Translation slightly adapted from Brink, *Thraldom*, p. 84.

Chapter 10: Endings

1 Watts, 'Kirkdale', p. 81.

2 Watts, 'Kirkdale', p. 81.

3 Rahtz, *St Gregory's Minster*, pp. 298–300.

4 Rahtz, *St Gregory's Minster*, p. 301.

5 Watts, 'Kirkdale', p. 86.

6 Rahtz, *St Gregory's Minster*, p. 304; Blair, 'Kirkdale Dedication Inscription', p. 143 and note 14.

7 Notker the Stammerer, *The Deeds of Charlemagne*, book 2, chapter 19. For a translation see Ganz, *Two Lives of Charlemagne*.

8 Brown, *Ivory Vikings*.

9 Finlay, *Snorri Sturluson. Heimskringla: Volume 1*, p. 10.

10 Gade, 'Sturla Þórðarson, *Hrafnsmál*', stanza 16, p. 741.

11 Skene, *John of Fordun's Chronicle*, p. 295.

12 Skene, *John of Fordun's Chronicle*, p. 295.

13 Gade, 'Sturla Þórðarson, *Hrafnsmál*', stanza 11, p. 736.

14 See Steinforth, *Thorvald's Cross*.

15 For more on this mixed language community see Russell, 'A Critical Afterword'.

16 Inscription recorded as MM 145 Maughold I. See Russell, 'A Critical Afterword', p. 268, and Barnes, *The Runic Inscriptions of the Isle of Man*, p. 205.

17 Inscription recorded as MM 130 Kirk Michael III. See Barnes, *The Runic Inscriptions of the Isle of Man*, p. 180.

18 Inscription recorded as MM 135 Braddan IV. See Barnes, *The Runic Inscriptions of the Isle of Man*, p. 141.

19 See Di Clemente, 'People and Personal Names'.

20 Personal communication with Brian Smith, Shetland Amenity Trust.

21 For a detailed description of Poul Nørlund's extraordinary excavation in the 1920s and the piecemeal discoveries that were made before, see Østergård, *Woven into the Earth*, pp. 17–18.
22 Østergård, *Woven into the Earth*, pp. 128, 144.
23 Slightly adapted from Kunz, *Saga of the Greenlanders*, pp. 19–20.
24 Kunz, *Saga of the Greenlanders*, p. 21.
25 See Sabo, 'Possible Thule Carving'.
26 See Gulløv, 'Eskimo's View'.
27 Barraclough, *Beyond the Northlands*, pp. 153–6.

Further Reading

Prologue

For more on the comb in the bog see Looijenga, *Texts and Contexts of the Oldest Runic Inscriptions* (2003), and for more on the relationship between Rome and Scandinavia see Grane, 'Did the Romans Really Know (or Care) about Southern Scandinavia?' (2007). For the Vimose sacrifices see Möller-Wiering, 'Vimose' (2011) and Mees, 'The Vimose Dedication as Ritual Language' (2015). On early runes see Imer, 'Runes and Romans in the North' (2010), and on the origin of runes see Barnes, *Runes: A Handbook* (2012).

Chapter 1: Introduction

For explorations of the geographical and chronological breadth of the Viking Age, see above all Jesch, *The Viking Diaspora* (2015) and Price, *Children of Ash and Elm* (2020). For sumptuously illustrated thematic, chronological and geographical overviews see Forte, *Viking Empires* (2005), Hall, *World of the Vikings* (2007) and Fitzhugh and Ward, *Vikings: The North Atlantic Saga* (2000). For two excellent discussions on the start of the Viking Age see Barrett, 'What Caused the Viking Age?' (2008) and Ashby, 'What Really Caused the Viking Age?' (2015).

Chapter 2: Beginnings

For more on the latest Ribe excavations see Sindbæk, *Northern Emporium I* (2022) and Sindbæk, *Northern Emporium II* (2023). For more background to Ribe and the early emporia see Feveile, 'Ribe' (2008) and Søvsø, 'Emporia, Sceattas and Kingship in 8th C. "Denmark"' (2018). For more on the Salme ships see Price, 'Human Remains, Context and Place of Origin for the Salme, Estonia, Boat Burials (2020)', and for more on the origins of the Salme dead see Price, 'Isotopic Provenancing of the Salme Ship burials in Pre-Viking Age Estonia' (2016). The Salme gaming pieces are analysed in Hall, 'Board Games in Boat Burials' (2016), and the antler combs are discussed in Luik, 'Antler Combs from the Salme Ship Burials' (2020). For more on the Inchmarnock Hostage Stone see Lowe, 'Image and Imagination' (2007) and Lowe, *Inchmarnock* (2008). For more on the question of sex ratios in the early Viking Age see Raffield,

'Male-biased Operational Sex Ratios and the Viking Phenomenon' (2017). On reliquaries that ended up in Norwegian graves see Heen-Pettersen, 'An Insular Reliquary from Melhus' (2018), Heen-Pettersen, 'The Earliest Wave of Viking Activity' (2019) and Mikkelsen, *Looting or Missioning* (2019). For Viking raids on the Scottish Isles see Downham, 'An Imaginary Raid on Skye in 795?' and for more on Viking raids recorded in the Irish annals see Downham, 'The Good, The Bad, and the Ugly' (2004).

Chapter 3: Love

For more on Bergen in the twelfth and thirteenth centuries see Helle, 'Bergen's Role in the Medieval North Atlantic Trade' (2019). For more on the runic inscriptions of Bergen see most importantly Knirk, 'Love and Eroticism in Medieval Norwegian Runic Inscriptions' (2017). See also Knirk, 'Learning to Write with Runes in Medieval Norway' (1994), Knirk, 'Runic Inscriptions Containing Latin in Norway' (1998), Liestøl, 'The Runes of Bergen: Voices from the Middle Ages' (1996), Zilmer, 'Words in Wood and Stone' (2016) and Zilmer, 'Runic Sticks and Other Inscribed Objects from Medieval Bergen' (2020). For a book-length discussion of how to access the emotions of the past see Síf Ríkharðsdóttir, *Emotion in Old Norse Literature* (2017) and also Airlie, 'The History of Emotions and Emotional History' (2003). The history of women in the Viking Age, their hidden lives and identities are explored particularly in Jesch, *Women in the Viking Age* (1991), Jochens, *Women in Old Norse Society* (1995) and Jóhanna Katrín Friðriksdóttir, *Valkyrie* (2020). For more on queer sexualities and gender fluidity, the classical study is Meulengracht Sørensen, *The Unmanly Man* (1983). See also in particular Jacobsen, 'Sexual Irregularities in Medieval Scandinavia' (1982) and Finlay, 'Monstrous Allegations' (2001). For more on gender identity see Gardeła, 'Warrior-Women in Viking Age Scandinavia?' (2013), Gardeła, 'Amazons of the Viking World' (2017) and Moen, 'Gender Archaeology' (2019). For more on fertility and reproduction see Jacobsen, 'Pregnancy and Childbirth in the Medieval North' (1984), Mitchell, 'Anaphrodisiac Charms in the Nordic Middle Ages' (1998) and Raffield, 'Polygyny, Concubinage, and the Social Lives of Women in Viking-Age Scandinavia' (2017). For inscribed runic amulets see Simek, *Runes, Magic and Religion* (2004) and Steenholt Olesen, 'Runic Amulets from Medieval Denmark' (2010). For more about St Margaret and her role in childbirth see Jón Steffensen, 'Margrétar saga and its History in Iceland' (1962–1965). For more on the development of Novgorod from Norse to Slavic see Melnikova, 'Runic Inscriptions as a Source for the Relation of Northern and Eastern Europe in the Middle Ages' (1998) and Melnikova, 'The Cultural Assimilation of the Varangians into Eastern Europe from the Point of View of Language and Literacy' (2003). Finally, for little Onfim and his drawings, see particularly Schaeken, 'Learning to Read and Write' (2019).

Chapter 4: Travel
For more on the little foot outlined on the Gokstad ship see Raffield, 'Playing Vikings' (2019), and for more on the Gokstad ship more generally see Łucejko, 'Textile Dyes from Gokstad Viking Ship's Grave' (2021) and Warming, 'The Viking Age Shields from the Ship Burial at Gokstad' (2023). For more on the ships and graffiti of Dublin see Christensen, 'Ship Graffiti and Models' (1988). For more on sea travel, real and imagined, see Jesch, *Ships and Men in the Late Viking Age* (2001), Jesch, 'Geography and Travel' (2005) and Forte, 'Water World', in their *Viking Empires* (2005), pp. 118–69. For more on Greenlandic walrus ivory see Star, 'Ancient DNA Reveals the Chronology of Walrus Ivory Trade from Norse Greenland' (2018) and Barrett, 'Walruses on the Dnieper' (2022). Information about glacial archaeology in Norway can be found on the Secrets of the Ice website, https://secretsoftheice.com, and in Pilø, 'Crossing the Ice' (2020). For more on skiing see Finstad, 'Prehistoric and Medieval Skis from Glaciers and Ice Patches in Norway' (2016) and for more on Norwegian petroglyphs see Sognnes, 'The Case of the Lone Reindeer' (2011). For analysis on the Mountain Woman, Icelandic speakers can read Rannveig Þórhallsdóttir's MA thesis, 'Fjallkonan' (2018), available online at https://skemman.is/handle/1946/31704. There is further discussion of this find in Jóhanna Katrín Friðriksdóttir's *Valkyrie* (2020), pp. 89–90. For more on Norse concepts of the afterlife see Ellis, *The Road to Hel* (1943), and for more on the underpinning mythology see Simek, *Dictionary of Northern Mythology* (1993). For more on the Oseberg ship burial see particularly Holck, 'The Oseberg Ship Burial, Norway' (2006).

Chapter 5: Belief
For more on the rituals that might have been going on in Surtshellir, see Smith, 'Ritual Responses to Catastrophic Volcanism in Viking Age Iceland' (2021) and Smith, 'All that Glitters is not Gold' (2023). For earlier publications from the same team that show how their theories developed in line with the evidence, see Guðmundur Ólafsson, 'Surtshellir' (2010) and Patel, 'The Blackeners Cave' (2017). For more on the eruption of Laki see Wieners, 'Haze, Hunger, Hesitation' (2020). For more about the Norse mythological world more generally, two good guides to the key figures are Simek, *Northern Mythology* (1993) and Lindow, *Norse Mythology* (2002). For more on *Bergbúa þáttr* (which contains the long poem spoken

by a cave giant) see Lindow, *Trolls* (2014), especially pp. 30–31, Ármann Jakobsson, 'Cave' (2017) and Ármann Jakobsson, 'Bergbúa þáttr' (2018). For more on the etymology of Tyr's name, see Sayers, '"ok er hann einhendr"' (2016), and for more on the Tyr medallion from Trollhättthen see Hultgård, *The End of the World in Scandinavian Mythology* (2022), at pp. 215–16. For more on theophoric place names see Brink, 'Mythologizing Landscape' (2001) and Brink, 'Myth and Ritual in Pre-Christian Landscape' (2013). For more on the Tjängvide picture stone and the Altuna stone see Hultgård, *The End of the World in Scandinavian Mythology* (2022), at pp. 150–52. For more on pagan Norse beliefs about the world around them and its supernatural inhabitants, see especially Price, *The Viking Way* (2019), and Price, 'The Making of Midgård', which is the first third of *Children of Ash and Elm* (2020). For more on the ambiguity of the 'Odin' figurine from Lejre in Denmark, see Christensen, 'A Silver Figurine from Lejre' (2013) and Arwill-Nordbladh, 'Negotiating Normatives' (2014). For more on Frösö see Magnell, 'Veitstu Hvé Blóta Skal?' (2010). For more on Hofstaðir see Lucas, 'Bloody Slaughter' (2007), for more on the Glavendrup stone see Cole, 'When Gods Become Bureaucrats' (2020) and for more about Thorvald's Cross see Steinforth, *Thorvald's Cross* (2022). For German speakers, for more on the grave at Thumby-Bienebek see Staecker, *Rex regnum et dominus dominorum* (1999), at pp. 132–4.

Chapter 6: Bodies

For more about Viking Age combs, the first port of call is always Ashby, *A Viking Way of Life* (2014), and also Ashby, 'Making a Good Comb' (2013). For more about the Danelaw see Holman, 'Defining the Danelaw' (2001), Abrams, 'Edward the Elder's Danelaw' (2001) and Abrams, 'King Edgar and the Men of the Danelaw' (2008). For more about the boundaries established by Alfred and Guthrum see Davis, 'Alfred and Guthrum's Frontier' (1982). For more on haircare see Arwill-Nordbladh, 'Viking Age Hair', and for more on the Salme combs see Luik, 'Antler Combs from the Salme Ship Burials' (2020). For more about the Hårby figurine see Gardeła, *Women and Weapons* (2021), and Jóhanna Katrín Friðriksdóttir, *Valkyrie*, at pp. 69–70. Information about the St John's massacre can be found in Pollard, 'Sprouting like Cockle Amongst the Wheat' (2012), and the link between the Oxford and Fyn bodies is discussed in Margaryan, 'Population Genomics of the Viking World' (2020). For more about grooved teeth see Arcini, 'The Vikings Bare Their Filed Teeth' (2005) and Arcini, 'Markers of Identity', in her *The Viking Age* (2018), at pp. 74–83. For more about the Ridgeway mass burial see Loe, *Given to the Ground* (2014) and for more about the Oseberg ship

burial see Holck, 'The Oseberg Ship Burial, Norway' (2006). For more
on runic inscriptions to ward off sickness see Steenholt Olesen, 'Runic
Amulets from Medieval Denmark' (2010) and Simek, 'Elves and Exorcism'
(2011). For more about the siblings with dwarfism see Arcini, 'Two
Dwarves from Sweden' (1996) and Arcini, 'Reconnecting Relationships'
(2022), which can be found online: https://the-past.com/feature/
reconnecting-relationships-uncovering-genealogy-in-archaeology/.

Chapter 7: Home

For more on the Farm under the Sand see Berglund, 'The Farm Beneath
the Sand' (2000) and Hebsgaard, 'The Farm Beneath the Sand' (2009).
For more on Greenland's natural resources see Lísabet Guðmundsdóttir,
'Driftwood Utilization and Procurement in Norse Greenland' (2022)
and Lísabet Guðmundsdóttir, 'Timber Imports to Norse Greenland'
(2023). For more on the homesteads built by the Norse Greenlanders
see Guldager, *Medieval Farmsteads in Greenland* (2002), Arneborg, *Saga
Trails* (2006) and Høegsberg, 'Continuity and Change' (2009). For more
on Viking Age dwellings more generally see Beck, 'Opening Doors'
(2014) and Croix, 'Houses and Households in Viking Age Scandinavia'
(2014). For more on relations between Norse Greenland and Europe
see Arneborg, 'Greenland and Europe' (2000). For more on walruses
see Frei, 'Was It for Walrus?' (2015) and Star, 'Ancient DNA Reveals the
Chronology of Walrus Ivory Trade from Norse Greenland' (2018). For
more on what Norse Greenlanders ate see Arneborg, 'Norse Greenland
Dietary Economy' (2012). Meanwhile, for more on what they ate and how
they lived on the Faroe Islands see Arge, 'Vikings in the Faroe Islands'
(2000), Church, 'Puffins, Pigs, Cod and Barley' (2005) and Arge, 'Pigs in
the Faroe Islands' (2009). For more about farming practices and shielings,
especially in Iceland, see Kupiec, 'Roles and Perceptions of Shielings and
the Mediation of Gender Identities in Viking and Medieval Iceland' (2015).
For more on the North Atlantic region see Buckland, 'The North Atlantic
Environment' (2000), and on settling Iceland see Orri Vésteinsson, 'The
Archaeology of *landnám*' (2000). For more on life in Viking Age towns see
Í, 'From Country to Town' (2013), Griffiths, 'Living in Viking-Age Towns'
(2013), Poole, 'More than Just Meat' (2013) and Williams, 'Towns and
Identities in Viking England' (2013). For investigations into specific Norse
Greenlandic sites in different areas of the colonies see McGovern, 'The
Arctic Frontier of Norse Greenland' (1985), Henriksen, 'Norse Agriculture
in Greenland' (2014), Ledger, 'Vatnahverfi' (2014), Madsen, 'Norse Pastoral
Farming and Settlement in the Vatnahverfi Peninsula, South Greenland'
(2014), Nyegaard, 'Dairy Farmers and Seal Hunters' (2018) and Madsen,

'Behind the Ice' (2022). For textile production see Østergård, *Woven into the Earth* (2009), Hayeur Smith, 'Dress, Cloth and the Farmer's Wife' (2014), Hayeur Smith, 'Weaving Wealth' (2015) and Cartwright, 'Making the Cloth that Binds Us' (2015). For gendered work spaces see Dommasnes, '"Spun on a wheel were women's hearts"' (2008), Milek, 'The Roles of Pit Houses and Gendered Spaces on Viking-Age Farmsteads in Iceland' (2012), Croix, 'Identifying "Occasions" of the Self in Viking-Age Scandinavia' (2020) and Hayeur Smith, *The Valkyries' Loom* (2020). For the runic inscriptions of Greenland see Imer, 'The Runic Inscriptions from Vatnahverfi and the Evidence of Communication' (2009), Imer, 'The Tradition of Writing in Norse Greenland' (2014) and most importantly Imer, *Peasants and Prayers* (2018). For domestic animals see Toplak, 'The Warrior and the Cat' (2019). For more about the collapse of Greenland see McGovern, 'The Demise of Norse Greenland' (2000), Dugmore, 'Norse Greenland Settlement: Reflections on Climate Change, Trade, and the Contrasting Fates of Human Settlements in the North Atlantic Islands' (2008) and Dugmore, 'Norse Greenland Settlement and Limits to Adaption' (2009).

Chapter 8: Play

For what they got up to in their spare time, see Gardeła, 'What Did the Vikings do for Fun?' (2012). For more on the musical instruments of early Scandinavia see Lund, 'The Archaeomusicology of Scandinavia' (1981). For more on Earl Rognvald and his many (nine) talents see Jesch, 'The Nine Skills of Earl Rögnvaldr of Orkney' (2006). For more on Gunnar playing the harp see Aðalheiður Guðmundsdóttir, 'Gunnar and the Snake Pit in Medieval Art and Legend' (2012). For more on the Greenlandic farm where the cat and the fiddle were found, see Nyegaard, 'Dairy Farmers and Seal Hunters' (2018). For the site at Ytre Fosse see 'Gaming in the Roman Iron Age', available online https://www.uib.no/en/culturalhistory/135652/gaming-roman-iron-age. On the knuckle bones from Pálstóftir in Iceland see Lucas, 'Pálstóftir' (2008). For more on the gaming boards at Buckquoy see Ritchie, 'Excavation of Pictish and Viking-Age Farmsteads at Buckquoy, Orkney' (1979), and for the gaming boards at Deerness see Barrett, 'New Excavations at the Brough of Deerness' (2009). For evidence for how children played see Callow, 'First Steps Towards an Archaeology of Childhood in Iceland' (2006), McAlister, 'Childhood in Viking and Hiberno-Scandinavian Dublin' (2013) and Raffield, 'Playing Vikings' (2019). For the information on ice skates see Edberg, 'Bone Skates and Young People in Birka and Sigtuna' (2016).

Chapter 9: Unfreedom

For a book-length study of slavery in the Viking Age see most importantly Brink, *Thraldom* (2021). See also Brink, 'Slavery in the Viking Age' (2008), Raffield, 'The Slave Markets of the Viking World' (2019), Kjellström, 'The Norm and the Subaltern' (2021), Roslund, 'Legacy of the Disowned' (2021) and Zachrisson, 'Bonded People' (2021). For more on slavery in Viking Age Britain and Ireland see Fontaine, 'Slave Resistance in Early Medieval England' (2020) and Fontaine, 'The Archaeology of Slave Trading in Viking-Age Britain and Ireland' (2021) and for slavery more broadly in the medieval and early modern periods see Iversen, 'Slavery and Unfreedom from the Middle Ages to the Beginning of the Early Modern Period' (2020). For more about the slave trade in Dublin see Holm, 'The Slave Trade of Dublin' (1986), and for more on the meaning of the word *kjafal* see Breeze, 'An Irish Etymology for *kjafal* "hooded cloak" in *Þorfinns saga*' (1998). For more on the work of the enslaved see Myrdal, 'Milking and Grinding, Digging and Herding' (2012). For more on slavery and human sacrifice see Naumann, 'Slaves as Burial Gifts in Viking Age Norway?' (2014) and Moen, 'Agents of Death' (2021). For possible connections between slavery and the Oseberg ship burial see Holck, 'The Oseberg Ship Burial, Norway' (2006). For more about freed people see Jón Hnefill Aðalsteinsson, 'The Position of Freed Slaves in Medieval Iceland' (1986) and Karras, 'Concubinage and Slavery in the Viking Age' (1990).

Chapter 10: Endings

For more about the Kirkdale sundial see Page, 'How Long did the Scandinavian Language Survive in England?' (1995), Watts, 'Kirkdale' (1997), Rahtz, 'Three Ages of Conversion at Kirkdale, North Yorkshire' (2003), Blair, 'The Kirkdale Dedication Inscription and its Latin Models' (2010), and Rahtz, *St Gregory's Minster, Kirkdale, North Yorkshire* (2021). For more about Orm Gamalsson and also *Domesday Book* see Fellows-Jensen, 'Of Danes – and Thanes – and *Domesday Book*' (1991) and Fletcher, *Bloodfeud* (2002). For more on Harald Hardrada see Bagge, *From Viking Stronghold to Christian Kingdom* (2010) and Finlay, 'History and Fiction in the Kings' Sagas' (2015). See also Krag, 'The Early Unification of Norway' (2003). For more on Tostig see Barlow, *The Godwins* (2002), and for more about Stamford Bridge as the ending of the Viking Age see Winroth, 'Epilogue, The End of the Viking Age' (2014). For discussions about the complex, expansive endings to the Viking Age see in particular Jesch, *The Viking Diaspora*, especially pp. 1–4 and 55–63, and Price, 'The Many Ends of the Viking Age', in his *Children of Ash and Elm* (2020), pp. 495–504. See also Somerville, 'The End of the Viking Age' in their *The Viking Age* (2014), pp. 455–82. For a specifically eastern perspective on this question see Mägi, 'The End of the Viking Age', in her *The Viking Eastern Baltic* (2020), pp. 72–92. For more about Sviatoslav's name see Barraclough, *Beyond the Northlands* (2016), p. 182, and for more about the origins of Greenlandic chess pieces see Star, 'Ancient DNA Reveals the Chronology of Walrus Ivory Trade from Norse Greenland' (2018). For more about the theory that the chess pieces were carved by Margrét in Iceland see Brown, *Ivory Vikings* (2015). For a selection of articles about the Lords of the Isles see Fell, *The Viking Age on the Isle of Man* (1983), Power, 'Meeting in Norway' (2005) and Etchingham, *Norse-Gaelic Contacts in a Viking World* (2019). For more about the runes and ogam on the Isle of Man see especially Barnes, *The Runic Inscriptions of the Isle of Man* (2019) and Page, 'The Manx Rune-Stones' (1995). For more about Ogam see McManus, *A Guide to Ogam* (1991) and Sims-Williams, *The Celtic Inscriptions of Britain* (2003). For more about the mixed names of the Isle of Man see Di Clemente, 'People and Personal Names from the Scandinavian Rune Stones of the Isle of Man' (2014) and Russell, 'A Critical Afterword' (2023). For more about the history of the Icelandic Commonwealth and the thirteenth-century civil war see Clunies Ross, 'Land-Taking and Text-Making in Medieval Iceland' (1998), Helgi Þorláksson, 'Historical Background', (2005) and Brégaint, 'Conquering Minds' (2012). For more about Norn in the Northern Isles see Jakobsen, *An Etymological Dictionary of the Norn Language in Shetland* (1928), Barnes, *The Norn Language of Orkney and Shetland* (1998) and the articles in McColl Millar, *Northern Lights, Northern Worlds* (2010). For more about Norse Greenlandic clothes see Østergård, *Woven into the Earth* (2009), and for the nitty-gritty of how these clothes can be reconstructed see Fransen, *Medieval Garments Reconstructed* (2011). Finally, for more about the 'Inuit' carvings see Gulløv, 'The Eskimo's View of the European (1983) and Sabo, 'A Possible Thule Carving of a Viking from Baffin Island, N.W.T.' (1978).

Bibliography

Primary sources

Attwood, K., 'Anonymous Poems, *Gyðingsvísur 5*', in *Poetry on Christian Subjects*, ed. M. Clunies Ross (Turnhout: Brepols, 2007), pp. 521–2.

Clunies Ross, M., 'Anonymous Poems, *Bjarkamál in fornu 7*', in *Poetry from Treatises on Poetics*, ed. K. E. Gade and E. Marold (Turnhout: Brepols, 2017), p. 505.

Cook, R., *Njal's Saga*, in *The Complete Sagas of Icelanders Including 49 Tales, Volume 3*, gen. ed. Viðar Hreinsson (Reykjavik: Leifur Eiríksson Publishing, 1997), pp. 1–220.

Cross, S. H., and O. P. Sherbowitz-Wetzor, ed. and transl., *The Russian Primary Chronicle. Laurentian Text* (Cambridge, MA: The Medieval Academy of America, 1953).

Einar Ól. Sveinsson, ed., *Brennu-Njáls saga*, Íslenzk fornrit 12 (Reykjavik: Hið íslenzka fornritafélag, 1954).

Faulkes, A., ed. and transl., *Snorri Sturluson: Edda* (London: J. M. Dent, 1995).

Faulkes, A., transl., *Hemings þáttr* (London: Viking Society for Northern Research, 2016).

Finlay, A., and A. Faulkes, transl., *Snorri Sturluson. Heimskringla: Volume 1. The Beginnings to Óláfr Tryggvason* (London: Viking Society for Northern Research, 2nd ed., 2017).

Finlay, A., and A. Faulkes, transl., *Snorri Sturluson. Heimskringla: Volume 2. Óláfr Haraldsson (The Saint)* (London: Viking Society for Northern Research, 2014).

Foote, P. G., *Olaus Magnus. A Description of the Northern Peoples 1555, Volume 1* (London: The Hakluyt Society, 1996).

Fulk, R. D., 'Anonymous Poems, *Eiríksmál*', in *Poetry from the Kings' Sagas 1: From Mythical Times to c. 1035*, ed. D. Whaley (Turnhout: Brepols, 2012), p. 1006.

Fulk, R. D., 'Sigvatr Þórðarson, *Austrfararvísur*', in *Poetry from the Kings' Sagas 1: From Mythical Times to c. 1035*, ed. D. Whaley (Turnhout: Brepols, 2012), p. 578.

Gade, K. E., 'Sturla Þórðarson, *Hákonarkviða* ', in *Poetry from the Kings' Sagas 2: From c. 1035 to c. 1300*, ed. K. E. Gade (Turnhout: Brepols, 2009), pp. 719–20.

Gade, K. E., 'Sturla Þórðarson, *Hrafnsmál*', in *Poetry from the Kings' Sagas 2: From c. 1035 to c. 1300*, ed. K. E. Gade (Turnhout: Brepols, 2009), pp. 727–45.

Gade, K. E., 'Valgarðr á Velli, Poem about Haraldr harðráði 9', in *Poetry from the Kings' Sagas 2: From c. 1035 to c. 1300*, ed. K. E. Gade (Turnhout: Brepols, 2009), pp. 307–8.

Ganz, D., transl., *Two Lives of Charlemagne* (London: Penguin, 2008).

Gem, S. H., *An Anglo-Saxon Abbot: Aelfric of Eynsham: A Study* (Edinburgh: T&T Clark, 1912).

Grønlie, S., transl., *Íslendingabók. Kristni Saga. The Book of the Icelanders. The Story of the Conversation* (London: Viking Society for Northern Research, 2006).

Hermann Pálsson and P. Edwards, ed. and transl., *The Book of Settlements. Landnámabók* (Winnipeg: University of Manitoba Press, 1972).

Kennedy, J., *The Saga of Finnbogi the Mighty*, in *The Complete Sagas of Icelanders Including 49 Tales, Volume 3*, gen. ed. Viðar Hreinsson (Reykjavik: Leifur Eiríksson Publishing, 1997), pp. 221–70.

Kunz, K., *Eirik the Red's Saga*, in *The Complete Sagas of Icelanders Including 49 Tales, Volume 1*, gen. ed. Viðar Hreinsson (Reykjavik: Leifur Eiríksson Publishing, 1997), pp. 1–18.

Kunz, K., *The Saga of the Greenlanders*, in *The Complete Sagas of Icelanders Including 49 Tales, Volume 1*, gen. ed. Viðar Hreinsson (Reykjavik: Leifur Eiríksson Publishing, 1997), pp. 19–32.

Kunz, K., *The Saga of the People of Laxardal*, in *The Complete Sagas of Icelanders Including 49 Tales, Volume 5*, gen. ed. Viðar Hreinsson (Reykjavik: Leifur Eiríksson Publishing, 1997), pp. 1–120.

Larrington, C., transl., *The Poetic Edda* (Oxford: Oxford University Press, rev. ed. 2014).

Larson, L. M., transl., *The King's Mirror (Speculum Regale – Konungs Skuggsjá)* (New York, NY: Twayne Publishers Inc., 1917).

Lunde, P., and C. Stone, *Ibn Fadlān and the Land of Darkness: Arab Travellers in the Far North* (London: Penguin Books, 2012).

Mynors, R. A. B., R. M. Thomson and M. Winterbottom, ed. and transl., *William of Malmesbury. Gesta Regum Anglorum, Volume 1* (Oxford: Clarendon Press, 1998).

Regal, M. S., transl., *Gisli Sursson's Saga*, in *The Complete Sagas of Icelanders Including 49 Tales, Volume 2*, gen. ed. Viðar Hreinsson (Reykjavik: Leifur Eiríksson Publishing, 1997), pp. 1–48.

Scudder, B., transl., *Egil's Saga*, in *The Complete Sagas of Icelanders Including 49 Tales, Volume 1*, gen. ed. Viðar Hreinsson (Reykjavik: Leifur Eiríksson Publishing, 1997), pp. 31–177.

Scudder, B., transl., *The Saga of Grettir the Strong*, in *The Complete Sagas of Icelanders Including 49 Tales, Volume 2*, gen. ed. Viðar Hreinsson (Reykjavik: Leifur Eiríksson Publishing, 1997), pp. 49–191.

Skene, W. F., ed., transl. F. J. H. Skene, *John of Fordun's Chronicle of the Scottish Nation* (Edinburgh: Edmonston and Douglas, 1972).

Somerville, A. A., and R. A. McDonald, *The Viking Age: A Reader* (Toronto: University of Toronto Press, 2nd ed., 2014).

Taylor, M., *The Tale of the Mountain-Dweller*, in *The Complete Sagas of Icelanders Including 49 Tales, Volume 2*, gen. ed. Viðar Hreinsson (Reykjavik: Leifur Eiríksson Publishing, 1997), pp. 444–7.

Thorpe, L., *Gerald of Wales. The Journey Through Wales and the Description of Wales* (Harmondsworth: Penguin, 1978).

Tolkien, C., transl., *The Saga of King Heidrek the Wise* (London: Thomas Nelson and Sons, 1960).

Townend, M., 'Óttarr svarti, *Hǫfuðlausn*', in *Poetry from the Kings' Sagas 1: From Mythical Times to c. 1035*, ed. D. Whaley (Turnhout: Brepols, 2012), p. 793.

Tschan, F. J., transl., *History of the Archbishops of Hamburg Bremen: Adam of Bremen* (New York, NY: Columbia University Press, 2005).

Vaughan, R., ed., *The Chronicle Attributed to John of Wallingford* (London: Royal Historical Society, 1958).

Waitz, G., ed., *Vita Rimberti*, in *Vitae Anskarii et Rimberti*, SS rer. Germ. 55 (Hannover: Hahn, 1884).

Warner, D., ed. and transl. *Ottonian Germany: The Chronicon of Thietmar of Merseburg* (Manchester: Manchester University Press, 2001).

Whitelock, D., ed., *English Historical Documents, Volume 1, c.500–1042* (London: Eyre Methuen, 2nd ed., 1979).

Secondary sources

Abels, R., 'Alfred the Great, the *micel hæðen here* and the Viking Threat', in *Alfred the Great. Papers from the Eleventh-Centenary Conferences* (London: Routledge, 2003) pp. 265–79.

Abram, C., *Myths of the Pagan North: The Gods of the Norsemen* (London: Continuum, 2011).

Abrams, L., 'Edward the Elder's Danelaw', in *Edward the Elder 899–924*, ed. N. J. Higham and D. H. Hill (London: Routledge, 2001), pp. 128–43.

Abrams, L., 'King Edgar and the Men of the Danelaw', in *Edgar King of the English 959–975*, ed. D. Scragg (Woodbridge: Boydell and Brewer, 2008), pp. 171–91.

Aðalheiður Guðmundsdóttir, 'Gunnar and the Snake Pit in Medieval Art and Legend', *Speculum* 87(4) (2012), pp. 1015–49.

Airlie, S., 'The History of Emotions and Emotional History', *Early Medieval Europe* 10(2) (2003), pp. 235–41.

Andersson, E. B., 'Tools, Textile Production and Society in Viking Age Birka', in *Dressing the Past*, ed. M. Gleba, C. Munkholt and M.-L. Nosch (Oxford: Oxbow Books, 2008), pp. 68–85.

Arcini, C., 'The Vikings Bare Their Filed Teeth', *American Journal of Physical Anthropology* 128(4) (2005), pp. 727–33.

Arcini, C., *The Viking Age: A Time of Many Faces* (Oxford: Oxbow Books, 2018).

Arcini, C., and P. Frölund, 'Two Dwarves from Sweden: A Unique Case', *International Journal of Osteoarchaeology* 6(2) (1996), pp. 155–66.

Arge, S. V., 'Vikings in the Faroe Islands', in *Vikings: The North Atlantic Saga*, ed. W. W. Fitzhugh and E. I. Ward (Washington, DC: Smithsonian Books, 2000), pp. 154–63.

Arge, S. V., M. J. Church and S. D. Brewington, 'Pigs in the Faroe Islands: An Ancient Facet of the Islands' Palaeoeconomy', *Journal of the North Atlantic* 2 (2009), pp. 19–32.

Ármann Jakobsson, 'Cave', in his *The Troll Inside You: Paranormal Activity in the Medieval North* (New York, NY: Punctum Books, 2017), pp. 37–42.

Ármann Jakobsson, 'Bergbúa þáttr: The Story of a Paranormal Encounter', in *Supernatural Encounters in Old Norse Literature and Tradition*, ed. D. Sävborg and K. Bek-Pedersen (Turnhout: Brepols, 2018), pp. 15–29.

Arneborg, J., 'Greenland and Europe' in *Vikings: The North Atlantic Saga*, ed. W. W. Fitzhugh and E. I. Ward (Washington, DC: Smithsonian Books, 2000), pp. 304–17.

Arneborg, J., *Saga Trails. Brattahlið, Garðar, Hvalsey Fjord's Church and Herjolfsnes: Four Chieftains' Farmsteads in the Norse Settlements of Greenland* (Copenhagen: Nationalmuseet, 2006).

Arneborg, J., N. Lynnerup et al., 'Human Diet and Subsistence Patterns in Norse Greenland ad c.980–AD c.1450', *Journal of the North Atlantic. Special Volume 3: Greenland Isotope Project: Diet in Norse Greenland AD 1000–AD 1450* (2012), pp. 119–33.

Arneborg, J., N. Lynnerup et al., 'Norse Greenland Dietary Economy ca. AD 980–ca. AD 1450: Introduction', *Journal of the North Atlantic. Special Volume 3: Greenland Isotope Project: Diet in Norse Greenland ad 1000–ad 1450* (2012), pp. 1–39.

Arwill-Nordbladh, E., 'Negotiating Normatives – "Odin from Lejre" as Challenger of Hegemonic Orders', *Danish Journal of Archaeology* 2(1) (2014), pp. 87–93.

Arwill-Nordbladh, E., 'Viking Age Hair', *Internet Archaeology* 42 (2016).

Ashby, S. P., 'Making A Good Comb: Mercantile Identity in 9th to 11th Century England', in *Everyday Life in Viking-Age Towns: Social Approaches to Towns in England and Ireland, c. 800–1100*, ed. D. M. Hadley and L. ten Harkel (Oxford: Oxbow Books, 2013), pp. 193–208.

Ashby, S. P., *A Viking Way of Life: Combs and Communities in Early Medieval Britain* (Stroud: Amberley Publishing, 2014).

Ashby, S. P., 'What Really Caused the Viking Age? The Social Content of Raiding and Exploration', *Archaeological Dialogues*, 22(1) (2015), pp. 89–106.

Bagge, S., *From Viking Stronghold to Christian Kingdom: State Formation in Norway c. 900–1350* (Copenhagen: Museum Tusculanum Press, 2010).

Barfod, G. H., C. Feveile and S. M. Sindbæk, 'Splinters to Splendours: From Upcycled Glass to Viking Beads at Ribe, Denmark', *Archaeological and Anthropological Sciences* 14 (2022), p. 180.

Barlow, F., *The Godwins: The Rise and Fall of a Noble Dynasty* (London: Routledge, 2002).

Barlow, L., J. P. Sadler et al., 'Interdisciplinary Investigations of the End of the Norse Western Settlement in Greenland', *The Holocene* 7(4) (1997), pp. 489–99.

Barnes, M. P., *The Norn Language of Orkney and Shetland* (Lerwick: The Shetland Times Press, 1998).

Barnes, M., *Runes: A Handbook* (Woodbridge: Boydell & Brewer, 2012).

Barnes, M., *The Runic Inscriptions of the Isle of Man* (London: Viking Society for Northern Research, 2019).

Barraclough, E. R., *Beyond the Northlands: Viking Voyages and the Old Norse Sagas* (Oxford: Oxford University Press, 2016).

Barrett, J. H., 'What Caused the Viking Age?', *Antiquity* 82 (2008), pp. 671–85.

Barrett, J. H., S. Bossenkool et al., 'Ecological Globalisation, Serial Depletion and the Medieval Trade of Walrus Rostra', *Quarternary Science Reviews* 229 (2020), 106122.

Barrett, J. H., N. Khamaiko et al., 'Walruses on the Dnieper: New Evidence for the Intercontinental Trade of Greenlandic Ivory in the Middle Ages', *Proceedings of the Royal Society B* 289 (2022), 20212773.

Barrett, J. H., and A. Slater, 'New Excavations at the Brough of Deerness: Power and Religion in Viking Age Scotland', *Journal of the North Atlantic* 2(1) (2009), pp. 81–94.

Beck, A. S., 'Opening Doors – Entering Social Understandings of the Viking Age Longhouse', in *Dwellings, Identities and Homes: European Housing Culture from the Viking Age to the Renaissance*, ed. M. Svart

Kristiansen and K. Giles (Aarhus: Aarhus University Press, 2014), pp. 127–38.

Berglund, J., 'The Farm Beneath the Sand' in *Vikings: The North Atlantic Saga*, ed. W. W. Fitzhugh and E. I. Ward (Washington, DC: Smithsonian Books, 2000), pp. 295–303.

Blair, J., 'The Kirkdale Dedication Inscription and its Latin Models: Romanitas in Late Anglo-Saxon Yorkshire', in *Interfaces between Language and Culture in Medieval England*, ed. A. Hall, O. Timofeeva et al. (Leiden: Brill, 2010), pp. 139–45.

Boyd, R., 'From Country to Town', in *Everyday Life in Viking-Age Towns: Social Approaches to Towns in England and Ireland, c. 800–1100*, ed. D. M. Hadley and L. ten Harkel (Oxford: Oxbow Books, 2013), pp. 73–85.

Breeze, A., 'An Irish Etymology for *kjafal* "hooded cloak" in *Þorfinns saga*', *Arkiv för nordisk filologi* 113 (1998), pp. 5–6.

Brégaint, D., 'Conquering Minds: Konungs skuggsjá and the Annexation of Iceland in the Thirteenth Century', *Scandinavian Studies* 84(4) (2012), pp. 439–66.

Brink, S., 'Mythologizing Landscape: Place and Space of Cult and Myth', in *Kontinuitäten und Brüche in der Religionsgeschichte. Feschrift für Anders Hultgård zu seinem 65. Geburtstag am 23.12.2001*, ed. M. Stausberg (Berlin: De Gruyter, 2001), pp. 76–112.

Brink, S., 'Myth and Ritual in Pre-Christian Landscape', in *Sacred Sites and Holy Places. Exploring the Sacralization of Landscape through Time and Space*, ed. S. Walaker Nordeide and S. Brink (Turnhout: Brepols, 2013), pp. 33–51.

Brink, S., 'Slavery in the Viking Age', in *The Viking World*, ed. S. Brink. and N. Price (London: Routledge, 2008), pp. 49–56.

Brink, S., *Thraldom: A History of Slavery in the Viking Age* (New York, NY: Oxford University Press, 2021).

Brown, N. M., *Ivory Vikings: The Mystery of the Most Famous Chessmen in the World and the Woman Who Made Them* (New York, NY: St Martin's Press, 2015).

Buckland, P. C., 'The North Atlantic Environment', in *Vikings: The North Atlantic Saga*, W. W. Fitzhugh and E. I. Ward (Washington, DC: Smithsonian Books, 2000), pp. 146–53.

Callow, C., 'First Steps Towards an Archaeology of Childhood in Iceland', *Archaeologica Islandica* 5 (2006), pp. 55–74.

Cartwright, B., 'Making the Cloth that Binds Us: The Role of Textile Production in Producing Viking-Age Identities', in *Viking Worlds: Things, Spaces and Movement*, ed. M. Hem Eriksen, U. Pedersen et al. (Oxford: Oxbow Books, 2015), pp. 160–78.

Christensen, A., E., 'Ship Graffiti and Models' in *Miscellanea 1, Medieval Dublin Excavations, 1962–81*, ed. P. F. Wallace (Dublin: Royal Irish Academy, 1988), pp. 13–26.

Christensen, T., 'A Silver Figurine from Lejre', *Danish Journal of Archaeology* 2(1) (2013), pp. 65–78.

Church, M. J., S. V. Arge et al., 'Puffins, Pigs, Cod and Barley: Palaeoeconomy at Undir Junkarinsfløtti, Sandoy, Faroe Islands', *Environmental Archaeology* 10(2) (2005), pp. 179–97.

Clayton, M., 'An Edition of Ælfric's Letter to Brother Edward', in *Early Medieval English Texts and Interpretations: Studies Presented to Donald G. Scragg*, ed. E. Treharne and S. Rosser (Tempe, AZ: Arizona Center for Medieval and Renaissance Studies, 2002), pp. 263–83.

Clunies Ross, M., 'Land-Taking and Text-Making in Medieval Iceland', in *Text and Territory: Geographical Imagination in the European Middle Ages*, ed. S. Tomasch and S. Gilles (Philadelphia, PA: University of Pennsylvania, 1998), pp. 159–84.

Cole, R., 'When Gods Become Bureaucrats', *Harvard Theological Review* 113(2) (2020), pp. 186–209.

Cole, R., 'Runes and Rye: Administration in Denmark and the Emergence of the Younger Futhark, 500–800', *Comparative Studies in Society and History* 65(4) (2023), pp. 1–25.

Croix, S., 'Houses and Households in Viking Age Scandinavia – Some Case Studies', in *Dwellings, Identities and Homes: European Housing Culture from the Viking Age to the Renaissance* ed. M. Svart Kristiansen and K. Giles (Aarhus: Aarhus University Press, 2014), pp. 113–26.

Croix, S., 'Identifying "Occasions" of the Self in Viking-Age Scandinavia: Textile Production as Gendered Performance in its Social and Spatial Settings', in *Approaches to the Medieval Self: Representations and Conceptualizations of the Self in the Textual and Material Culture of Western Scandinavia, c. 800–1500*, ed. S. G. Eriksen, K. Langsholt Holmqvist and B. Bandlien (Berlin: De Gruyter, 2020), pp. 235–54.

Davis, R. H. C., 'Alfred and Guthrum's Frontier', *The English Historical Review* 97 (1982), pp. 803–10.

Di Clemente, V., 'People and Personal Names from the Scandinavian Rune Stones of the Isle of Man', *Itinerari* 3 (2014), pp. 219–45.

Dommasnes, L. H. '"Spun on a Wheel were Women's Hearts": Women between Ideology and Life in the Nordic Past', in *Engendering Social Dynamics: The Archaeology of Maintenance Activities*, ed. S. Montón-Subías and M. Sánchez-Romero (Oxford: Archaeopress, 2008), pp. 87–95.

Downham, C., 'An Imaginary Raid on Skye in 795?', *Scottish Gaelic Studies* 20 (2000), pp. 192–96.

Downham, C., 'The Good, the Bad, and the Ugly: Portrayals of Vikings in "The Fragmentary Annals of Ireland"', in *The Medieval Chronicle III. Proceedings of the 3rd International Conference on the Medieval Chronicle. Doorn/Utrecht 12–17 July 2002*, ed. E. Kooper (Leiden: Brill, 2004), pp. 28–40.

Dugmore, A. J., C. Keller and T. H. McGovern, 'Norse Greenland Settlement: Reflections on Climate Change, Trade, and the Contrasting Fates of Human Settlements in the North Atlantic Islands', *Arctic Anthropology* 44(1) (2007), pp. 12–37.

Dugmore, A. J., C. Keller et al., 'Norse Greenland Settlement and Limits to Adaption', in *Adapting to Climate Change: Thresholds, Values, Governance*, ed. W. N. Adger, I. Lorenzoni and K. L. O'Brien (Cambridge: Cambridge University Press, 2009), pp. 96–114.

Edberg, R., and J. Karlsson, 'Bone Skates and Young People in Birka and Sigtuna', *Journal of Swedish Antiquarian Research* 111 (2016), pp. 6–16.

Einarsson, Árni, 'Viking Age Fences and Early Settlement Dynamics in Iceland', *Journal of the North Atlantic* 27 (2015), pp. 1–21.

Ellis, H. R., *The Road to Hel: A Study of the Conception of the Dead in Old Norse Literature* (Cambridge: Cambridge University Press, 1943).

Etchingham, C., Jón Viðar Sigurðsson and E. A. Rowe, ed., *Norse-Gaelic Contacts in a Viking World: Studies in the Literature and History of Norway, Iceland, Ireland and the Isle of Man* (Turnhout: Brepols, 2019).

Fell, C., P. Foote et al., ed., *The Viking Age on the Isle of Man. Select Papers from The Ninth Viking Congress, Isle of Man, 4–14 July 1981* (London: Viking Society for Northern Research, 1983).

Fellows-Jensen, G., 'Of Danes – and Thanes – and *Domesday Book*', in *People and Places in Northern Europe 500–1600: Essays in Honour of Peter Hayes Sawyer*, ed. I. Wood and N. Lund (Woodbridge: Boydell & Brewer, 1991), pp. 107–21.

Feveile, C., 'Ribe', in *The Viking World*, ed. S. Brink and N. Price (London: Routledge, 2008), pp. 126–30.

Fiddyment, S., N. J. Goodison et al., 'Girding the Loins? Direct Evidence of the Use of a Medieval English Parchment Birthing Girdle from Biomolecular Analysis', *Royal Society Open Science* 8(3) (2021), 1202055.

Finlay, A., 'Monstrous Allegations: An Exchange of *ýki* in *Bjarnar saga Hítdœlakappa*', *alvíssmál* 10 (2001), pp. 21–44.

Finlay, A., 'History and Fiction in the Kings' Sagas: The Case of Haraldr Harðráði', *Saga-Book of the Viking Society* 39 (2015), pp. 72–102.

Finstad, E., J. Martinsen et al., 'Prehistoric and Medieval Skis from Glaciers and Ice Patches in Norway', *Journal of Glacial Archaeology* 3(1) (2016), pp. 43–58.

Fitzhugh, W. W., and E.I. Ward, ed., *Vikings: The North Atlantic Saga* (Washington: Smithsonian Institution Press, 2000).

Fletcher, R., *Bloodfeud: Murder and Revenge in Anglo-Saxon England* (London: Allen Lane, 2002).

Fontaine, J. M., 'Slave Resistance in Early Medieval England', *Anglo-Saxon England* 49 (2020), pp. 253–84.

Fontaine, J. M., 'The Archaeology of Slave Trading in Viking-Age Britain and Ireland: A Methodological Approach', in *The Archaeology of Slavery in Early Medieval Northern Europe: The Invisible Commodity*, ed. F. Biermann and M. Jankowiak (Cham: Springer, 2021), pp. 53–63.

Forsyth, K., and C. Tedeschi, 'Text-inscribed Slates', in *Inchmarnock: An Early Historic Island Monastery and its Archaeological Landscape*, ed. C. Lowe (Edinburgh: Society of Antiquaries of Scotland, 2008), pp. 128–50.

Forte, A., R. Oram and F. Pedersen, *Viking Empires* (Cambridge: Cambridge University Press, 2005).

Fransen, L., A. Nørgård and E. Østergård, *Medieval Garments Reconstructed: Norse Clothing Patterns* (Aarhus: Aarhus University Press, 2011).

Frei, K. M., A. N. Coutu et al., 'Was It for Walrus? Viking Age Settlement and Medieval Walrus Ivory Trade in Iceland and Greenland', *World Archaeology* 47(3) (2015), pp. 439–66.

Gardeła, L., 'What Did the Vikings Do for Fun? Sports and Pastimes in Medieval Northern Europe', *World Archaeology* 44(2) (2012), pp. 234–47.

Gardeła, L., '"Warrior-women" in Viking Age Scandinavia? A Preliminary Archaeological Study', *Analecta Archaeologica Ressoviensia* 8 (2013), pp. 273–339.

Gardeła, L., 'Amazons of the Viking World: Between Myth and Reality', *Medieval Warfare* 7(1) (2017), pp. 8–15.

Gardeła, L., *Women and Weapons in the Viking World: Amazons of the North* (Oxford: Oxbow Books, 2021).

Graham-Campbell, J., 'The Vikings in Orkney', in *The Faces of Orkney: Stones, Skalds and Saints*, ed. D. J. Waugh (Edinburgh: Scottish Society for Northern Studies, 2003), pp. 128–37.

Grane, T., 'Did the Romans Really Know (or Care) about Southern Scandinavia? An Archaeological Perspective', in *Beyond the Roman Frontier: Roman Influences on The Northern Barbaricum*, ed. T. Grane (Rome: Edizioni Quasar, 2007) pp. 7–30.

Griffiths, D., 'Living in Viking-Age Towns', in *Everyday Life in Viking-Age Towns: Social Approaches to Towns in England and Ireland, c. 800–1100*, ed. D. M. Hadley and L. ten Harkel (Oxford: Oxbow Books, 2013), pp. 1–13.

Grove, J. P., 'The Place of Greenland in Medieval Icelandic Saga Narrative', *Journal of the North Atlantic. Special Volume 2: Norse Greenland – Selected Papers from the Hvalsey Conference 2008* (2009), pp. 30–51.

Grönvold, K., Níels Óskarsson et al., 'Ash Layers from Iceland in the Greenland GRIP Ice Core Correlated with Oceanic and Land Sediments', *Earth and Planetary Science Letters* 135 (1995), pp. 149–55.

Guðmundur Ólafsson, K. P. Smith and T. McGovern, 'Surtshellir: A Fortified Outlaw Cave in West Iceland', in *The Viking Age: Ireland and the West – Proceedings of the Fifteenth Viking Congress, Cork, 2005* (Dublin: Four Courts Press, 2010), pp. 283–97.

Guldager, O., S. Stummann Hansen and S. Gleie, *Medieval Farmsteads in Greenland: The Brattahlid Region 1999–2000* (Copenhagen: Danish Polar Centre, 2002).

Gulløv, H. C., 'Natives and Norse in Greenland', in *Vikings: The North Atlantic Saga*, ed. W. W. Fitzhugh and E. I. Ward (Washington, DC: Smithsonian Books, 2000), pp. 318–26.

Gulløv, H. C., *Grønlands Forhistorie* (Copenhagen: Gyldendal, 2004).

Gulløv, H. C., and A. M. Jensen, 'The Eskimo's View of the European: The So-Called Norse Dolls and Other Questionable Carvings', *Arctic Anthropology* 20(2) (1983), pp. 121–29.

Hall, M. A., 'Board Games in Boat Burials: Play in the Performance of Migration and Viking Age Mortuary Practice', *European Journal of Archaeology* 19(3) (2016), pp. 439–55.

Hall, R., *World of the Vikings* (New York: Thames and Hudson, 2007).

Hayeur Smith, M., 'Dress, Cloth and the Farmer's Wife: Textiles from Ø172 Tatsipataa, Greenland, with Comparative Data from Iceland', *Journal of the North Atlantic. Special Volume 6: In the Footsteps of Vebæk Vatnahverfi Studies 2005–2011* (2014), pp. 64–81.

Hayeur Smith, M., 'Weaving Wealth: Cloth and Trade in Viking Age and Medieval Iceland', in *Textiles and the Medieval Economy: Production, Trade, and Consumption of Textiles, 8th–16th Centuries*, ed. A. Ling Huang and C. Jahnke (Oxford: Oxbow Books, 2015), pp. 23–40.

Hayeur Smith, M., *The Valkyries' Loom: The Archaeology of Cloth Production and Female Power in the North Atlantic* (Gainesville, FL: University Press of Florida, 2020).

Hebsgaard, M. B., M. T. P. Gilbert et al., '"The Farm Beneath the Sand" – An Archaeological Case Study on Ancient "Dirt" DNA', *Antiquity* 83 (2009), pp. 430–44.

Heen-Pettersen, A. M., 'The Earliest Wave of Viking Activity? The Norwegian Evidence Reconsidered', *European Journal of Archaeology* 22(4) (2019), pp. 523–41.

Heen-Pettersen, A. M., and G. Murray, 'An Insular Reliquary from Melhus: The Significance of Insular Ecclesiastical Material in Early Viking-Age Norway', *Medieval Archaeology* 62(1) (2018), pp. 53–82.

Heide, E., 'Loki, the *Vätte*, and the Ash Lad: A Study Combining Old Scandinavian and Late Material', *Viking and Medieval Scandinavia* 7 (2011), pp. 63–106.

Helgi Þorláksson, 'Historical Background: Iceland 870–1400', in *A Companion to Old Norse-Icelandic Literature and Culture*, ed. R. McTurk (Oxford: Blackwell, 2005), pp. 136–54.

Helle, K., 'Introduction', in *The Cambridge History of Scandinavia I, Prehistory to 1520*, ed. K. Helle (Cambridge: Cambridge University Press, 2003), pp. 1–14.

Helle, K., 'Bergen's Role in the Medieval North Atlantic Trade', *AmS-Skrifter* 27 (2019), pp. 43–51.

Henriksen, P. S., 'Norse Agriculture in Greenland – Farming at the Northern Frontier', in *Northern Worlds: Landscapes, Interactions and Dynamics*, ed. H. C. Gulløv (Odense: University Press of Southern Denmark, 2014), pp. 423–48.

Holck, P., 'The Oseberg Ship Burial, Norway: New Thoughts on the Skeletons from the Grave Mound', *European Journal of Archaeology* 9(2–3) (2006), pp. 185–210.

Holm, P., 'The Slave Trade of Dublin, Ninth to Twelfth Centuries', *Peritia* 5 (1986), pp. 317–45.

Holman, K., 'Defining the Danelaw', in *Vikings and the Danelaw*, ed. J. Graham-Campbell et al. (Oxford: Oxbow, 2001), pp. 1–11.

Hultgård, A., *The End of the World in Scandinavian Mythology: A Comparative Perspective on Ragnarök* (Oxford: Oxford University Press, 2022).

Høegsberg, M. S., 'Continuity and Change: The Dwellings of the Greenland Norse', *Journal of the North Atlantic. Special Volume 2: Norse Greenland – Selected Papers from the Hvalsey Conference 2008* (2009), pp. 82–101.

Imer, L. M., 'The Runic Inscriptions from Vatnahverfi and the Evidence of Communication', *Journal of the North Atlantic. Special Volume 2: Norse Greenland – Selected Papers from the Hvalsey Conference 2008* (2009), pp. 74–81.

Imer, L. M., 'Runes and Romans in the North', *Futhark: International Journal of Runic Studies* 1 (2010), pp. 41–64.

Imer, L. M., 'The Tradition of Writing in Norse Greenland – Writing in an Agrarian Community', in *Northern Worlds: Landscapes, Interactions and Dynamics*, ed. H. C. Gulløv (Odense: University Press of Southern Denmark, 2014), pp. 339–52.

Imer, L. M., *Peasants and Prayers: The Inscriptions of Norse Greenland* (Odense: Odense University Press, 2017).

Imer, L. M., 'Lumps of Lead: New Types of Written Sources from Medieval Denmark', in *The Meaning of Media: Texts and Materiality in Medieval Scandinavia*, ed. A. C. Horn and K. G. Johansson (Berlin: De Gruyter, 2021), pp. 19–38.

Iversen, T., 'Slavery and Unfreedom from the Middle Ages to the Beginning of the Early Modern Period', in *Peasants, Lords and State: Comparing Peasant Conditions in Scandinavia and the Eastern Alpine Region, 1000–1750*, ed. T. Iversen, J. R. Myking and S. Sonderegger (Leiden: Brill, 2020), pp. 41–87.

Jacobsen, G., 'Sexual Irregularities in Medieval Scandinavia', in *Sexual Practices and the Medieval Church*, ed. V. L. Bullough and J. Brundage. (Buffalo, NY: Prometheus, 1982), pp. 72–85.

Jacobsen, G., 'Pregnancy and Childbirth in the Medieval North: A Topology of Sources and a Preliminary Study', *Scandinavian Journal of History* 9 (1984), pp. 91–111.

Jakobsen, J., *An Etymological Dictionary of the Norn Language in Shetland* (London: D. Nutt, 1928).

Jarman, C. L., M. Biddle et al., 'The Viking Great Army in England: New Dates from the Repton Charnel', *Antiquity* 92 (2018), pp. 183–99.

Jesch, J., *Women in the Viking Age* (Woodbridge: Boydell & Brewer, 1991).

Jesch, J., *Ships and Men in the Late Viking Age: The Vocabulary of Runic Inscriptions and Skaldic Verse* (Woodbridge: Boydell & Brewer, 2001).

Jesch, J., 'Geography and Travel', in *A Companion to Old Norse-Icelandic Literature and Culture*, ed. R. McTurk (Oxford: Blackwell, 2005), pp. 119–35.

Jesch, J., 'The Nine Skills of Earl Rögnvaldr of Orkney', *Occasional Papers of the Centre for the Study of the Viking Age: 3* (Nottingham: Centre for the Study of the Viking Age, University of Nottingham, 2006), pp. 1–16.

Jesch, J., *The Viking Diaspora* (London: Routledge, 2015).

Jochens, J., *Women in Old Norse Society* (Ithaca, NY: Cornell University Press, 1995).

Jóhanna Katrín Friðriksdóttir, *Valkyrie: The Women of the Viking World* (London: Bloomsbury, 2020).

Jón Hnefill Aðalsteinsson, 'The Position of Freed Slaves in Medieval Iceland', *Saga-Book of the Viking Society* 22 (1986), pp. 33–49.

Jón Steffensen, '*Margrétar saga* and its History in Iceland', *Saga-Book of the Viking Society* 16 (1962–1965), pp. 273–82.

Jón Viðar Sigurðsson, 'Viking Age Scandinavia: A "Slave Society?', in *Viking-Age Slavery*, ed. M. Toplak, H. Østhus and R. Simek (Vienna: Fassbender, 2021), pp. 59–74.

Jørgensen, L. B., 'The Introduction of Sails to Scandinavia: Raw Materials, Labour and Land', in *N-TAG TEN: Proceedings of the 10th Nordic TAG Conference at Stiklestad, Norway, 2009*, ed. R. Berge, M. E. Jasinski and K. Sognnes (Oxford: BAR Publishing, 2012), pp. 173–81.

Karras, R. M., 'Concubinage and Slavery in the Viking Age', *Scandinavian Studies* 62(2) (1990), pp. 141–62.

Kjellström, A., 'The Norm and the Subaltern: Identifying Slaves in an Early Medieval Scandinavian Society', in *The Archaeology of Slavery in Early Medieval Northern Europe: The Invisible Commodity*, ed. F. Biermann and M. Jankowiak (Cham, Springer: 2021), pp. 67–79.

Knirk, J. E., 'Learning to Write with Runes in Medieval Norway', in *Medeltida skrift- och språkkultur: Nordisk medeltidsliteracy i ett diglossisk och digrafisk perspektiv II: Nio föreläsningar från ett symposium i Stockholm våren 1992 med en inneledning av Barbro Söderberg* (Stockholm: Sällskapet Runica et Mediævalia, 1994), pp. 169–212.

Knirk, J. E., 'Runic Inscriptions Containing Latin in Norway', in *Runeninschriften als Quellen interdisziplinärer Forschung: Abhandlungen des Vierten Internationalen Symosiums über Runen und Runeninschriften in Göttingen vom 4.–9. August 1995*, ed. K. Düwel and S. Nowak (Berlin: De Gruyter, 1998), pp. 476–508.

Knirk, J. E., 'Love and Eroticism in Medieval Norwegian Runic Inscriptions', in *Die Faszination des Verborgenen und Seine Entschlüsselung: Rāði sār kunni*, ed. J. Krüger, V. Busch et al. (Berlin: De Gruyter, 2017), pp. 217–32.

Krag, C., 'The Early Unification of Norway', in *The Cambridge History of Scandinavia, Volume 1: Prehistory to 1520*, ed. K. Helle (Cambridge: Cambridge University Press, 2003), pp. 184–201.

Kuitems, M., B. L. Wallace et al., 'Evidence for European Presence in the Americas in AD 1021', *Nature* 601 (2022), pp. 388–91.

Kupiec, P., and K. Milek, 'Roles and Perceptions of Shielings and the Mediation of Gender Identities in Viking and Medieval Iceland', in

Viking Worlds: Things, Spaces and Movement, ed. M. Hem Eriksen, U. Pedersen et al. (Oxford: Oxbow Books, 2015), pp. 102–23.

Larsen, E. B., 'The Ribe Skull Fragment. Toolmarks and Surface Textures', in *Ribe Excavations 1970–76*, ed. M. Bencard, L. Bender Jørgensen and H. Brinch Madsen (Esbjerg: Sydjysk Universitetsforlag, 2004), pp. 43–59.

Ledger, P. M., K. J. Edwards and J. E. Schofield, 'Vatnahverfi: A Green and Pleasant Land? Palaeoecological Reconstructions of Environmental and Land-use Change', *Journal of the North Atlantic. Special Volume 6: In the Footsteps of Vebæk Vatnahverfi Studies 2005–2011* (2014), pp. 29–46.

Lethbridge, E. 'Medieval to Modern: Using Spatial Data from the Digital Projects Icelandic Saga Map and Nafnið.is to Explore the Interaction Between Narrative and Place in Iceland', in *Digital Spatial Infrastructures and Worldviews in Pre-Modern Societies*, ed. A. Petrulevich and S. Skovgaard Boeck (Leeds: Arc Humanities Press, 2023), pp. 59–90.

Liestøl, A., 'Correspondence in Runes', *Medieval Scandinavia* 1 (1968), pp. 17–27.

Liestøl, A., 'The Runes of Bergen: Voices from the Middle Ages', *Minnesota History* 40(2) (1996), pp. 49–58.

Lindow, J., *Norse Mythology: A Guide to Gods, Heroes, Rituals, and Beliefs* (Oxford: Oxford University Press, 2002).

Lindow, J., *Trolls: An Unnatural History* (London: Reaktion Books, 2014).

Lindow, J., 'Old Norse Mythology as Sacred Narrative: Þórr's Fishing Expedition', in his *Old Norse Mythology* (New York, NY: Oxford Academic, 2021), pp. 65–159.

Lísabet Guðmundsdóttir, 'Driftwood Utilization and Procurement in Norse Greenland', *Acta Borealia* 39(2) (2022), pp. 138–67.

Lísabet Guðmundsdóttir, 'Timber Imports to Norse Greenland: Lifeline or Luxury?', *Antiquity* 97 (2023), pp. 454–71.

Loe, L., A. Boyle et al., *Given to the Ground. A Viking Age Mass Grave on Ridgeway Hill, Weymouth* (Oxford: Oxford Archaeology, 2014).

Lonnert, L., 'Harpan i ormgropen – om källor till vikingatidens stränginstrumet', CD-uppsats i musikvetenskap, Växjö universitet (2006).

Looijenga, T., *Texts and Contexts of the Oldest Runic Inscriptions* (Leiden: Brill, 2003).

Lowe, C., 'Image and Imagination: The Inchmarnock "Hostage Stone"', in *West over Sea: Studies in Scandinavian Sea-Borne Expansion and Settlement before 1300. A Festschrift in Honour of Dr Barbara Crawford,* ed. B. Ballin Smith, S. Taylor and G. Williams (Leiden: Brill, 2007), pp. 53–67.

Lowe, C., ed., *Inchmarnock: An Early Historic Island Monastery and its Archaeological Landscape* (Edinburgh: Society of Antiquaries of Scotland, 2008).

Lowe, C., 'Non-text-inscribed Slates' in *Inchmarnock: An Early Historic Island Monastery and its Archaeological Landscape*, ed. C. Lowe (Edinburgh: Society of Antiquaries of Scotland, 2008), pp. 151–74.

Lucas, G. 'Pálstóftir: A Viking Age Shieling in Iceland', *Norwegian Archaeological Review* 41(1) (2008), pp. 87–100.

Lucas, G., and T. McGovern, 'Bloody Slaughter: Ritual Decapitation and Display at the Viking Settlement of Hofstaðir, Iceland', *European Journal of Archaeology* 10(1) (2007), pp. 7–30.

Łucejko, J. J., M. Vedeler and I. Degano, 'Textile Dyes from Gokstad Viking Ship's Grave', *Heritage* 4(3) (2021), pp. 2278–86.

Luik, H., J. Peets et al., 'Antler Combs from the Salme Ship Burials: Find Context, Origin, Dating and Manufacture', *Estonian Journal of Archaeology* 24(1) (2020), pp. 3–44.

Lund, C., 'The Archaeomusicology of Scandinavia', *World Archaeology* 12 (1981), pp. 246–65.

Macleod, M., and B. Mees, *Runic Amulets and Magic Objects* (Woodbridge: Boydell and Brewer, 2006).

Madsen, C. K., 'Norse Pastoral Farming and Settlement in the Vatnahverfi Peninsula, South Greenland', in *Northern Worlds: Landscapes, Interactions and Dynamics*, ed. H. C. Gulløv (Odense: University Press of Southern Denmark, 2014), pp. 95–114.

Madsen, C. K., and A. E. Lennert, 'Behind the Ice: The Archaeology of Nunatarsuaq, Southwest Greenland', *Journal of the North Atlantic* 42 (2022), pp. 1–32.

Magnús Á. Sigurgeirsson, U. Hauptfleisch et al., 'Dating of the Viking Age Landnám Tephra Sequence in Lake Mývatn Sediment, North Iceland', *Journal of the North Atlantic* 21 (2013), pp. 1–11.

Mägi, M., *The Viking Eastern Baltic*, transl. P. Ruustal (Amsterdam: Amsterdam University Press, 2020).

Magnell, O., and E. Iregren, '*Veitstu Hvé Blóta Skal*: The Old Norse *Blót* in the Light of Osteological Remains from Frösö Church, Jämtland, Sweden', *Current Swedish Archaeology* 18(1) (2010), pp. 223–50.

Margaryan, A., D. J. Lawson et al., 'Population Genomics of the Viking World', *Nature* 585.7825 (2020), pp. 390–96.

Mathers, D., 'A Fourteenth-Century Description of Greenland', *Saga-Book of the Viking Society* 33 (2009), pp. 67–94.

McAlister, D., 'Childhood in Viking and Hiberno-Scandinavian Dublin, 800–1100', in *Everyday Life in Viking-Age Towns: Social Approaches to Towns in England and Ireland, c. 800–1100*, ed. D. M. Hadley and L. ten Harkel (Oxford: Oxbow Books, 2013), pp. 86–102.

McColl Millar, R., ed., *Northern Lights, Northern Worlds. Selected Papers from the FRLSU Conference, Kirkwall 2009* (Aberdeen: Publications of the Forum for Research on the Languages of Scotland and Ulster, University of Aberdeen, 2010).

McGovern, T., 'The Arctic Frontier of Norse Greenland', in *The Archaeology of Frontiers and Boundaries*, ed. S. Green and S. Perlman (New York, NY: Academic Press, 1985), pp. 275–323.

McGovern, T. H., 'The Demise of Norse Greenland' in *Vikings: The North Atlantic Saga*, ed. W. W. Fitzhugh and E. I. Ward (Washington, DC: Smithsonian Books, 2000), pp. 327–39.

McGovern, T. H., T. Amorosi et al., 'Vertebrate Zooarchaeology of Sandnes V51: Economic Change at a Chieftain's Farm in West Greenland', *Arctic Anthropology* 33(2) (1996), pp. 94–122.

McManus, D., *A Guide to Ogam* (Maynooth: Maynooth Monographs, 1991).

Mees, B., 'The Vimose Dedication as Ritual Language', *NOWELE* 68(2) (2015), pp. 129–51

Melnikova, E., 'Runic Inscriptions as a Source for the Relation of Northern and Eastern Europe in the Middle Ages', in *Runeninschriften als Quellen interdisziplinärer Forschung:Abhandlungen des Vierten Internationalen Symposiums über Runen und Runeninschriften in Göttingen vom 4.–9. August 1995*, ed. K. Düwel and S. Nowak (Berlin: De Gruyter, 1998), pp. 647–59.

Melnikova, E., 'The Cultural Assimilation of the Varangians into Eastern Europe from the Point of View of Language and Literacy', in *Runica – Germanica – Mediaevalia*, ed. W. Heizmann and A. van Nahl (Berlin: De Gruyter, 2003), pp. 454–65.

Meulengracht Sørensen, P., *The Unmanly Man: Concepts of Sexual Defamation in Early Northern Society*, transl. J. Turville-Petre (Odense: Odense University Press, 1983).

Mikkelsen, E., *Looting or Missioning: Insular and Continental Sacred Objects in Viking Age Contexts in Norway* (Oxford: Oxbow Books, 2019).

Milek, K., 'The Roles of Pit Houses and Gendered Spaces on Viking-Age Farmsteads in Iceland', *Medieval Archaeology* 56:1 (2012), pp. 85–130.

Milis, L., 'Children and Youth. The Medieval Viewpoint', *Paedagogica Historica* 29(1) (1993), pp. 15–32.

Mitchell, S. A., 'Anaphrodisiac Charms in the Nordic Middle Ages: Impotence, Infertility and Magic', *Norveg* 38 (1998), pp. 19–42.

Mitchell, S. A., *Witchcraft and Magic in the Nordic Middle Ages* (Philadelphia, PA: University of Pennsylvania Press, 2011).

Moen, M., 'Gender Archaeology: Where Are We Now?', *Archaeologies* 15(2) (2019), pp. 206–26.

Moen, M., and M. Walsh, 'Agents of Death: Reassessing Social Agency and Gendered Narratives of Human Sacrifice in the Viking Age', *Cambridge Archaeological Journal* 31(4) (2021), pp. 597–611.

Myrdal, J., 'Milking and Grinding, Digging and Herding: Slaves and Farmwork 1000–1300', in *Settlement and Lordship in Viking and Early Medieval Scandinavia*, ed. B. Poulsen and S. M. Sinbæk (Turnhout: Brepols, 2012), pp. 293–308.

Möller-Wiering, S., 'Vimose', in *War and Worship: Textiles from 3rd to 4th-Century AD Weapon Deposits in Denmark and Northern Germany* (Oxford: Oxbow Books, 2011), pp. 30–39.

Naumann, E., M. Krzewińska et al., 'Slaves as Burial Gifts in Viking Age Norway? Evidence from Stable Isotope and Ancient DNA Analyses', *Journal of Archaeological Science* 41 (2014), pp. 533–40.

Nordström, J., 'Dvärgen på Ribekraniet', *Arkiv för nordisk filologi* 136 (2021), pp. 5–24.

Nyegaard, G., 'Dairy Farmers and Seal Hunters: Subsistence on a Norse Farm in the Eastern Settlement, Greenland', *Journal of the North Atlantic* 37 (2018), pp. 1–80.

Orri Vésteinsson, 'The Archaeology of *landnám*: Early Settlement in Iceland', in *Vikings: The North Atlantic Saga*, ed. W. W. Fitzhugh and E. I. Ward (Washington, DC: Smithsonian Books, 2000), pp. 164–74.

Page, R. I., 'The Manx Rune-Stones', in *The Viking Age in the Isle of Man. Select Papers from The Ninth Viking Congress, Isle of Man, 4–14 July 1981*, ed. C. Fell et al. (London: Viking Society for Northern Research, 1983), pp. 133–46.

Page, R. I., 'How Long Did the Scandinavian Language Survive in England? The Epigraphical Evidence', in his *Runes and Runic Inscriptions: Collected Essays on Anglo-Saxon and Viking Runes* (Woodbridge: Boydell & Brewer, 1995), pp. 181–224.

Page, R. I., 'The Icelandic Rune Poem', *Nottingham Medieval Studies* 42 (1998), pp. 1–37.

Patel, S. S., 'The Blackeners Cave', *Archaeology* 70(3) (2017), pp. 36–41.

Pilø, L., E. Finstad and J. H. Barrett, 'Crossing the Ice: An Iron Age to Medieval Mountain Pass at Lendbreen, Norway', *Antiquity* 94 (2020), pp. 437–54.

Pollard, A. M., and P. Ditchfield et al., 'Sprouting like Cockle Amongst the Wheat: The St Brice's Day Massacre and the Isotopic Analysis of Human Bones from St John's College, Oxford', *Oxford Journal of Archaeology* 31(1) (2012), pp. 83–102.

Poole, K., 'More Than Just Meat', in *Everyday Life in Viking-Age Towns: Social Approaches to Towns in England and Ireland, c. 800–1100*, ed. D. M. Hadley and L. ten Harkel (Oxford: Oxbow Books, 2013), pp. 144–56.

Power, R., 'Meeting in Norway: Norse-Gaelic Relations in the Kingdom of Man and the Isles, 1090–1270', *Saga-Book of the Viking Society* 29 (2005), pp. 5–66.

Price, N., *The Viking Way: Magic and Mind in Late Iron Age Scandinavia* (Oxford: Oxbow Books, 2nd ed., 2019).

Price, N., *Children of Ash and Elm: A History of the Vikings* (New York, NY: Basic Books, 2020).

Price, T. D., J. Peets et al., 'Isotopic Provenancing of the Salme Ship Burials in Pre-Viking Age Estonia', *Antiquity* 90(325) (2016), pp. 1022–37.

Price, T. D., J. Peets et al., 'Human Remains, Context, and Place of Origin for the Salme, Estonia, Boat Burials', *Journal of Anthropological Archaeology* 58 (2020), 101149.

Raffield, B., 'Playing Vikings: Militarism, Hegemonic Masculinities and Childhood Enculturation in Viking Age Scandinavia', *Current Anthropology* 60(6) (2019), pp. 813–35.

Raffield, B., 'The Slave Markets of the Viking World: Comparative Perspectives on an "Invisible Archaeology"', *Slavery and Abolition* 40(4) (2019), pp. 682–705.

Raffield, B., N. Price and M. Collard, 'Male-biased Operational Sex Ratios and the Viking Phenomenon: An Evolutionary Anthropological Perspective on Late Iron Age Scandinavian Raiding', *Evolution and Human Behavior* 38(3) (2017), pp. 315–24.

Raffield, B., N. Price and M. Collard, 'Polygyny, Concubinage, and the Social Lives of Women in Viking-Age Scandinavia', *Viking and Medieval Scandinavia* 13 (2017), pp. 165–209.

Rahtz, P. A., and L. Watts, 'Three Ages of Conversion at Kirkdale, North Yorkshire', in *The Cross Goes North*, ed. M. Carver (York: York Medieval Press, 2003), pp. 289–309.

Rahtz, P. A., and L. Watts, *St Gregory's Minster, Kirkdale, North Yorkshire: Archaeological Investigation and Historical Context* (Oxford: Archaeopress, 2021).

Rannveig Þórhallsdóttir, 'Fjallkonan. "Sér hún hátt og vítt um veg' – hinsta hvíla konu frá 10. öld á Vestdalsheiði. Sið-fræðileg rannsókn á mannvistarleifum og gripum' (MA thesis, University of Iceland, 2018). https://skemman.is/handle/1946/31704.

Reséndez, A., *The Other Slavery: The Uncovered Story of Indian Enslavement in America* (Boston: Houghton Mifflin Harcourt, 2016).

Ritchie, A., B. Noddle et al., 'Excavation of Pictish and Viking-Age Farmsteads at Buckquoy, Orkney', *Proceedings of the Society of Antiquaries of Scotland* 108 (1979), pp. 174–227.

Rodríguez-Varela, R., K. H. S. Moore, et al., 'The Genetic History of Scandinavia from the Roman Iron Age to the Present', *Cell* 186(1) (2023), pp. 32–46.

Roslund, M., 'Legacy of the Disowned. Finding *ambátts* in High Medieval Scania and Östergötland Through Ceramic Production' in *The Archaeology of Slavery in Early Medieval Northern Europe: The Invisible Commodity*, ed. F. Biermann and M. Jankowiak (Cham: Springer, 2021), pp. 81–98.

Russell, R., 'A Critical Afterword', in *Languages and Communities in the Late-Roman and Post-Imperial Western Provinces*, ed. A. Mullen and G. Woudhuysen (Oxford: Oxford University Press, 2023), pp. 268–76.

Sabo, D., and G. Sabo, 'A Possible Thule Carving of a Viking from Baffin Island, N.W.T.', *Canadian Journal of Archaeology* 2 (1978), pp. 33–42.

Sayers, W., '"ok er hann einhendr": Tyr's Enhanced Functionality', *Neophilologus* 100(2) (2016), pp. 245–55.

Schaeken, J., 'Learning to Read and Write', in his *Voices on Birchbark: Everyday Communication in Medieval Russia* (Leiden: Brill, 2019), pp. 109–16.

Schulte, M., 'Runology and Historical Sociolinguistics: On Runic Writing and its Social History in the First Millennium', *Journal of Historical Sociolinguistics* 1(1) (2015), pp. 87–110.

Síf Ríkharðsdóttir, *Emotion in Old Norse Literature: Translations, Voices, Contexts* (Woodbridge: Boydell & Brewer, 2017).

Simek, R., *Dictionary of Northern Mythology*, transl. A. Hall (Woodbridge: Boydell and Brewer, 1993).

Simek, R., J. McKinnell and K. Düwel, *Runes, Magic and Religion: A Sourcebook*, Verlag Fassbaender, (2004).

Simek, R., 'Elves and Exorcism: Runic and Other Lead Amulets in Medieval Popular Religion', in *Myths, Legends and Heroes: Essays on Old Norse and Old English Literature*, ed. D. Anlezark (Berlin: De Gruyter, 2011) pp. 25–52.

Sims-Williams, P., *The Celtic Inscriptions of Britain: Phonology and Chronology, c. 400–1200* (Oxford: Blackwell, 2003).

Sindbæk, S. M., 'Glass Beads and Beadmaking', in his *Northern Emporium II: The Networks of Viking-Age Ribe* (Aarhus: Aarhus University Press, 2023), pp. 239–82.

Sindbæk, S. M., ed., *Northern Emporium I: The Making of Viking-Age Ribe* (Aarhus: Aarhus University Press, 2022).

Sindbæk, S. M., ed., *Northern Emporium II: The Networks of Viking-Age Ribe* (Aarhus: Aarhus University Press, 2023).

Skre, D., 'The Development of Urbanisation in Scandinavia', in *The Viking World*, ed. S. Brink. and N. Price (London: Routledge, 2008), pp. 83–92.

Smiarowski, K., 'Preliminary Report on the 2012 Archaeofauna from E47 Gardar in the Eastern Settlement, Greenland', NABO HERC Laboratory Report 61, pp. 1–24.

Smith, K. P., Guðmundur Ólafsson and Albína Hulda Pálsdóttir, 'Ritual Responses to Catastrophic Volcanism in Viking Age Iceland: Reconsidering Surtshellir Cave through Bayesian Analyses of AMS Dates, Tephrochronology, and Texts', *Journal of Archaeological Science* 126 (2021), 105316.

Smith, K. P., and Guðmundur Ólafsson, 'All that Glitters is not Gold: Multi-instrumental Identification of Viking Age Orpiment (As2S3) from Surtshellir Cave, Iceland', *Journal of Archaeological Science: Reports* 47 (2023), 103724.

Soffia Guðný Guðmundsdóttir and Laufey Guðnadóttir, 'Book Production in the Middle Ages', in *The Manuscripts of Iceland*, ed. Gísli Sigurðsson and Vésteinn Ólason (Reykjavik: The Árni Magnússon Institute in Iceland, 2004), pp. 45–61.

Sognnes, K. J., 'The Case of the Lone Reindeer: The Bøla Rock Art Site in Trøndelag, Norway', *Acta Archaeologica* 82 (2011), pp. 81–95.

Spurkland, T., *Norwegian Runes and Runic Inscriptions* (Woodbridge: Boydell and Brewer, 2005).

Staecker, J., *Rex regum et dominus dominorum: die wikingerzeitlichen Kreuz- und Kruzifixanhänger als Ausdruck der Mission in Altdänemark und Schweden* (Stockholm: Almquist & Wiksell International, 1999).

Star, B., J. H. Barrett et al., 'Ancient DNA Reveals the Chronology of Walrus Ivory Trade from Norse Greenland', *Proceedings of the Royal Society B* 285 (2018), 20180978.

Steenholt Olesen, R., 'Runic Amulets from Medieval Denmark', *Futhark 1 (2010)*, pp. 161–76.

Steinforth, D. H., *Thorvald's Cross: The Viking-Age Cross-Slab 'Kirk Andreas MM 128' and its Iconography* (Oxford: Archaeopress, 2022).

Søvsø, M., 'Emporia, Sceattas and Kingship in 8th C. "Denmark"', in *The Fortified Viking Age: 36th Interdisciplinary Viking Symposium*, ed. J. Hansen and M. Bruus (Odense: University Press of Southern Denmark, 2018), pp. 75–86.

Toplak, M., 'The Warrior and the Cat: A Re-evaluation of the Roles of Domestic Cats in Viking Age Scandinavia', *Current Swedish Archaeology* 27 (2019), pp. 213–45.

Thomav, T., 'Four Scandinavian Ship Graffiti from Hagia Sophia', *Byzantine and Modern Greek Studies* 38(2) (2014), pp. 168–84.

Tuckley, C., 'The Vikings of JORVIK: 40 Years of Reconstruction and Re-enactment', in *Digging into the Dark Ages: Early Medieval Public Archaeologies* (Oxford: Archaeopress, 2020), pp. 76–100.

Van der Plicht, J., C. Bronk Ramsey, et al., 'Recent Developments in Calibration for Archaeological and Environmental Samples', *Radiocarbon* 62(4) (2020), pp. 1095–1117.

Vedeler, M., and L. Bender Jørgensen, 'Out of the Norwegian Glaciers: Lendbreen – A Tunic from the Early First Millennium AD', *Antiquity* 87 (2013), pp. 788–801.

Warming, R. F., 'The Viking Age Shields from the Ship Burial at Gokstad: A Re-examination of their Construction and Function', *Arms and Armour* 20(1) (2023), pp. 11–34.

Watts, L., P. A. Rahtz, et al., 'Kirkdale: The Inscriptions', *Medieval Archaeology* 41 (1997), pp. 51–99.

Wieners, C. E., 'Haze, Hunger, Hesitation: Disaster Aid after the 1783 Laki Eruption', *Journal of Volcanology and Geothermal Research* 406 (2020), 107080.

Williams, G., 'Towns and Identities in Viking England', in *Everyday Life in Viking-Age Towns: Social Approaches to Towns in England and Ireland, c. 800–1100*, ed. D. M. Hadley and L. ten Harkel (Oxford: Oxbow Books, 2013), pp. 14–34.

Winroth, A., 'Epilogue, The End of the Viking Age', in his *The Age of the Vikings* (Princeton, NJ: Princeton University Press, 2014), pp. 241–52.

Zachrisson, T., 'Bonded People: Making Thralls Visible in Viking-Age and Early Medieval Sweden', in *The Archaeology of Slavery in Early Medieval Northern Europe: The Invisible Commodity*, ed. F. Biermann and M. Jankowiak (Cham: Springer, 2021), pp. 99–110.

Zilmer, K., 'Words in Wood and Stone: Uses of Runic Writing in Medieval Norwegian Churches', *Viking and Medieval Scandinavia* 12 (2016), pp. 199–227.

Zilmer, K., 'Runic Sticks and Other Inscribed Objects from Medieval Bergen: Challenges and Possibilities', *Maal og Minne* 112(1) 2020, pp. 65–101.

Østergård, E., *Woven into the Earth: Textile Finds in Norse Greenland* (Aarhus: Aarhus University Press, 2009).

Databases and websites

CELT. Corpus of Electronic Texts', https://celt.ucc.ie/.

Downham, C., 'Vikings in Irish Chronicles, 794–902', currently

available at https://www.celt.dias.ie/publications/online/
vikings-temporarily-removed/.

Gersum Project: www.gersum.org.

Gramoty birch bark database: http://gramoty.ru/birchbark/.

RuneS-project database, 'Runic Writing in the Germanic Languages':
https://www.runesdb.eu/project/.

Secrets of the Ice: https://secretsoftheice.com.

Articles

Arcini, C., 'Reconnecting Relationships: Uncovering Genealogy in
Archaeology', The Past, 16 January 2022, https://the-past.com/
feature/reconnecting-relationships-uncovering-genealogy-in-
archaeology/.

'Gaming in the Roman Iron Age', Department of Cultural History,
University of Bergen, https://www.uib.no/en/culturalhistory/
135652/gaming-roman-iron-age.

Jeffery, S., 'Museum's broken treasure not just any old shit', Guardian,
6 June 2003, https://www.theguardian.com/uk/2003/jun/06/
artsandhumanities.arts1.

Jesch, J., 'What does the word "Viking" really mean?', The Conversation,
5 April 2017, https://theconversation.com/what-does-the-word-viking-
really-mean-75647.

McKenzie, S., 'Face of Orkney's St Magnus Reconstructed', BBC News,
8 February 2017, https://www.bbc.co.uk/news/uk-scotland-north-
east-orkney-shetland-38892669.

'The People of Jorvik', Jorvik Viking Centre, https://www.jorvikviking
centre.co.uk/the-vikings/the-people-of-jorvik/.

Orange, R., 'Norwegian youths who "ruined" 5,000-year-old rock
carving could face prosecution', Daily Telegraph, 31 July 2016,
https://www.telegraph.co.uk/news/2016/07/31/norwegian-youths-
who-ruined-5000-year-old-carving-could-face-pro/.

Pilø, L., The Best-Preserved Pair of Skis from Prehistory', Secrets of the
Ice, 5 October 2021, https://secretsoftheice.com/news/2021/10/05/
the-best-preserved-pair-of-skis-from-prehistory/.

Pilø, L., 'The Hunt for the Lost Mountain Pass', Secrets of the Ice,
16 April 2020, https://secretsoftheice.com/news/2020/04/16/
mountain-pass/.

'Westness Brooch-Pin', National Museum of Scotland,
https://www.nms.ac.uk/explore-our-collections/stories/
scottish-history-and-archaeology/westness-brooch-pin/.

List of Illustrations

Glass gaming pieces for *hnefatafl*, Birka, Sweden, 9th century. Photo: ©
Getty Images

The Sundial from St Gregory's Minster, England, early 11th century.
Photo: © Alan Curtis / Alamy Stock Photo

A gown from Ikigaat, Greenland, c. 1380-1530. Photo: Peter Danstrom /
National Museum of Denmark

Black-and-white illustrations

p. vi Map of Scandinavia, © Martin Lubikowski, ML Design, London, UK

Prologue: Kindling

p. 6 Comb from Vimose, Denmark, 2nd century. Photo: Roberto Fortuna
and Kira Ursem / National Museum of Denmark

Chapter 2: Beginnings

p. 48 Brain shell with incised runes, Ribe, Denmark, 8th century. Photo:
Lennart Larsen / National Museum of Denmark

Chapter 3: Love

p. 68 Rune inscription stick, Bergen, Norway, c. 1200 (Bf_DiA_003130).
Photo: Svein Skare, Universitetsmuseet i Bergen, Attribution-
ShareAlike (CC BY-SA)

p. 81 Carving of a baby in amber, Hedeby, Denmark, c. 9th-11th century.
Photo: Landesmuseen Schleswig-Holstein, inv. SH1930-3.289

p. 83 Amulet of silver with runes, Østermarie, Denmark, 11th century.
Photo: John Lee / National Museum of Denmark

p. 85 Opening page from *Margrétar saga*, Iceland, 1540-1560, from the Arni
Magnusson Institute for Icelandic Studies (AM 431 12mo). Photo: ©
The Arni Magnusson Institute for Icelandic Studies

p. 88 A gilt bronze mount featuring a lion or wolf, Rousay, Orkney
Islands, c. 850-900. Photo: © National Museums Scotland

p. 91 Sketches showing two examples of Onfim's birch bark artwork
(Novgorod, Russia, c.13th Century). Image: © Cecily Gayford /
Profile Books 2024

Chapter 4: Travel

p. 94 Photo and sketch of a wooden board from the Viking ship
collection ship Gokstad. Museum of Cultural History, University of
Oslo (C10384). Photo: Vegard Vike / Museum of Cultural History,
University of Oslo (CC BY-SA 4.0).

p. 173 Filed teeth from a skeleton buried at Trelleborg, Denmark, 10th century, from *The Viking Age: A Time with Many Faces* (Caroline Ahlström Arcini, Oxbow Books, 2018) Photo: Staffan Hyll

p. 175 Carved wooden head from the Oseberg ship, Norway, 834. Photo: © Album / Alamy Stock Photo

p. 176 Reconstruction of the Funen skeleton at the National Museum of Denmark. Photo: Arnold Mikkelsen / National Museum of Denmark

p. 178 Fossilised coprolite, York, England, 9th century. Photo: © York Archaeology

p. 184 Pair Of Ancient Viking Shoes from Viking Ship Museum, Oslo, Norway, 834. Photo: © Graham Mulrooney / Alamy Stock Photo

p. 185 Comb made of elk antler, Skåmsta, Sweden, 11th century. Photo: Caroline Ahlström Arcini

Chapter 7: Home

p. 201 A woven loop of human hiar, from the weaving room at the Farm Under the Sand in Greenland's Western Settlement (Hårkrans, Gården under Sandet). Photo: Peter Danstrom / National Museum of Denmark

p. 203 Sketch of a whalebone object found at Austmannadal, Greenland. Photo: Lisbeth Imer / National Museum of Denmark

p. 210 Ancient Norse ruins at Igaliku, Greenland. Photo: © ARCTIC IMAGES / Alamy Stock Photo

p. 213 Ivory carving of a polar bear, Eastern Settlement, Greenland. Photo: © Georg Nyegaard / The Greenland National Museum & Archives.

p. 214 Wooden chopping board with walrus heads, Eastern Settlement, Greenland. Photo: © Georg Nyegaard / The Greenland National Museum & Archives.

Chapter 8: Play

p. 223 Stave church carving from Hylestad, Norway, 12th century. Photo: © Getty Images

p. 227 Boxwood pan pipes, York, England, 10th century. Photo: © York Archaeology

p. 229 Musical notation and runes from the *Codex Runcius*, Denmark, c. 1300. Photo: © Alamy

p. 237 Gaming board, pieces and die from Vimose, Denmark. Photo: Roberto Fortuna and Kira Ursem / National Museum of Denmark

p. 239 Illustration of the golden horn of Gallehus. Photo: © Florilegius / Alamy Stock Photo

Acknowledgements

It takes a village to raise a book. My village is wonderful and widespread, and I am very lucky to be part of it.

Starting with my academic community, I am indebted to Judith Jesch and Neil Price, both of whom read the entire book with such kindness and close attention to detail. Warmest thanks also to Georg Nyegaard, who went through my Greenland material so carefully, and gave his knowledge and experiences so generously. Massive thanks to the other archaeologists who shared the fruits of their research with me: Kevin P. Smith on Surtshellir, Ellen Marie Næss on Oseberg, Kevin Edwards on Norse Greenland, Søren M. Sindbæk and Sarah Croix on Ribe, Lars Pilø and Espen Finstad on Lendbreen, Bastiaan Star on walrus ivory, Rannveig Þórhallsdóttir on the Mountain Woman and Caroline Arcini on filed teeth and the siblings with dwarfism. Thank you to Gale Owen-Crocker, Nancy Spies, Michael Lerche Nielsen, Steve Ashby, Chris Tuckley, Lia Lonnert and David Petts, all of whom were kind enough to answer my questions on everything from weaving tablets to place names, combs, facial reconstructions, musical instruments and gaming pieces. I'm very grateful to Jóhanna Katrín Friðriksdóttir, Leszek Gardeła and Carolyne Larrington for being so openhearted with their knowledge of Viking Age women, manuscripts, burials, grammar, and so much more. Enormous thanks also to Lisbeth Imer, who not only helped me with the runes of Norse Greenland but also posted a copy of her book to me across the North Sea. And thank you to Jos Schaeken, who shared his vast knowledge of a little Novgorodian artist with me because, as he put it, 'there's always time for Onfim'.

This book would have had far fewer pictures and far less underpinning scholarship were it not for the expertise and tenacity of the librarians, archivists, researchers and curators who helped me track down all sorts of elusive items. The heroic Hannah Clinton and Katie Rickard at Bath Spa University Library went above and beyond more times than I can count. So did Jamie Copeland from the Bodleian Library in Oxford, who tracked down and emailed me all the Old English references I needed when the British Library went down in a cyber-attack. Meanwhile, Siobhan Cooke-Miller from the Orkney Museum didn't let a snowstorm stop her from getting me the images I needed, quite literally. Warmest thanks to Guðvarður Már Gunnlaugsson and Sigurður Jónsson at the Arni Magnusson Institute for Icelandic Studies (Árnastofnun), and to Anne Spears and Robert Paterson at the Bute Museum. Many thanks also to Christian Koch Madsen from the Greenland National Museum and Archives, Lembi Lõugas from Tallinn University, Volker Hilberg from Landesmuseum Schleswig-Holstein, Hanne Lovise Aannestad from the Museum of Cultural History in Oslo, Marie T. Laursen and Emilie Sommer Jappe from the National Museum of Denmark in Copenhagen, Ellie Drew from the York Archaeological Trust and Brian Smith from the Shetland Amenity Trust.

My spheres of writing, researching and broadcasting intersect in all sorts of serendipitous ways, and radio producers are often my first companions as I set out to discover more about the world. Warmest thanks are due to my fellow adventurer Alasdair Cross, who joined me on a quest to learn about Viking music, and to Einar Selvik of Wardruna, who guided us along our path. Many thanks also to Leonie Thomas, who traversed chambered cairns and stone circles with me in Orkney so that we could learn more about runes.

Amongst my dearest friends are many academics, researchers and writers who have been generous enough to read big chunks of the book, honest enough to tell me what worked and what didn't, and kind enough to let me lean on them when I needed moral support or a kick up the backside. My love and thanks to Paul Russell, Cressida Peever, Kevin Waite, Denis Casey, Rosie Bonté, Pamela Welsh, Mandy Green, Allyson Edwards, Emma Firestone and Matthias Wivel.

On the subject of moral support, kicks up the backside, honest feedback and generous reading, I owe a huge debt of gratitude to Matthew Marland at RCW. The job title 'Literary Agent' doesn't even begin to do justice to the enormity of a role that runs the gamut from creative collaborator to cheerleader, therapist and deal negotiator. This man has dragged baby buggies up and down the steps of the London underground for me, not batted an eyelid when a hungry infant needed breastfeeding during meetings, and matched me with the editor of my dreams. And my thanks to Cecily Gayford for being exactly that. You are an extraordinary human, and this book would be an entirely different beast without your unerring guidance and patient support. Thank you also to the rest of the wonderful team at Profile, including Jon Petre, Emily Frisella, Valentina Zanca, Rosie Parnham and Audrey Kerr. Thanks to copywriter Seán Costello for his eagle eye, creativity and patience, and to Joe McLaren for the wonderful cover artwork. Over in the USA, I am very grateful to Alane Mason, YJ Wang and Mo Crist at Norton.

Closest to home, special thanks to my mum Lindsey, who read every chapter. Thanks also to my family support team: my dad Richard, my siblings Imogen, Christian, Rowena and Benjamin, and my wonderful network of siblings' partners and siblings-in-law, especially Fred and Abi, who helped hugely when I was trying to keep the work wheels on the wagon through pandemic and pregnancies. Thanks also to the fabulous staff at One Nine Seven Early Years Nursery, who went above and beyond on so many occasions to make our lives easier. And warmest thanks to Elizabeth Archibald, Richard Holt and Bjørg Kosmo, my colleagues who became then confidants, then friends, then family. There is so much to thank you for, both in bringing this book to life, and in my life beyond this book.

Which brings me to John, without whom this book would never have been started or, indeed, finished. In fair or foul weather, you are our *leiðarstjarna*. My deepest love and thanks to you, and also to Magnus and Wulfie, without whom this book would have been written ten times faster but also far less reflectively. You shape my thoughts, my writing and my world beyond all measure.

Index

Z